Hollywood's

Fatal Feng Shui

An In-Depth Examination of 10 Celebrity Homes
with a Tragic History

Master Jennifer Bonetto
Master Denise Liotta Dennis

Ω
Moon Gate Press
The Woodlands, Texas

Hollywood's Fatal Feng Shui
An In-Depth Examination of 10 Celebrity Homes with a Tragic History

Copyright© 2018 by Jennifer Bonetto and Denise Liotta Dennis
First Edition, First Printing

Photography & Illustrations
Celebrity photos are from Wikipedia Commons, Flickr Commons, Google and Bing selections tagged *for commercial use with modifications, free to share and use* or *public domain*. Additional photos are from Unsplash, Pixaby and other photographers; with thanks and credit to: John Wiley, Mona Eshaiker, Shazari Casto, Crassula ovate Florero, Vinnie Zuffante, Jennifer Bonetto, Arin Djuhic, Artiom Vallat, Bill Anastas, Bruno Martins, Douglas Sheppard, Emanuel Hahn, Haley Phelps, Ima Geedit, Iris Papillon, Jamie Street, Jean Philippe-Delberghe, Leland Stanford, Martin Jernberg, Nathan Dumlao, Sasha, Vita Vilcina, Nathan Dumlao, Alice Elizabeth and www.MarilynMonroe Collection.com

Special thanks to *Pacific Coast News* for the photos of the following celebrity homes: Anna Nicole Smith, Phil Spector and Brittany Murphy. Thanks to Google Maps for the street/house and ariel views. Illustrations and charts created by Denise Liotta Dennis. Ancient Chinese images are public domain.

Floor plans and site plans of the celebrity homes were recreated by architect, Brandon Broadstone (2008).

Cover/Book Designer: Denise Liotta Dennis; photos from Unsplash and Pixabay. Interior book layout and designed by Denise Liotta-Dennis. Senior Editor: Linda Dennis.

Published by Moon Gate Press (713-897-1719) and Create Space (www.createspace.com)

ISBN-13: 978-1986981965

John Ox – 6
JV – Ox – 6
AL Horse – 1
PJ Dragon 3
MJ Snake 4

This book is dedicated to Jennifer's parents
Alfredo and Alicia Bonetto

*'You came here, from another country, with nothing,
and ironically you left and went to heaven with nothing. But your
spirits' of determination, persistence and steadfastness,
will live in me forever. Thank you with all my heart and soul.'*

Stove faces 210 SW
House Faces ~~H2 East~~ 148 SE
Period 7
SE–3 Exact direct

Table of Contents

SECTION ONE
Classical Feng Shui

Introduction

Feng Shui and Hollywood have a simpatico relationship. They're both unique and can truly impact lives. Hollywood has attracted people from all walks of life and from every part of the world. Los Angeles is a valley that is dynamically surrounded on three sides by mountain ranges. This makes the *City of Angels* both hilly and flat. The Pacific Ocean is also a major feature of the city. Generally speaking, the city has very vibrant, yang energy because of the water, mountains, and sunny climate.

However, even with these extraordinary environmental features, not everyone is guaranteed a perfect or blessed life. The focus of this book is to examine the lives of 10 celebrities who attained riches, fame, adoration, and forever, a place in history. More precisely, we'll put their homes under the Feng Shui microscope. With over 30 years' combined experience, conducting thousands of assessments for homes and businesses, we have examined these celebrity homes in meticulous and compassionate detail.

These particular stories were selected because they *still* break our hearts. Some are very old, indeed. Regardless of the passing years, we remain shocked, appalled and fascinated with the disastrous ending of their

lives. How was it possible that their lives fell into the depths of hell? Why did their homes attract murder, drugs, violence,

suicide, affairs, bankruptcy, fatal illness, and loss of reputation? The answer is that these homes violate not only the *basic* tenets of Classical Feng Shui, but some deadly and rare ones as well. Their tragic lives confirm the power of the extraordinary findings discovered by the ancient Chinese millenniums ago. In modern-day life, these Feng Shui principles for 'superior living' are as valid and needed as ever.

Without a doubt, you'll notice the many similarities between the celebrities' properties. Their homes, in fact, share many of the same negative features that brought about the astonishing and bizarre events that unfolded. Depending on the circumstances, homes can have energy that's benevolent, malevolent, or mixed. Some buildings are more susceptible to attracting disastrous events, while others will provide a mix of good and bad luck. Amazingly, there are structures where people enjoy one good event after another. None of these scenarios are a coincidence but, rather, a natural manifestation of environmental energy.

Feng Shui tells a tale so deep that the most important aspects of a person's life are revealed through their home. We attract homes on an energetic, subconscious level depending on where we are in life at the moment. The house is often a mirror to consciousness, what we wish to experience, and how we want to evolve.

Feng Shui is all about energy – unseen, yet powerful. Astoundingly, the energy of a home can influence and impact human behavior. Some environments can manifest negative experiences such as divorce, bankruptcy, lawsuits, cancer, murder, or anything we might consider disastrous. Through hundreds of years of research and by simply observing how people experienced life, the ancient Chinese were able to devise a plan in which people could thrive. This systematic, esoteric approach to life and setting up your home came to be known as Feng Shui.

While Classical Feng Shui is well over 3,000 years old, most Americans are not familiar with it. Up until this point in time, most of the Western cultures of the world believe the Feng Shui introduced about 30 years ago is authentic. Hopefully, this book will foster appreciation for the art and science of *real* Feng Shui. It is through this powerful lens that we will examine the 10 celebrity homes.

We've made every effort to present accurate information regarding our famous stars. Rest assured that every site was visited. The two homes outside of Los Angeles were also inspected, Michael Jackson's Neverland Ranch in Los Olivos, and Phil Spector's home in Alhambra. However, security would not permit getting too close. Jennifer spent over a year traipsing all over Los Angeles on various quests. She took compass directions of the homes and

snapped photos like a tourist. She spent endless hours investigating public records and collecting accurate floor plans and land surveys. Like Sherlock Holmes, she never gave up until the mystery was solved.

The evaluations/critiques are comprehensive and, in the Feng Shui business, referred to as a full-scale audit. This means not only examining the home's floor plan, but everything [human-made or natural] surrounding it. Additionally, we use the person's birthday to get a complete picture. All Classical Feng Shui systems, formulas and methods were used to perform the audits. If you're not familiar with these classic systems, no worries. We have described them in Chapters 3, 4 and 5. You may also want to make some changes to your own home based on this information.

Due to the fact that we weren't able to see inside the properties, we had to make some assumptions and educated guesses. For example, we might say 'the bed was likely on the North wall according to the room's layout'. Or, 'they probably renovated the home after 2004 to put their stamp on it'. Also, we can make these assumptions because we know the ending; a bit of reverse engineering, if you will. In the case of Michael Jackson, his Neverland Ranch was featured in the October 2009 Architectural Digest issue. The article, *Inside Michael*

Jackson's Private Kingdom, featured several photographs of the home's furnishings, including the kitchen. Some episodes of *The Anna Nicole Show* were filmed in her Studio City home, so furniture layout and rooms are visible on *YouTube*.

We were unable to locate floor plans for Phil Spector's 'castle' (a murder) or Phil Hartman's home (a murder-suicide), although much effort was made to do so. However, the property features were so compelling, and *telling*, we wanted to include them. The energy of these sites contributed to the horrific events that took place there and, we again, made some educated guesses. In Classical Feng Shui, landforms (e.g., roads, water, mountains, electrical towers, land elevations, canyons, huge drains, and house shapes) are so potent; they may override *Flying Stars* and *Eight Mansions*. These are the two most popular systems for interior spaces. Also a *Flying Star Chart* can look good on paper but, once the structure is thrust into a negative setting, all hell can break loose.

And, lastly, we are part of the 400-year old *Wu Chang Pai* lineage of Feng Shui Grandmaster Yap Cheng Hai. This means that we are faithful in sharing, teaching, and practicing the classic systems per his teachings, interpretations and implementation techniques.

Now, let's take a peek at the basic principles and bones of Feng Shui in Chapter One. You'll be intrigued with what the ancients discovered.

Chapter One
Feng Shui Basic Concepts

The principles and concepts found in this chapter have all been used in the critiques of the 10 celebrity homes. These are the bones of Feng Shui.

The art and science of Feng Shui has been part of the Chinese culture for thousands of years, going in and out of fashion and favor. It came to America and other Western countries almost 40 years ago. However, it was a faux, Hollywood version reducing Feng Shui to placing tchotkies here and there with a New Age twist. From its inception, Feng Shui was designed to support the human experience, that of prosperity, health, and relationships. After hundreds of years of experimentation and careful documentation, Feng Shui morphed into a sophisticated art/science that is composed of numerous formulas, techniques and methods.

The Five Metaphysical Arts

Mountain (Shan or Xian Xue): This category encompasses philosophy (e.g. the teachings of the fourth-century B.C. philosophers Lao Tzu and Zhuang Zi), Taoism, martial arts, Qi Gong, Tai Chi Chuan, meditation, healing, and diet. It also includes the study of Alchemy—the science of prolonging life through specific rituals and exercises, which are deeply rooted in Taoism.

Medicine (Yi): The Chinese follow an integrated, holistic, and curative approach to medicine and healing such as acupuncture, herbal prescriptions, and massage.

Divination (Po): The Chinese are acknowledged for their intuitive skills and abilities to read and interpret symbols. The divination techniques of Da Liu Ren, Tai Yi Mystical Numbers, Qi Men, Mei Hua Xin Yi (Plum Blossom oracle) employ numbers to predict everything from wars or missing persons, to the details of one's past and future.

Destiny (Ming): Most forms of Chinese augury seek to interpret fate and determine the timing of life events. The ancient sages devoted much time and research to this study. The most popular methods of Chinese fortune-telling include Zi Wei Dou Shu (Purple Star Astrology) and BaZi (literally means 'eight characters' but is also commonly known as the Four Pillars of Destiny), both of which examine a person's destiny and potential based on their date and time of birth. A complimentary form of Ming is the Science of Divination (Bu Shi), which is analogous to the mathematics of probability.

Physiognomy (Xiang Xue): Grandmaster Yap Cheng Hai refers to this category as *Sow*, and it involves making predictions based on the image, form, and features of the landscape, the human face and palms, architecture, and gravesites. Feng Shui is the fortune-telling of a building by rendering an accurate observation of the structure's appearance, shape, direction, and other surrounding environmental features.

Feng Shui Concepts

The concepts of Feng Shui are how the ancients viewed the universe and energy. Virtually, every book on Feng Shui introduces the famous precepts of the Ba Gua, five elements, yin-yang theory, Luo Shu, and He Tu. This often leaves the reader confused as how to apply them. These tools are *principles* and not stand alone formulas or techniques. You may already be familiar with these concepts, but it's worth skimming over them. If this is your first Feng Shui book, take a few minutes to peruse these important ideas.

There continues to be a certain mysticism surrounding the practice of Feng Shui. Understanding its many principles and canons requires the acceptance of fundamental theories about the universe. This may, at first glance, seem alien in the context of how the modern world works. At any rate, Feng Shui is part of Chinese metaphysics which is a huge body of knowledge comprised of five major categories of study. All five categories (aka the 'five arts') have their foundation in the same energy tools [the two Ba Guas, five elements, yin-yang, and so forth] and then develop into different branches of study.

Classical Feng Shui is just one of the five (5) main art-sciences of Chinese metaphysics. Deeply rooted in the I Ching and the Tao, these philosophical tenets—mountain, medicine, divination, destiny, and physiognomy—are the origins of the Chinese culture developed over 5,000 years. It is said that if you are able to master just one of these studies it would be a significant life-accomplishment. Now let's briefly discuss the Feng Shui precepts one by one.

The Nature of Chi

Chi simply means energy. The ancient Chinese was one of the first cultures to discover that humans and our entire universe are comprised of pure energy. Modern-day science now confirms this. Chi also spelled *qi*, (either spelling is pronounced *chee*) is the life-force energy of the universe, heaven, earth, and man. Sometimes it is also referred to as the *cosmic breath*, which is present in every living and non-living entity. It can be auspicious, inauspicious, or benign. Chi is the life-force energy that pervades mankind's existence. It is the unseen force that moves through the human body and the environment. Feng Shui's main objective is to attract and harness auspicious energy to support the human experience. It is energy that determines the shape and form of the landscape as well as the vitality of all living things. The famous Tai  Chi symbol, which resembles two interlocking fish demonstrate the polarity of energy which is either yin (female) or yang (male).

The Eight Guas or Trigrams

The Guas, also known as trigrams, date back to Chinese antiquity. These important symbols give a macro, inclusive perspective of our universe, energy and direction. Each of the eight Guas is comprised of three lines either solid or broken. The broken lines indicate yin/female energy while the solid lines represent yang/male energy. The three lines also represent the cosmology of heaven, earth and man. The famous Ba Gua includes all eight trigrams; "Ba" means *eight*, and "Gua" means the *result of divination.*

The Eight Trigrams (Guas)	
Chien Gua	**Kun Gua**
The "Creative" and Heaven Family Member: The Father Element: *Big Metal* Represents the Northwest Color: Gold, Silver, White Body Part: Head & Lungs Luo Shu Number: 6	The "Receptive" Family Member: Mother Element: Earth Represents the Southwest Color: Brown and Yellow Body Part: Stomach, Abdomen Luo Shu Number: 2
Chen Gua	**Xun Gua**
"Arousing" and Thunder Family Member: Oldest Son Element: Big Wood Represents the East Color: Jade Green Body Part: Liver, Feet Luo Shu Number: 3	"Gentle" and the Wind Family Member: Oldest Daughter Element: *Small Wood* Represents the Southeast Color: Green Body Part: Liver, Thighs, Buttocks Luo Shu Number: 4
Kan Gua	**Li Gua**
The "Abysmal" and Water Family Member: Middle Son Element: Water Represents the North Color: Black, Blue Body Part: Kidneys, Blood Luo Shu Number: 1	"Clinging" and Fire Family Member: Middle Daughter Element: Fire Represents the South Color: Red, Purple, Orange, Pink Body Part: Heart, Eyes Luo Shu Number: 9
Gen Gua	**Dui Gua**
"Stillness" and Earth Family Member: Youngest Son Element: *Mountain* Earth Represents the Northeast Color: Brown, Yellow Body Part: Bones, Hands/Fingers Luo Shu Number: 8	"Joyful" and the Marsh Family Member: Youngest Daughter Element: *Small Metal* Represents the West Color: Gold, Silver, White Body Part: Mouth, Throat, Lungs Luo Shu Number: 7

The eight Guas, in addition to representing the eight directions, have several layers of information that becomes useful in assessing the energy of land, homes or buildings. The Chinese related this information to everyday life, resulting in each Gua representing the Father, Mother, Eldest Son, Eldest Daughter and so forth. In the end, each Gua represents yin or yang energy, relates to a family member, an element, a body part, a possible illness, a season, a number, human personality types, and direction. Additionally, they have numerous interpretations and slight distinctions that

can be overwhelming for a novice of Feng Shui. All the same, these implications and interpretations have great significance in Feng Shui and other Chinese metaphysical studies. The eight Guas are Kan, Gen, Chen, Xun, Li, Kun, Dui, and Chien representing North, Northeast, East, Southeast, South, Southwest, West, and Northwest respectively[1].

In modern-day language, the trigrams are the eight binary numbers of 111, 110, 101, 100, 011, 010, 001 and 000. The *solid lines* represent the 1 digit, while the *broken lines* represent the digit 0; they are read from the bottom up. It's been said that the Chinese were the first to use binary arithmetic. Binary codes are the 'language' of computers.

Tien-Di-Ren

"Heaven Luck is the boat given to you by God. Earth Luck is the wind that fills the sails and the currents of the ocean. Man Luck is the way in which you use the wind and the currents to steer your boat." – Grandmaster Yap Cheng Hai

The three types of luck or opportunities, known as Tien-Di-Ren, are Heaven Luck, Earth Luck, and Man Luck. Each one of these categories will champion you in a very different way. This aspect of Feng Shui is called the Cosmic Trinity. In other words all three areas will influence your life and living space.

Heaven Luck (Tien)
This category of luck is often referred to as destiny or karma. The Chinese believe that what goes around comes around; that past deeds, for good or evil, will visit you again in this life. They also contend that this area

---

[1] Please note all directions are capitalized throughout the book as they are part of Classical Feng Shui formulas and teachings.

of luck is fixed and may not be influenced; it counts as 1/3 of your overall luck and opportunities in life.

Earth Luck (Di)

This category is the dominion of Feng Shui. If your home site and living space has auspicious and harmonious energy, you will reap the rewards. Additionally, life will support your efforts, goals, relationships, health, and prosperity if this aspect is taken care of. In Earth Luck, you have total control and it can exceed the normal 1/3 associated with it if you have superior energy at home and work. Grandmaster Yap purports that it can be raised to 2/3.

Man Luck (Ren)

This category of luck is another area you have total control over. This is created by you own efforts and the choices you make in life. This may include your education, morals, hard work, beliefs, and your ability to seize and exploit good opportunities that may present themselves. This area accounts for approximately 1/3 of your overall luck.

He Tu and Luo Shu

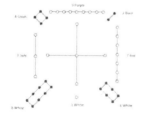 

These two very distinct mathematical diagrams representing universal energy are so ancient and intrinsic in the Chinese culture that its people are often referred to as the He-Luo culture. Together they form the foundation of Chinese philosophy and are the genesis of Classical Feng Shui. These famous diagrams are frequently mentioned

in ancient Chinese literature and are shrouded by legend and mystery. There are a series of lines connected with black and white dots in both diagrams. Most scholars believe the He Tu chronicles the cycle of birth, while the Luo Shu represents the process of death: yin and yang.

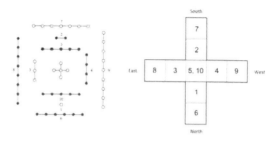

Ancient lore surrounding the He Tu began with the reign of the shaman king Fu Xi, who was born in the 29th century B.C., witnessed a mythical dragon-horse bearing strange, unusually patterned markings on its back emerging from the mighty Yellow River. This design became known as the He Tu (pronounced *hur too*). As Fu Xi examined these markings, valuable information pertaining to cosmic laws of the universe was revealed. The dots (black are yin and white are yang) of the He Tu illustrate several concepts; including direction, the five elements of Feng Shui and the flow of chi.

Following Fu Xi's life, succeeding scholars meticulously preserved and passed down the mysteries of the He Tu. Even today, it is found in written texts and ancient scrolls which pervade Eastern ideologies, including traditional Chinese medicine and some of the initial principles of Feng Shui. The five element (water, wood, fire, earth, and metal) have its basis in the He Tu. These elements indentify, interpret, and predict natural phenomena. Later to arrive on the scene would be the Guas or trigrams. Therefore, the theories and principles of the He Tu gave birth to the first Ba Gua, known as the Early Heaven Ba Gua (Xien Tien Ba Gua).

The Luo Shu is also surrounded by legend and myth. Emperor Yu of the Xia Dynasty, while sitting next to the River Lo saw a giant turtle emerge in or around 2100 B.C. It too, had a pattern and series of black and white dots on its back. The Luo Shu is a nine square grid containing nine numbers. Each of the nine numbers represents a trigram, body organ, family member, direction, or element and it is either male or female energy. Interestingly, no matter which way you add the numbers in the grid they total 15. The Luo Shu is often referred to as the Magic Square of 15. This arrangement of numbers became part of the Later Heaven Ba Gua (LHB). The Luo Shu is used extensively in all methods and applications of Classical Feng Shui.

The Luo Shu and He Tu are coded maps that represent the cosmology of heaven and earth; they are energy tools which are used to assess buildings, living spaces, and land sites. These ancient oracles are considered the backbone of Chinese metaphysics. Unlocking their mysteries takes many years of study, contemplation and a learned teacher. Please note that South is placed at the top, not North in the He Tu and Luo Shu images. This may take some getting used to.

The Five Elements (Wu Xing)

All categories of Chinese metaphysics explain the world and the universe, in terms of the five elements. As with most brilliant discoveries made by humans, nature served as the inspiration. In ancient China, they paid close attention to the predicable cycles of energy, fire burns wood, and metal comes from the Earth. By associating this information in everyday life and events, the Five Element theory was created.

The Chinese knew that energy was part of everything. Therefore, by placing energy into five different categories offered a viable solution in which to assess their interaction. These five categories or five phases of energy are known as Wu Xing. The five elements are metal (jin-literally the word for gold), wood (mu), water (shui), fire (ho), and earth (tu). Each element is a representation of matter and energy as it coalesces from one form to the next. The five element theory simply elucidates the relationship among different types of energy. It is understood as both figurative and literal in Feng Shui applications.

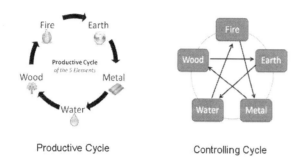

Productive Cycle   Controlling Cycle

The premise of the five elements is used in every study of Chinese metaphysics—Feng Shui, astrology, traditional Chinese medicine, and martial arts. If you wish to master Feng Shui, you must master the five elements. The five elements have three cycles: productive, weakening, and controlling.

Productive Cycle: It represents the productive force that drives the smooth flow of events in their natural order. This important cycle produces or gives birth to something. Wood feeds fire. Fire produces ash and creates earth. Earth gives birth to metal. Metal melts into a fluid and becomes water, which in turn produces wood.

The Weakening/Reductive Cycle: This cycle represents the retarding force that inhibits and reverses the natural flow of events. This process is the reverse of the productive cycle, because what we give birth to weakens us. Wood stokes fire, therefore, fire weakens wood. Fire generates ash and creates earth, therefore, earth weakens fire. Earth produces metal, therefore, metal weakens earth. Metal melts to a fluid and produces water, therefore, water weakens metal. Water produces wood, therefore, wood weakens water.

The Controlling Cycle: This cycle describes conflict. Constructive conflict is referred to as controlling, while destructive conflict is called killing energy. This process can conquer, control or destroy. Water extinguishes fire, fire melts metal, and metal cuts wood. Wood, in the form of plants or tree roots, controls the Earth by breaking it apart or keeping it together. Earth is big enough to hold water, without earth water would have no boundary.

Reductive Cycle

The Two Ba Guas

Likely the second most recognized image after the Tai Chi symbol is the Ba Gua; however most are not aware that there are two. The Ba Gua literally appears in all

Feng Shui books; it is an octagonal map that depicts the eight trigrams. The two Ba Guas are the Early Heaven Ba Gua—Fu Xi or Xien Tien Ba Gua and Later Heaven Ba Gua (Ho Tien or Wen Wang Ba Gua). Both are used in the practice of Classical Feng Shui as all formulas, methods, and techniques are born from the two arrangements of the Guas.

The Early Heaven Ba Gua (EHB), which dates back approximately 6,000 years, depicts the polarities in nature. It reflects an ideal world of harmony in which chi is in a constant, perfect state of polarization. The eight Guas, or trigrams, create a conceptual model that marks the changes in energy. The Early Heaven Ba Gua, representing a 'perfect' world, can be commonly seen over doorways to repel negative energy. It is used extensively in Westernized styles of Feng Shui. It has more profound implications and uses in Classical Feng Shui as it is the basis of complex formulas, such as water/road formulas.

The Later Heaven Ba Gua (*Ho Tien* or *Wen Wang Ba Gua)*, was the brilliant work of King Wen, a Chou Dynasty ruler who elaborated on Fu Xi's earlier diagrams. This arrangement was done to represent the cyclical forces of nature. The Later Heaven Ba Gua (LHB) describes the patterns of environmental changes. Unlike the Early Heaven Ba Gua, the LHB is dynamic, not static. It represents the ever-changing structure of the universe and the circular nature of life. Many Feng Shui applications stem from the

understanding of the Later Heaven Ba Gua. For instance, the Luo Shu is the numerical representation of the Later Heaven Ba Gua.

The Celestial Animals: Essential Topographical Landform Configurations

Gently sloping landforms, rolling hills, and undulating contours are considered excellent Feng Shui. Land that is too steep, completely flat, or severe in any way is regarded as unbalanced and void of vibrant, life-giving energy. Extreme, high, or jagged mountain ranges do not emit benevolent chi either. Not everyone is fortunate enough to find the perfect landforms, so it is often necessary to simulate them. And that's where celestial animals come into play.

To the Chinese, Feng Shui is strongly connected to the celestial animals, namely the Green Dragon, the White Tiger, the Black Turtle, and the Red Phoenix. The celestial animals symbolize important, key *land formations* that should immediately surround your home site. This is especially important when examining landforms for luck value.

Identifying the needed celestial animals land forms in relation to your house or business is easy. As you look out your front door, the left-hand side is known as the Green Dragon; the right-hand side is called White Tiger. The Black Turtle (or Dark Warrior) resides at the back of your property, while the Red Phoenix (or Vermillion Bird) occupies the front edge of your property. The open space in front of the house is called *Ming Tang,* or bright hall: this is where chi collects near your main entrance.

Figure 1: This is an example of a good 'turtle'. The back is supported by tall, solid fencing.

Ideally, the celestial animals should be represented by certain landforms. High ground, such as soft rolling hills and ridges, should define the Dragon side—same goes for the Tiger side, but not as pronounced. The Turtle in the back of the property can be a high mountain, but it should not overwhelm the site. The Phoenix, like a low footstool, calls for low ground or a distant mountain. If no ideal landforms surround your living space, or you live in a relatively flat area, other homes can serve as invaluable substitutes. The easiest way to emulate the support needed by landforms is to select a house flanked by other residences. In other words, houses on the left and right sides offer protection. Most modern-day neighborhoods are divided by fences, especially at the back of the property. If your site does not have one, simply create a strong, high backing. You want to be embraced within your home site; this not only protects you but keeps the chi or energy contained. Where energy can collect, pool or be retained—people can thrive.

For a business to be successful the left-hand side must be represented; remember this is as you are looking out your front door, not facing the building. If you do not have support on this side, you could experience serious cash-flow issues or bankruptcy. People in positions of authority, such as judges, high-powered lawyers, or CEOs, should make sure the right side is higher than the left side, e.g. a two-story home. Without support on the left-hand side, the man of the house could be bullied at work. The celestial animals are Feng Shui Landforms 101—basic but extremely accurate and necessary to prosper.

The Chinese Luo Pan

Hundreds of years before the Europeans, the ancient Chinese had discovered the magnetic compass. There is an intriguing legend in how they acquired this enormous gift as part of their culture—it's the ancient legend of the *Warrior-Goddess of the Nine Heavens*. When China's first ruler, the Yellow Emperor Huangdi (2698 to 2598 BC), was asleep one night, there appeared a bright light from heaven in which the Goddess emerged. She held in her hand a 9 by 8 inch jade box. The Yellow Emperor received the jade box from the Goddess and found that it contained a magic scroll written on dragon skin. It is said that by following the secrets written on the 'dragon scroll' that the Emperor defeated the  evil wizard (Chi You) in the famous Battle of Zhuolu; thus began the start of the great Han Chinese civilization. Other stories tell about Huangdi's unique invention, a compass cart which leads to victory. Either way, the Luo Pan soon became the quintessential tool for a Feng Shui master or practitioner. Throughout its illustrious and long history, the Luo Pan has been re-designed and refined many times over so that it would align with the latest discoveries relating to landforms, techniques, and directional energy. There are two standard types of Luo Pans—San He and San Yuan—designed to include formulas of these two main disciplines of Feng Shui. The third standard Luo Pan is the Chung He, which combines the most important information of the San He and San Yuan Luo Pans.

Figure 2: This is an example of a Zhung He Luo Pan. They will feature rings from the San Yuan and San He Luo Pans.

The purpose of the Luo Pan is the same as a conventional compass—to locate direction. However, the Luo Pan contains some very important differences. A typical compass may display four or eight directions. A Luo Pan divides up the 360 degrees into 24 sectors; this is derived by dividing the forty-five degrees of the eight directions into three, fifteen degree increments (3x 8=24). This is very fundamental in Classical Feng Shui, and this ring on the Luo Pan is known as the 24 mountain ring (not actual mountains, just a term). The Luo Pan is an impressive and beautiful instrument, truly a work of art and well worth the several hundred dollars it commands. Here are the three types of Luo Pans:

San Yuan Luo Pan: Used in the Flying Stars and the Xuan Kong systems, the San Yuan Luo Pan is readily indentified by the 64 hexagrams of the I Ching ring. It has only one 24 mountain ring. The first ring of this Luo Pan is always the Later Heaven Ba Gua arrangement of trigrams.

San He Luo Pan: The San He Luo Pan, used for San He (aka San Hup) formulas and schools, is easily identified by its *three* 24 mountain rings. These rings are used to measure direction, mountains, and water as each of these elements has distinctly different energy; however, these rings also relate to the *three harmonies* associated with this branch of Classical Feng Shui.

Chung He Luo Pan: Also spelled or referred to as Zong He, Zhung He, or Chong He. This Luo Pan is an amalgamation of the San He and San Yuan compasses. This is a great instrument for practitioners who employ both systems. Though some rings have been eliminated for size considerations, all essential rings are intact.

This extraordinary instrument is often called the '*Universe on a Plate*' by Feng Shui masters and practitioners; for more information on the Luo Pan and its history, refer to Stephen Skinner's book entitled *Guide to the Feng Shui Compass*, it is the most comprehensive book ever written on the subject.

Authentic Feng Shui is always compass-based. This is not so with the Westernized version that stormed America and other countries in the 1970's. Let see what the differences are in the next chapter.

Chapter Two
Classical vs Western Feng Shui

The power of Feng Shui cannot be found in crystals, candles, bamboo flutes, red walls, picture frames, artwork, and other decorative items.

Classical Feng Shui provides a powerful collection of people-thriving tools if executed in accordance with ancient principles. That's not, however, the case when it comes to contemporary, popular applications. Like the shag carpets and the avocado dining sets of the seventies, Feng Shui is a trend; once again, it's all the rage. But when the amulets, crystals, and candles fail to bring fame, fortune—even a bit of serenity—consumers are left spiritually bankrupt and with a houseful of expensive tchotkies.

Figure 3: Feng Shui is not a religion or spiritual practice. Its roots are from the I Ching, not Buddhism.

To successfully implement Feng Shui as the Eastern world does, Westerners should

ౚౚౚ

There is so much confusion surrounding Feng Shui, it's hard to keep it all straight. Once it was introduced to the non-Asian world, it was either embraced or dished. No matter the sentiment, Feng Shui is either authentic or commercial.

Westernized Feng Shui is often linked to the Eight Life Aspirations or Black Sect (aka Black Hat Sect Tantric Buddhist or BHTB), brought over to America in the 1970's.

They are heavy on cures such as mirrors, crystals, bamboo flutes, red ribbons, fu dogs, coin-chocked frog, fish tanks, lighting, paintings/pictures, bells, and plants. These types of Feng Shui cures were created in order to sell 'things'.

ౚౚౚ

understand this venerable doctrine as a comprehensive approach to a balanced life. That is why it is important to grasp what Feng Shui is not. Turn on the television, surf the web, or read any book about this subject and you'll discover plenty of DIY Feng Shui tips and tricks from self-proclaimed digital gurus. These so-called experts have distilled Feng Shui from an all-encompassing science to color and object placement—banish TVs from the bedroom, avoid sofa sets, open the doors, don't open the doors, paint those southern walls red, and so on. Hawkers of modern-style Feng Shui sell it as either an Asian-inspired interior design contrivance or a sustainable, eco-friendly approach to living in harmony with the environment.

Perhaps part of the problem lies in mainstream media's simplistic and uninformed presentation of Feng Shui. Television programs, such as Dateline, HGTV (Home & Garden Television), and Oprah, carve it into delicious pieces of information, easily digested by the viewing audience. And voila! A hip, new morsel of pop culture for public consumption—a Westernized and diluted version of ancient, scientific principles. Classical Feng Shui is far more complex than that.

Classical Feng Shui

The English translation of Feng Shui—wind and water—aptly describes society's relationship over the eons with this dynastic relic. Wind changes direction; water ebbs and flows. Like most trends, Feng Shui, throughout its 4,000-year history, has fallen in and out of vogue with the public. But that's only part of it. Political doctrines, too, have suppressed, even endangered, the popularity and the practice of Feng Shui in China.

Communism, in little more than half century, has thwarted the progress of a metaphysical movement that has evolved over thousands of years. The disintegration of Feng Shui in Chinese culture started in 1966 with the Great Proletarian Cultural Revolution. Communist Party leader Mao Zedong demanded an end to Chinese antiquity, and with the help of the Red Army, launched a zealous massacre of all things created before 1949.

He called these edifices of Chinese culture the Four Olds: Old Custom, Old Culture, Old Habits, and Old Ideas. Many masters fled the People's Republic of China during these dark days of despotic oppression. They found refuge in Taiwan and Hong Kong, at the time a British colony. Today, this autonomous territory—the unofficial seat of Classical Feng Shui—provides shelter to a thriving hub of the Four Olds. Other members of the Feng Shui community followed the defeated Chinese General Chiang Kai-shek to the island of Taiwan. Some say that the Chinese Nationalists who joined the deposed leader smuggled a treasure trove of

Figure 4: These are typical Westernized Feng Shui cures, not part of authentic Feng Shui.

ancient Feng Shui books from the Forbidden City in Beijing. Taiwan, east of Hong Kong, also defines its bustling business culture through the power of Feng Shui. There, the discipline flourishes as an integral aspect of design and construction, transforming this once agrarian society into an international financial powerhouse. In his early twenties,

Grand Master Yap Cheng Hai traveled there to study Feng Shui with several learned scholars.

Though the Cultural Revolution eased up after Chairman Mao's death in 1976, the practice of Feng Shui is still illegal in the People's Republic of China, but it has suffered greatly in disrespecting the natural environment with the 'Iron Man' mentality. Restrictions against Feng Shui, however, continue to relax as Communist tenets fail to meet the demands of a financially sophisticated and environmentally savvy younger generation (Spencer 2008). Case in point: Beijing Capital International Airport. Designers incorporated Classical Feng Shui elements into this ultra-modern, Olympic-friendly hub to greet the global sporting community for the 2008 Summer Games (Seattle Times 2008).

Figure 5: Hong Kong is the 'un-official' capital of Classical Feng Shui.

But even the Chinese want in on the action, if it means a promotion or not losing a job. Some members of the Iron Rice Bowl—mostly civil servants and military personnel who once enjoyed airtight job security—are paying consultants top dollar to reconfigure their offices with the prosperity-enhancing energy of Feng Shui (Reuters 2007).

Thus, West meets East. As the Orient gains financial momentum in the global market, you can bet your bottom dollar that Asian investors will want some of that good chi Chinese, Taiwanese, and other Far Eastern financiers are increasingly nudging their overseas business partners—including plenty of United States mega firms—to espouse Classical Feng Shui in the architecture of their buildings. Even as far back as the early nineties, this mixing of Eastern capital with American moxie has been reported by the media. Everyone, from local real estate brokers to major celebrities, is receiving the Asian treatment: no Feng Shui, no money.

Mainstream Faux Feng Shui

Feng Shui is often mistaken as a religion; it is not. That is why it is so important that the brazen pioneers of industry, such as Steve Wynn, and Adelson, Sir Richard Branson and Oprah publicly embrace it. Their enthusiasm has energized the resurgence of Feng Shui among practitioners and the public.

In the mid-1980s, internationally renowned Professor Thomas Lin Yun, a Tibetan Buddhist monk, founded Tibetan Black Hat Tantric Feng Shui (TBHT) and introduced it to the Western world. Like most monks (or nuns), Lin Yun possesses a working knowledge of Chinese medicine, martial arts, and Feng Shui. TBHT focuses specifically on the Ba Gua, one of the basic tenets of Feng Shui. Lin Yun relied on his extensive teachings in the healing arts and Eastern philosophy to simplify the Ba Gua—a diagram that identifies the profound mysteries of energy in the eight directions, for a Western palate.

Stephen Skinner, author of the *Keep it Simple Series*, described Lin Yun's American debut in his book, *K.I.S.S. Guide to Feng Shui*:

"The arrival of Professor Lin Yun in the United States from Taiwan via Hong Kong in the 1980s, and the work of his pupil Sarah Rossbach, put Feng Shui on the map in the U.S. Initially, Lin Yun taught a fairly traditional style of Feng Shui, but soon found, at that early stage, that a simpler form of Feng Shui was required. Accordingly, he modified the Ba Gua and launched it in 1985 as Tibetan Black Hat Tantric Buddhist (TBHT) Feng Shui. By allying Feng Shui with Buddhism, he gave Feng Shui a cloak of spiritual respectability and by adding in the mystery of the Black Hat Tibetan Lamaism, he distanced it from its Chinese

roots. And 'tantric' was the final seductive addition that made Feng Shui far more popular in the United States than it would have been otherwise."

Lin Yun called his revision of the Ba Gua as the *Eight Life Stations* or the *Eight Life Aspirations*. It served as the mainstay of

Feng Shui in America for many years and perhaps the reason behind the widely held perception of Feng Shui as a religious practice. When words such as "holiness," "sect," and "temple" are tossed in the popular vernacular, all sorts of assumptions take place. Furthermore, most of Lin Yun's students are also trained in Buddhist invocations and chanting as part of a consultation. Though these rituals can be wonderful experiences, they are not a part of the study or practice of Classical Feng Shui.

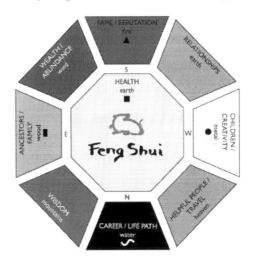

Figure 6: This is a Ba Gua retro-fitted for Western Feng Shui's Eight Life Aspirations.

Regardless of the unorthodox nature of TBHT, Feng Shui in general may not have been as well known if it hadn't been for Lin Yun's work.

Over the years, variations of Lin Yun's newfangled Feng Shui, though not considered TBHT, have cropped up everywhere and are Westernized versions. Western Feng Shui achieved mainstream status in the late 1990s, when it was featured extensively in books and on popular television programs. Feng Shui even found its way into commercials. Western schools of practice, including TBHT, employ similar Feng Shui ideas and cures—Lin Yun's Eight Life Stations, symbols of fortune, coin-choked frogs, clever lighting arrangements, unique colors and wall hangings, live plants and animals, and aesthetically pleasing furniture arrangement.

Feng Shui is not a spiritual pursuit; it does not spawn miracles, create magic, or bring overnight results. Its true purpose will help attract success, protect against misfortune, generate opportunities, enhance the quality of life, create a supportive space, and maximize potential. Be careful about experts, books, and other resources that make outlandish claims or promises. Feng Shui is not by any means a quick fix. Rather, good Feng Shui evolves over time to generate deep, lasting results. The outcomes will depend on the quality of energy near and around your home or property.

Many schools, textbooks, and manuscripts have documented Eastern or Classical Feng Shui. Basically, Classical Feng Shui has three main functions—corrective, to remedy existing problems; constructive, to enhance wealth or health or create specific outcomes; and predictive, to expose the past, accurately describe the present, and foretell the future. Outcomes are infinite because people are complex, and so are the structures we live in. The scholars of old China embraced this secret school of knowledge and developed it into a sustainable, scientific, and practical cultural canon. The genesis of this ancient form of Feng Shui dates back at least 4,000 years. Its present-day incarnation of complexity, however, includes the past 1,500 years. Many cultures have something akin to Feng Shui.

For instance, the Hindus follow Vastu Shastra, a set of metaphysical design principles that maximize the flow of energy. Though Feng Shui is also widely practiced in Tibet, Vietnam and Korea, the Chinese took it to unparalleled heights of sophistication. In ancient times, Feng Shui

was considered too potent for the common citizenry, so it was reserved for royalty, the powerful, and the privileged. Later, thanks to the charitable work of Master Yang Yun Song, everyone had access to this information and could help himself or herself. Yang, known as the *savior of the poor*, developed his own school of Feng Shui during the Tang Dynasty, which lasted from 618 to 907 AD.

Modern-day masters and pioneers, such as Grandmaster Yap Cheng Hai (1927-2014), Grandmaster Joseph Yu, Master Larry Sang, Master Peter Leung, Master Raymond Lo, Master Eva Wong, Stephen Skinner, and the prolific author Lillian Too, introduced authentic Classical Feng Shui to the Western world, particularly North America, which was still attached to Black Hat and Western Feng Shui.

In essence, Feng Shui was born out of the observation of the environment. Some people experienced fantastic success, while others faced great difficulty, depending on where they lived. The ancients deduced that the energy of a location had something to do with it, so they posed questions. Would living near water or close to mountains affect people's luck and the events of their lives? The Chinese were tenacious in documenting the results of their studies. Over thousands of years they formulated the sophisticated body of knowledge that is the Feng Shui of today.

Figure 7: In Classical Feng Shui roads and highways are 'rivers' of chi (energy).

Directional energy dictates the quality of a homesite. Therefore, Classical Feng Shui relies on a compass known as a Luo Pan to determine physical orientation. Once a compass direction of a property is ascertained, a wealth of information is revealed. The Western styles of Feng Shui do not use the Luo Pan. Its deliberate exclusion is what author Stephen Skinner likes to call the "dumbing down" of Feng Shui.

These two, very different approaches *cannot* be mixed together in a responsible way. Classical Feng Shui, including all its various techniques, is a living science, deeply rooted in the traditional texts and practices based on thousands of years of empirical observation and knowledge. Tossing a few amulets and colored walls into the mix only cheapens the experience.

The External Environment and How Energy Works

Energy is everywhere; it is the foundation of the practice of Classical Feng Shui. We humans are pure energy, our entire universe is energy, and all things around us emit an energy field. Even the chair you are sitting on, perhaps to read this book will look like Swiss cheese under a microscope. It actually comprises more space than solid matter. Quantum physics tells us this and more.

Figure 8: Tall human-made structures are considered 'urban' mountains.

In Elizabeth Moran's book, *The Complete Idiot's Guide to Feng Shui*, authors Masters Joseph Yu and Val Biktashev describe energy this way: "Chi moves. It is in perpetual process of change. Chi accumulates, disperses, expands and condenses. It moves fast, slow, in, out, up and down. Chi meanders and spirals. It flows along straight, angular and curved pathways. It rides with the wind (feng) and is retained by water (shui). There's no escaping chi's influence. We are all products of and subject to, the enormous power of chi".

In the language of Feng Shui, modern contrivances, too, imitate Mother Nature. Roads become powerful, fast-moving rivers of energy. Tall, heavy, and still, high-rise buildings emulate virtual mountains by exuding the power and the stature of the real thing. Throughout this book, keep the concepts of real water and virtual water, and real mountains and virtual mountains in mind. It will deepen your understanding of how energy and Feng Shui work together. Not only do environmental features release powerful energy, they can also affect luck regarding wealth, health, and relationships. How could living next to a cemetery (dead energy), a police station, a huge mountain, a skyscraper, a river, or a major highway not influence you?

The Two Classic Disciplines of Feng Shui

At its core, Classical Feng Shui is based on the keen observations of the heavens (time), earthly forces (exterior environments and interior spaces), and how these elements exchange energy or chi. The origins of Feng Shui date back thousands of years; some sources say it began around 4000 B.C. Kan Yu is the old term for Feng Shui. In fact, the term *Feng Shui* has only been in use for a little more than a hundred years, since the Ching Dynasty. The golden era of Feng Shui occurred during the Tang Dynasty between the seventh and tenth centuries A.D.

Over time, two main schools of practice emerged, San He and San Yuan. These ideologies form the foundation of Classical Feng Shui. It is important to understand that Feng Shui is highly dynamic and constantly developing, even today. Most modern-day Feng Shui masters will combine these schools into one big body of knowledge. But, there are a few who use one or the other exclusively; this is not bad, but rather unusual.

All Feng Shui systems share a common set of principles and theories. For example, all schools refer to the principles of yin-yang, the five elements, the Ba Gua, and the four factors, direction, occupants, time, and location. San He and San Yuan both use a Luo Pan when evaluating landforms and topography. Many popular Feng Shui books mistakenly describe these two schools as 'form school' and 'compass school'.

The notions of compass school and form school came about, no doubt, from the different approaches each theory takes. San He places emphasis on examining form, shape, contour, appearance, flow, and confirmation whereas San Yuan places its focus on time; it considers the influence, qualities and types of chi and time dimension. Despite the fact that the strategies of these ideologies are slightly different, the objectives are the same, to examine the energy of the site using form, shape, direction, timing, a compass, and the individual themselves that will rent, own, occupy, or develop it.

The San He School

San He, also known as San Hup, means three harmonies, three unities, or three combinations, depending on the Mandarin or Cantonese translation. It is considered the oldest form of Classical Feng Shui. The San He School gives great importance and consideration to environmental qualities, such as mountains and topography. In Neolithic China, Feng Shui was first used to select the ideal location for a home, a village, or the perfect gravesite for an ancestor, known as the practice of Yin Feng Shui. By the Tang Dynasty, Feng Shui had blossomed into a science, sophisticated and complex.

Since San He focuses on the environment, mountains, rivers, and landforms, it strives to understand how the environment shapes and creates chi. San He techniques are focused on finding the most advantageous or strategic location in which to extract the chi from the environment. This school recognizes that chi is dynamic and changes through time. This notion is based on immutable yin energy, such as mountains, to counter fluctuating yang energy, such as time cycles. San He systems do not try to adapt to cycles of chi. Rather, this approach attempts to insulate against and outlive any unfavorable energy cycles by selecting or creating superior landforms.

San He also relies on extensive systems and formulas to assess formations for disaster, wealth potential, and good luck. For example, a *Peach Blossom Sha* formation indicates bad romance and illicit affairs; an *Eight Roads of Destruction* causes bankruptcy, divorce, and disasters; and an *Eight Killing Mountain Forces* suggests death, crimes of passion, money-loss, and bad romance. Other formulas such as the *Five Ghost Carry Treasure*, a well-guarded secret from Taiwan, and the *Three Harmony Doorways, He Tu Roads, Assistant Star Water Method, Court Official* and *Sky Horse* are used to enhance wealth.

Water Dragons fall under this school and are considered the most powerful of the wealth-producing formulas. There are still other techniques such as the *72 Dragons, 120 Gold Divisions, the 60 Dragons, Goat Blade Water, Four Destructions and Six Harms*--all with various methods of analyzing, enhancing or adjusting the Feng Shui of a site. Our 10 celebrity homes had many of these formations, the good and the bad.

San Yuan School

Also known as Three Cycles, San Yuan is the contemporary cousin of San He. In San Yuan, chi is understood as dynamic with the disposition to cycle. Nothing in our universe is stagnating; everything is constantly in motion. Even so, it is possible to identify certain dependable trends. That's why it is necessary to regularly update your Feng Shui to stay current with the time cycles of energy. Both San Yuan and San He take into consideration the factors of time and form. The main difference between the two systems is that San He gives great credence to *forms* and San Yuan has an extreme focus on *time*.

The *Flying Stars* system (Xuan Kong Fei Xing) and *Eight Mansions* system (Pa Chai or Ba Zhai) fall under the San Yuan School. These are two of the more popular Feng Shui systems used today, especially for interior Feng Shui. In Flying Stars, an energy map of the property is derived from calculations and used to determine the quality of chi in each sector of the home. Eight Mansions, by contrast, is concerned with harmonizing the occupants with the distinctive energies of the house.

Flying Stars explains why no structure will forever enjoy good or bad Feng Shui as it cycles through time. Every structure has its own unique natal Flying Star Chart, which gives vital clues to the energy held there. Some Flying Star charts are special and indicate exceptional auspiciousness, including *Pearl String Formations* (Lin Cu San Poon Gua), *Parent String Formations* (Fu Mo San Poon Gua), and *Combinations of 10*. All three are famous for bringing great money or relationship luck. Other techniques, such as the *Castle Gate Theory* (Sent Mun Kuet), are used to tap the energy of a natural body of water for greater prosperity.

Other Feng Shui techniques that fall under the San Yuan method include *Zi Bai* (Purple-White Flying Stars); *Xuan Kong Da Gua* (Big 64 Hexagrams Method), which is used for date selection and precision; and *Xuan Kong Shui Fa* (Time-Space Water Method), used to enhance the site through wealth-producing water features. The *Dragon Gate Eight* (Long Men Ba Da Ju) method is part of the San Yuan School and is used to attract wealth and enhance career luck. The San Yuan system also developed and adopted techniques from the San He School, which assess annual visiting negative energies.

The *Three Killings*, *Grand Duke Jupiter*, and the *Year Breaker* can cause disastrous outcomes by disturbing the earth with a digging project, such as a pool construction or major landscaping. The annual visit of the *5 Yellow Star* is also disturbed by digging and construction. The *Great Sun Position* is a technique devised to counter the affect of these negative energies by selecting a good date to begin your construction or digging project and offers protection from harmful results. The *Robbery Mountain Sha*, the calculation of the daily, monthly, and yearly stars are other techniques used to assess the Feng Shui, and are part of the San Yuan School.

Both San Yuan and San He take into consideration the factors of time and form. The main difference between the two systems is that San He gives great credence to *forms* while San Yuan focuses on *time*. But neither school is superior over, both are needed to get the complete picture. At the end of the day, San He and San Yuan have common denominators; they both agree that the factor of *time* must always be considered and that *landforms* cannot be ignored. Ultimately, San He and San Yuan have one goal: to extract the chi of the environment to support the occupants and enhance the human experience. Let's now examine some very serious and negative features and formations that all 10 of our celebrities had at their homes and property.

Figure 9: Landforms, human-made or natural rate extremely high when evaluating a home site. In this photo land is slopping sharply down at the back. It does have excellent retaining walls however to capture and retain the energy. Without the walls, energy would slip away and the occupants would struggle to thrive.

Chapter Three
Detrimental Formations

These unfortunate formations can attract illicit affairs, death, drug abuse, crimes and violence, fatal attractions, murder, serious diseases, and other devastating life-events. The 10 celebrity homes had several of these formations which created the 'perfect storm'.

The Feng Shui formations described in this portion of the book can indeed cause devastation. However, in order for that to happen, several features need to be present and active. In other words, it is unlikely that a T-Juncture road will cause a death or murder in a household. While an *Eight Roads of Destruction* formation is extremely negative, it too would have to be augmented with other negative features to completely devastate a life.

Due to the fact that there are so many formations, and that each is activated by very different energy, they have been placed into major categories. They are Road/Water, Form/Shape, Mountains, Degrees, and Energy Vortexes.

I. Negative Roads and Water
Roads are considered 'virtual' water and the following formations involve either real or virtual water on the property. They are a considered a major purveyor of energy!

T-Juncture or T-Road formations
Indicates accidents, discord, divorce, and diseases

A *T-juncture* or T-road formation is when there is a road that is directly aligned with your front door or, perhaps even the garage door. In Feng Shui, this is considered one of the most toxic formations as will cause a host of negative events for the householders. While energy is good, too much will have the opposite, desired effect.

Figure 10: A road coming directly to a house can bring money loss, divorce, illness and marital discord.

This intense, direct energy is called sha or 'killing' chi; in almost all cases, it will lead to discord, money loss, divorce, illness, accidents, and other mishaps depending on how fast and close the road is to the property. If this formation is present, block off the *T-Juncture* with a stucco wall, a solid gate near the front door, boulders, or dense landscaping. While shopping for a new home, pass on these residences; even when cured they can cause issues.

Homes Surrounded by Too Many Roads
Accidents with the body, divorce, affairs, alcoholism, and drugs

Roads are fast-moving purveyors of energy and they act much like a raging river. It is extremely inauspicious to be too close or have too many roads surrounding your site. Numerous roads near a home can make it vulnerable and unstable.

Think about the stories in the news where someone is describing a car crashing into their bedroom or living room where they barely escaped with their life! Roads near the back of the property can be the worst.

Figure 11: Homes should not have too many roads surrounding it. It may cause host of problems such as divorce and money loss.

A virtual 'road' may also be a ditch or huge, open drain located in cities where monsoons and frequent rains will cause flooding. These sites can be so unstable they will activate affairs, divorce, illness and all types of misfortunes. If you have this scenario, create a strong backing at the rear of the property. Also, insulate the site on the left- and right-hand sides from the roads. Consider moving if you have experienced very bad events in your life, such as money-loss, disease, affairs, or lots of sickness.

Celebrity homes with this formation: Michael Jackson's luxury rental (Holmby Hills) and Phil Spector's castle (Alhambra).

Eight Roads of Destruction
Indicates money-loss, divorce, extreme disharmony, and violence

The *Eight Roads of Destruction* formation is also known as Yellow Springs, Eight Roads to Hell and Eight Roads to Disaster and Misfortune. No matter what you choose call it, the consequences are the same: devastating. The Chinese refer to the waters of the underworld, or hell, as *Yellow Springs.*

These devastating scenarios are formed by an important *exterior* door and a *water exit.* An important door would be a front or back door. The water exit could be a road, driveway or sidewalk (virtual water) or real water (drain, stream, ravine, or a natural wash). They involve a 15-degree increment for the door direction and a 15-degree increment for the exit. Driveways and sidewalks are not as detrimental or impactful as a busy road. A huge drain is more serious than a small one; see Figure 12. If an *Eight Roads of Destruction* is present, people can encounter bankruptcy, and other catastrophic experiences.

Here's an example of an *Eight Roads of Destruction*; the front door of a home faces *Southwest* (217.6° and 232.5°) and the road is *South* (157.6°-172.5°). Remember they are very specific to 15-degree increments. It won't apply to *all* Southwest-facing homes. The road doesn't include the entire 45

Figure 12: This huge drain could be an *Eight Roads of Destruction* exit.

degrees of South either. It only involves a specific 15-degree increment. There are only eight possible formations, one for each direction (N, S, E, W, NW, NE, SE and SW).

Celebrity homes with this formation: Nicole Brown Simpson (Bundy Drive), Anna Nicole Smith (Studio City), Michael Jackson (Neverland Valley Ranch), José & Kitty Menendez (Beverly Hills), Phil Hartman (Encino) and Brittany Murphy (Hollywood Hills).

Peach Blossom Sha Formations
Indicating affairs, adultery, incest, and fatal attractions

The *Peach Blossom Sha* formations are extremely negative for relationships, particularly romantic ones. They cause issues with reputation, sexual problems, illicit affairs, adultery, sexting, incest and all types of inappropriate sexual behavior. At a homesite, they are created by an important *exterior* door and a *water/road*. An important door would be a front or back door.

The water/road can be real water (pool, stream, lake, pond, or fountain) or virtual water (sidewalk, driveway or an actual road). The door and the water are restricted to specific 15-degree increments.

The formula includes twelve (12) possible *door* facings with four (4) offending *water/roads*. The door and the water must be in specific 15-degree increments to be a bona fide *Peach Blossom Sha* formation. Here's an example of a *Peach Blossom Sha* formation; the door faces South (172.6° to 187.5°) and the road is from the East (82.6° to 97.5°). These formations should be corrected as they can usher in several of the following results when there is a road or too much water in certain directions or locations:

- Turns the family upside down
- Soils the reputation of the house
- Scandals that are made public
- The female runs away
- Sexual problems
- Sex maniacs
- Disloyalty
- Incest
- Exile

It's interesting that nowadays the news is filled with scandalous behavior involving politicians either 'sexting", placing lewd pictures on the internet or sexually harassing women. It's highly probable they have a *Peach Blossom Sha* formation with 'scandals made public'. Tilting the door a few degrees is usually the way a Feng Shui expert will take care of it. Re-angling the door a few degrees forces the door to receive chi or energy differently. Door tilts are hugely popular in Southeast Asia and they take care of the problem very effectively. See Appendix III for photos.

Celebrity homes with this formation: O. J. Simpson (Rockingham), Michael Jackson (Holmby Hills and Neverland Valley Ranch) and Sharon Tate (Cielo Drive).

Goat Blade Water Formation
Indicates adultery, gambling, and drug abuse

A *Goat Blade Water* formation is very similar to The *Peach Blossom Sha* and they can bring a host of harmful events that can drive couples apart. There are eight (8) possible door facings with eight (8) offending roads or virtual water like a road or driveway that will cause a variety of negative results regarding relationships.

For example, if the home faces West between 277.6° to 292.5° and there is water or a road coming from Southwest between 232.6° to 247.5°, then it has a *Goat Blade Water* formation. Just like the *Peach Blossom Sha* formations, if there is too much water in that sector such as a pool, waterfall, river, lake or stream, they render negative events. These features can be human-made or natural and either way they may cause problems for the family. The 'roads' that are the offending *Goat Blade Water* formation is confined to 15-degree increment.

This should be corrected as they can bring on any of the following results:

- Divorce
- Adultery
- Gambling
- Alcohol abuse
- Drug abuse
- Family break-ups
- Overindulgence in sex
- Illegal activities leading to failure in business

Celebrity homes with this formation: Michael Jackson (Neverland Valley Ranch) and Phil Hartman (Encino).

Four Destructions and Six Harms
Indicate hassles and no peace

These formations involve a road and door and can bring clashes and hassles in the household and there will be no peace. Not all doors have the same importance or weight; it would involve a well-used, exterior door. This is usually a front or back door. An example of a *Four Destructions* is a door facing North (352.6°-7.5°) and a road from the East (82.6°-97.5°). A *Six Harms* formation is created by a door facing Northeast 52.6°-67.5°) and a road from the Southeast direction (142.6°-157.5°).

Celebrity homes with this formation: O.J. Simpson (Rockingham) and Michael Jackson (Holmby Hills and Neverland Valley Ranch).

Cutting Feet Formation
Indicates great instability and money loss

This is when a road or real water is too close to the house or its foundation (the 'feet' it stands on). Homes, townhomes or commercial buildings with the foundation too close to a busy road, lake, river, canal, bayou or the ocean can cause financial woes or health issues.

Celebrity home with this formation: Anna Nicole Smith (Studio City).

II. How Form and Shape Can Harm

Anything extreme in Feng Shui is basically taboo and is likely to spell disaster; this is particularly true for the overall design or shape of the house or building. The shapes that best support health, wealth and relationships are, in general, square or rectangular, referred to as the 'four point gold'. These 'golden' shapes allow energy to flow harmoniously throughout the home.

Extreme Designs

Figure 13: Extreme designs can harm the occupants or owners in every way. *The Walt Disney Concert Hall* **in Los Angles has a history of massive money loss.**

It would be impossible to list every type of extreme design that would indicate harm. However here are some of the worst and most common seen in cities, communities, and neighborhoods around the world:

- Triangular-shaped homes
- U-shaped buildings
- L-shaped homes or structures
- Half-circle designs

- Space-ship designs
- Huge missing sectors, especially in the center such as an atrium
- Designs with heavy tops and small 'legs' or foundation
- Designs with irregular angles
- Homes or office buildings with 'leaning' designs
- Offices or homes that look like a jail or garrison
- Extreme metal and glass designs that appear unstable
- Office or homes with knife-like attached objects or designs
- Split or multi-level homes that go in several directions
- Homes or offices that appear they may be falling or the design elements are asymmetrical or disproportional
- Homes shaped like weapons—sword, axe, guns or rifles
- Any design that would make the building appear to be unstable, odd or weird-shaped, sharp or with pointed edges, stepped designs or that has a harsh, repelling appearance

Extreme designs will bring weird diseases, money-loss, hurt the householders/workers' health and bring disharmony to the home and workplace. For example, buildings with excessive, sharp metal designs indicate that the occupants could experience violence with knives or lots of surgery involving 'cutting' the body. It is best not to occupy such buildings or select these types of designs for your living space.

Celebrity homes with this formation: O. J. Simpson (Rockingham), Nicole Brown Simpson (Bundy), Michael Jackson (Neverland Valley Ranch), José & Kitty Menendez (Beverly Hills), Phil Hartman (Encino), Phil Spector (Alhambra), Marilyn Monroe (Brentwood), and Brittany Murphy (Hollywood Hills).

Land Sites/ Lot Shapes
Indicates bankruptcy and spirits haunting the land

Land plots that have odd shapes will usually indicate loss of money, poor health and with triangular corner/s—ghosts or spirits will haunt the land. The best lot shapes and where the energy is distributed evenly is square or rectangular; both are 'golden' in Feng Shui.

Celebrity home with this formation: Phil Spector's castle (Alhambra).

Split-level Homes
Indicates headaches and confusion

This is not the same as a regular two-story or three-story home. No indeed, this is where the home design splits off in several different directions and levels. One of the worst that we've seen was in Salt Lake City, UT where the home had seven (7) different levels splintering off in several directions starting with the main entrance.

Celebrity home with this formation: Brittany Murphy (Hollywood Hills).

Sickle-shaped Driveways
Indicates rare and unusual diseases

This shape is like an extreme arch; regular, circular driveways are not necessarily bad. The arch must be an extreme design like a short U-shape to bring harm to the occupant's health, money and relationships.

Celebrity home with this formation: José & Kitty Menendez (Beverly Hills).

Extremely Narrow-Shaped Homes
Indicates the feeling of being confined or jailed, and loss of money/debt

Extremely narrow homes have what is known as "squeezed chi," which will prevent the accumulation of wealth. Sure, you might be able to earn money, but these types of structures make it difficult to retain. Here's the general rule to determine whether a building has squeezed-chi: the length of the structure is three to four times that of its width. For example, a space that is twenty feet wide and sixty feet long is considered squeezed chi. Townhomes and brownstones are notorious for harboring this design flaw, and people often experience bankruptcy and debt in them. Though not all multifamily dwellings are bad, many do prevent occupants from holding on to their cash.

Celebrity home with this formation: Nicole Brown Simpson (Bundy).

The Three Taboos
Indicates heart attacks, kidney, blood, and bone issues

It is taboo to have water, mountain or fire in the EXACT center of a home. This area is the 'heart of the home' or central palace. These 'forms' will activate extremely bad health. Fire (kitchen, stove or fireplace) will indicate high blood pressure, excessive heartburn and heart attacks. A mountain (staircase) will cause scoliosis, bone and skeleton issues. Water (toilet, atrium, or fountain) will cause blood and kidney issues.

Celebrity homes with this formation: Nicole Brown Simpson (Bundy) Michael Jackson (Neverland Ranch), José & Kitty Menendez (Beverly Hills) and Brittany Murphy (Hollywood Hills).

III. Mountains

How can a mountain affect human events and luck? However, they most certainly can in the most interesting ways—both good and devastating.

Robbery Mountain Sha
Indicates getting hurt by knives, strange diseases and disasters

This negative formation will rob vital energy from a house, though money loss is merely one aspect of the trouble you might encounter. The *Robbery Mountain Sha* technique does not use the door direction or the facing of your home. Rather, it is based on the back of the property, which is referred to as the sitting direction.

For example, if a home sits East (97.6°-112.5°) and there is a negative feature located in the Southwest (262.6°-277.5°), this forms a *Robbery Mountain Sha*. Negative features, such as high-tension electrical towers; a broken mountain (one that has been excavated, scarred, or marred); a quarry; a jagged cliff; lampposts; or a huge dead tree will activate the *Robbery Mountain* position. A jagged or broken

mountain, however, is the most detrimental to the occupants. These attributes emit noxious and poisonous energies. When this unfortunate formation exists, family members could contract a strange disease, get hurt by knives, or encounter all sorts of disasters, including loss of wealth.

Celebrity home with this formation: Nicole Brown Simpson (Bundy).

Eight Killing Mountain Forces
Death, murder, and blood-related accidents

The *Eight Killing Mountain Forces* is a very serious formation. The energy of the mountain and door are in conflict which causes a host of negative events for the householders including loss of life and blood-related accidents. These formations involve specific 15-degree increments for both the door direction and the mountain. If you live in an area of the world without mountains, tall buildings must be considered as well. Here is an example of this formation; a door faces Northeast (52.6°-67.5°) and a real mountain or tall building is located in the Northeast (37.6°-52.5°). There are only eight of these formations possible, one for each direction (N, S, E, W, NW, NE, SE and SW).

Celebrity homes with this formation: Sharon Tate (Cielo), Phil Hartman (Encino) and Brittany Murphy (Hollywood Hills).

IV. Energy Vortexes and Void Lines

Death and Empty Lines or Void Lines
Indicates ghosts, bankruptcy, and discord

Figure 14: DELs are common in homes that sit on the market empty for months at a time.

A long-time secret of Feng Shui masters was that the facing direction of doors and entrances should never lie exactly on the cardinal lines. These are referred to as Kong Wang or Kun Mang; *Death and Empty Lines* (DEL) or Void Lines. Now, 'death' does not mean dying rather that the property is *void of energy* and will bring all sorts of extreme misfortune and loss such as sickness, bankruptcy, and other forms of bad luck.

These degrees may also explain why some buildings don't sell and languish on the market. There are *lesser* DELs where, for example, west changes to Northwest (292.5) or South ends and Southwest begins (202.5). All DELs are inauspicious degrees and will attract ghost and spirits, which are *never* appropriate for homes or businesses. Benevolent spirits belong in churches and holy places. Listed below are the most serious void/empty lines:

Major Void Lines
90° (East), 180° (South), 270° (West), and 360/0° (North)

Emptiness Lines
202.5°, 247.5°, 292.5°, 337.5°, 22.5°, 67.5°, 112.5°, and 157.5°

When this inauspicious scenario is present, measures should be taken to correct them. A temporary solution is to remove the door from its hinges for an hour, and then re-hang it. This will take a door out of the DEL, at least for a while. A more permanent cure is to re-angle the door within its frame; this will require carpenter skills. Metal on or near the door may also help, but give it some time and then take another compass direction in a month or so. Since compass degrees are based on the *magnetic energies* of the earth, metal can reduce this negative affliction.

Celebrity home with this formation: Phil Spector (Alhambra).

Energy Vortexes and Lei Lines
Indicates nervousness, dizziness, alcoholism, and ghosts

Energy vortexes and lei lines have been quite a mystery to humans; in 1921 an Englishmen named Alfred Watkins was the first to notice that ancient sites/ruins such as Stonehenge, were built on straight lines and he began to call them 'ley' or lei lines. He also noted that hilltops, churches, standing stones, castles, and buried mounds seemed to be connected to these lines. His study of Ordnance Survey maps convinced him that these places were built intentionally along straight lines. He wrote about his findings in a book entitled *"The Old Straight Track"*, but ley lines were relegated to psychic phenomena and not taken seriously.

On January 25, 1987, Research Director, Joe Parr, conducted a field survey for Bethe Hagens (Professor of Anthropology) at

Governors State University, Illinois.[2] He was the first to bring scientific verification that these lines exist and can be quantified using scientific equipment. The results of the study were fascinating. They discovered that ley lines could be like a magnets field, but it doesn't work until you cross it! For example, a ley line may never indicate its location unless you cross it fast enough to induce a voltage into a large enough coil. Dr. Hagens herself indicated that some of the 'lines' could be miles across.

When homes are built over vortexes of energy it will lead to nervousness, dizziness, money loss, confusion, instability, alcoholism, drug use, and ghosts will visit. Paired with other negative features such as a *Death and Empty Line*, it would spell disaster.

Celebrity home with this formation: Phil Hartman (Encino).

Figure 15: Even estate homes may have a *Death and Empty Line* degree. Phil Spector's castle in Alhambra is an example of a luxury home with this inauspicious energy. Phil Hartman's home is likely built over a vortex of energy. Either of these scenarios may bring ghosts, money loss, illness, and disastrous events.

[2] See more about the study in **"Comments on Lei Lines"** by Joe Parr, J.D. at http://www.gizapyramid.com/parr/lei-lines.htm

Chapter Four
Popular Systems of Modern Feng Shui: Eight Mansions and Flying Stars

These systems were used extensively when critiquing the celebrities' homes. The Eight Mansions and Flying Stars are the most popular Classical Feng Shui systems for interior spaces.

Eight Mansions Feng Shui

Figure 16: Sharon Tate, an actress and model, was a 2 Life-Gua in the Eight Mansions system.

The Eight Mansions system dates back to the Tang Dynasty. While Eight Mansions is not as complex as Flying Stars, it is amazing. The Eight Mansions system's focus is on the *people* aspect, while Flying Stars' on the *structure*.

When the Eight Mansions formula is applied correctly, it can bring dazzling prospects for love and romance, business opportunities, health, promotions at work, flourishing investments, and money-luck. It can help identify negative energy, which will be apparent when people suffer from disease, poor health, a crippling divorce, bad relationships, accidents, disastrous events, and bankruptcy. In addition, it is the *only* system which has a 'personality type' aspect which is extremely useful for home and working relationships.

Eight Mansions has five (5) aspects: The Life-Gua Number; East and West Groups; 4 Good and 4 Bad Directions; Advanced Eight Mansions; and 8 Personality types.

Classical Feng Shui systems, including Eight Mansions, are all compass-based methods. Which means you'll need to take a compass direction of certain things in your space if you wish to use it. This is why compass-based methods are more powerful than the one-size-fits-all types; they are specific to the person and their unique space. Although Eight Mansions concerns itself with both direction and location, direction is the most important.

Locating Your Life-Gua Number

According to this Feng Shui system, based on your birthday and gender, you will be influenced in positive and negative ways by the eight directions: four will support you and four won't. The lucky directions will augment wealth and money luck, health, good relationships, and stability; the other four can set into motion divorce, bankruptcy, betrayals, lawsuits, cancer, and so forth. The idea is to use and activate your good directions and diminish the negative ones. Before you can begin using this great system, you will need to determine your personal Life-Gua number.

To find your personal Life-Gua number, refer to the Eight Mansions chart; make sure you're in the right column as there is one for males and one for females. There is a specific calculation to arrive at this number, but we have included the quick reference chart for ease. If you were born prior to February 4th in any given year, use the previous year to get your Life Gua number.[3] For example, if you were born January 28, 1970, use the year 1969 to get the year's begin-date in order to find the correct Life Gua number. The 10 celebrities, perpetrators and victims' Life-Gua numbers will appear in the descriptions. See if you or a family member shares the same Life-Gua Number of any of the stars.

Figure 17: Grandmaster Yap Cheng Hai devised the 'code' as a quick reference tool.

1933-1963			
Animal	Year	Male ♂	Female ♀
Rooster	1933	4	2
Dog	1934	3	3
Pig	1935	2	4
Rat	1936	1	8
Ox	1937	9	6
Tiger	1938	8	7
Rabbit	1939	7	8
Dragon	1940	6	9
Snake	1941	2	1
Horse	1942	4	2
Goat	1943	3	3
Monkey	1944	2	4
Rooster	1945	1	8
Dog	1946	9	6
Pig	1947	8	7
Rat	1948	7	8
Ox	1949	6	9
Tiger	1950	2	1
Rabbit	1951	4	2
Dragon	1952	3	3
Snake	1953	2	4
Horse	1954	1	8
Goat	1955	9	6
Monkey	1956	8	7
Rooster	1957	7	8
Dog	1958	6	9
Pig	1959	2	1
Rat	1960	4	2
Ox	1961	3	3
Tiger	1962	2	4
Rabbit	1963	1	8

1964-1994			
Animal	Year	Male ♂	Female ♀
Dragon	1964	9	6
Snake	1965	8	7
Horse	1966	7	8
Goat	1967	6	9
Monkey	1968	2	1
Rooster	1969	4	2
Dog	1970	3	3
Pig	1971	2	4
Rat	1972	1	8
Ox	1973	9	6
Tiger	1974	8	7
Rabbit	1975	7	8
Dragon	1976	6	9
Snake	1977	2	1
Horse	1978	4	2
Goat	1979	3	3
Monkey	1980	2	4
Rooster	1981	1	8
Dog	1982	9	6
Pig	1983	8	7
Rat	1984	7	8
Ox	1985	6	9
Tiger	1986	2	1
Rabbit	1987	4	2
Dragon	1988	3	3
Snake	1989	2	4
Horse	1990	1	8
Goat	1991	9	6
Monkey	1992	8	7
Rooster	1993	7	8
Dog	1994	6	9

1995-2025			
Animal	Year	Male ♂	Female ♀
Pig	1995	2	1
Rat	1996	4	2
Ox	1997	3	3
Tiger	1998	2	4
Rabbit	1999	1	8
Dragon	2000	9	6
Snake	2001	8	7
Horse	2002	7	8
Goat	2003	6	9
Monkey	2004	2	1
Rooster	2005	4	2
Dog	2006	3	3
Pig	2007	2	4
Rat	2008	1	8
Ox	2009	9	6
Tiger	2010	8	7
Rabbit	2011	7	8
Dragon	2012	6	9
Snake	2013	2	1
Horse	2014	4	2
Goat	2015	3	3
Monkey	2016	2	4
Rooster	2017	1	8
Dog	2018	9	6
Pig	2019	8	7
Rat	2020	7	8
Ox	2021	6	9
Tiger	2022	2	1
Rabbit	2023	4	2
Dragon	2024	3	3
Snake	2025	2	4

Figure 18: Locate your Life-Gua Number with this chart. There is a column for males and females.

Life Groups and GMY Codes

Now that you have your personal Life Gua Number, let's examine the chart, it has a good deal of information. First, based on your Life Gua Number, you will be part of the *East Life Group* or the *West Life Group*. Those who are a 1, 3, 4 or 9 Guas are part of the East group, and those who are a 2, 6, 7, or 8 belong to the West group. As opposites attract, it's not unusual for couples to belong to a different group.

---

[3] In Feng Shui, the Chinese solar calendar is used exclusively. Additionally, the New Year usually begins on February 4th. On rare occasions, it starts on the 3rd or 5th.

EAST Grov #4 +90 N
80 S   70 E

Hollywood's Fatal Feng Shui   39

Next, notice the GMY Code column. This is the clever creation of Grandmaster Yap Cheng Hai when referring to the good and bad directions without using the Chinese words associated with them. For example your best direction will be +90 which indicate prosperity or wealth luck. The +80 will help you to secure vital health. The +70 direction is your personal direction to and harmony and so forth. We will use the GMY code from now on throughout the book. Once you have located your personal *Life-Gua Number* on the chart, just follow down that column to see all good and bad directions and a brief description of what they'll indicate if you use them; below are the detailed indications.

Eight Mansions Chart for Life-Gua Numbers

	East Life Group				West Life Group			
	Kan (Water)	Chen (Big Wood)	Xun (Small Wood)	Li (Fire)	Kun (Mother Earth)	Chien (Big Metal)	Dui (Small Metal)	Gen (Lit. Earth)
Good Directions:	1	3	4	9	2	6	7	8
+90 Best for Money (Sheng Chi)	SE	S	N	E	NE	W	NW	SW
+80 Best for Health (Tien Yi)	E	N	S	SE	W	NE	SW	NW
+70 Relationships (Yen Nen)	S	SE	E	N	NW	SW	NE	W
+60 Stability (Fu Wei)	N	E	SE	S	SW	NW	W	NE
Bad Directions:								
-60 Nothing Goes Smooth (Wu Hai)	W	SW	NW	NE	E	SE	N	S
-70 Lawsuits & Bad Romance (Wu Gwei)	NE	NW	SW	W	SE	E	S	N
-80 Bad Health/Betrayals (Liu Sha)	NW	NE	W	SW	S	N	SE	E
-90 Divorce & Failures (Chueh Ming)	SW	W	NE	NW	N	S	E	SE

Figure 19: This chart shows your good and bad directions and what Life Group you belong to. East Life-Guas are 1, 3, 4 and 9. The West-Life Guas are 2, 6, 7, and 8.

The Life-Gua Number is highly significant, not only can you derive the directions that support you but give you important clues about your personality and key relationships. It's also used to determine the capability of spouses, the relationship between parents and children, the dynamic between siblings, work mates and business partners. The following are the Eight Mansions descriptions. They include Grandmaster Yap's code along with a one or two word summary of what they indicate if you activate or use these directions.

Your Four GOOD Directions:

+90 MONEY! Sheng Chi: Life-giving chi, growing chi and generating breath. Great wealth, great success and millionaire chi. This is the best direction to use for money-luck; also good for timing and opportunities. The Sheng Chi direction is good for the managing director, promotion, wealth, health, and children. Use this direction to set up a high position of power/politics. For wealth-luck set doors, stove knobs, bed direction, and face this direction! Activating this direction with the stove or bed may produce fives sons or lots of children who are very successful and good. *Stove:* If you suppress your Sheng Chi with the stove placement, the women in the household cannot conceive. If you do succeed in having children they will be foolish, and there will be no money. If the firemouth (stove knobs, button or controls) or the bed is to this direction, it will bring great success and harmony!

+80 HEALTH! Tien Yi: Good for wealth and health; the *Heavenly Doctor* protects you. Using this direction brings good friends, the power of speech, social standing and a long life. By activating this direction, a VIP and the government support you. For health-luck set doors, stove knobs, bed direction, and face this direction! You will have gentle and good children, expect three sons when this direction is activated. *Stove:* If you suppress this direction with a stove, you will encounter sickness, disease and there will be no harmony in the household. If the firemouth (stove knobs, buttons or controls) activates this direction, it will bring riches very quickly, a high position of authority and less illness.

+70 RELATIONSHIPS! Yen Nien: The *Yen Nien* direction supports relationships, longevity, health, family, harmonious families, love, romance, and networking. While this direction may indicate a slightly lower income than the +90 or +80, you will have wealthy descendants, conceive children quickly, or children who become specialized, rich and famous; four sons are possible. Place children or young adults in the father's Yen Nien for harmony. Using this direction indicates a very successful, middle class life. This direction may indicate a life less than 70 years, or if exceeding 70 years, the death is celebrated with a party. *Stove:* If you suppress this direction there will be quarrels and a short

life. If the firemouth (stove knobs, button or controls) or bed face this direction it indicates lots of harmony, being upper middle class, almost a millionaire, having powerful connections, good relationships, and love.

+60 STABILITY! Fu Wei: Using the *Fu Wei* direction brings stability and peace that can mirror your own energy, moderate happiness/wealth, a middle class family-life,

and can protect you from bad luck. Use this direction for adult children living at home so that they may 'move on'. You'll have less children, perhaps only one daughter and one son. For stability-luck set doors, stove knobs, bed direction, and face this direction. *Stove:* If you suppress this direction a short life is indicated. If the firemouth (stove knobs, buttons or controls) or bed face this direction brings less sons, living under 70 years, but a good middle class life.

Your Four BAD Directions:

-90 BANKRUPTCY! Chueh Ming: By activating the *Chueh Ming* direction, you will attract the worst things to you! It indicates bankruptcy, divorce, extremely bad health, fatality, business failures, loss of wealth, no harmony, family break-ups, accidents, and no descendants. Using this direction can bring the worst events ever, including death in the family. This is a good location for a toilet or stove. Marriages that are of the –90, the second wife can have two sons. *Stove:* Burning up this area with a stove will bring a long life, lots of money and kids.

-80 BAD HEALTH & BETRAYALS! Lui Sha: The *Six Killings* brings back-stabbing, thievery, injury, loss of wealth, ill health, bad money-luck, accidents, the wife leaves the family, lawsuits by the government, gossip, lingering/ongoing problems, legal issues, couples divorce or separate, no children, bad romance, grievous harm to the family, self-inducing disabilities, being unrecognized in the world, unfortunate accidents (even death), and betrayals. This location is good for a stove or toilet. Old age can be ok or pleasant. *Stove:* Burning up this area with a stove can bring money, children, no lawsuits, and no disasters or sickness.

-70 LAWSUITS & BAD ROMANCE! Wu Gwei: The *Five Ghosts* direction will activate lawsuits, bad romance, difficulty in conceiving, disobedient/rebellious children, fighting, gambling, drug use, petty people, robbery, bad health, fire hazards, career failures, betrayals, bad tempers, annoyances, undermining, no employee support, gossip, hot arguments, no harmony or peace. This is a good location for a stove or toilet. The son is not supporting the family. *Stove:* No fires, no sickness, no money problems, good employers and support.

Figure 20: The stove placement can 'burn up' your bad luck. A stove is the most important fire in the house.

-60 SETBACKS! Wo Hai: Activating this direction will indicate that *nothing* goes smooth, things turns out badly, irritating events, obstructions, accidents, afflictions, loss of investments, constant set-backs, and mild disasters. You can win a court case but lose money or lose the court case altogether if you use this direction for doors, beds, stove knobs or by facing it. *Stove:* Suppress or 'burn' this sector with a stove and there will be very little sickness in the household.

Advanced Eight Mansions for Fine-Tuning for Opposite Life Groups

What happens if partners belong to different Life Groups? Actually, this happens all the time; opposites attract. However, there is a solution. The Eight Mansions system has two levels; basic Eight Mansions and *Advanced Eight Mansions* (AEM). Here you're allowed to use certain 15-degree increments. This is really important in the 'shared space' (the bed). For more information on how to apply the Eight Mansions system, refer to the book *Feng Shui That Rocks the House* on page 202.

The Eight Life Gua Personalities

Now let's explore another aspect of Eight Mansions, the *Life-Gua Personalities*. Since you know your personal Life-Gua number, you now have information on which directions support you and those that can bring trouble. Also, based on your Life Gua, you're assigned certain personality traits, energy, and characteristics. Do keep in mind that they are general and not meant to be definitive. The personality narratives work very similar to astrology; each Life Gua will have an element (water, wood, fire, earth or metal) and this energy will influence the person's behavior, habits, physical looks, health issues, attraction to specific occupations, thinking process, and sexual desires, both negative and positive in all these areas.

1 Life-Gua Personalities
Secretive • Emotional • Scholarly

Famous 1 Guas: Steve Martin, **Nicole Brown Simpson**, Tom Selleck, **Brittany Murph**y, Emma Thompson, **Kitty Menendez,** James Cameron, Ron Howard, Lucy Lui, Jerry Seinfeld, Jet

Li, Ashley Judd, Kevin Costner, Mike Meyers, Jeff Bezos, Faye Dunaway, Li Ka-shing, Hugh Bonneville, Brittany Murphy, Greg Kinear, Amanda Bynes, Quentin Tarantino, Mischa Barton, Justin Timberlake, Jackie Chan, Billy Baldwin, David Lee Roth, Lee Shau Kee, Michael Bolton, Amanico Ortega, Ben Affleck, Catherine Bell, Goran Visnjic, Liv Tyler, Yanni, Nora Ephron, Dennis Quaid, Lady Gaga, and Rosanna Arquette.

Personality: The 1 Gua's are highly intellectual and can be studious or even scholarly. To the outside world, they appear calm and cool, however inside they have a rich emotional makeup. As a result, at times they can be overly emotional, moody, anxious and high strung. They are full of brilliant ideas and concepts, and are usually very good at making and holding onto money. The 1 Gua's are skilled at sizing up people using their natural, intuitive abilities. Since their element is water, they can be hard to pin down. They are sensual and can be highly sexual. Tending to keep secrets below the surface, 1 Guas are known to have secret and arcane lives.

2 Life-Gua Personalities
Calm • Reclusive • Dependable

Famous 2 Guas: Nick Nolte, **Sharon Tate**, Beau Bridges, **José Menendez**, Madeline Kahn, Ryan O'Neal, Sandra Dee, Stacy Keach, Wesley Snipe, Anjelicia Huston, Lakshmi Mittal, Peter Coyote, Julianne Moore, Wolfgang Peterson, Daryl Hannah, Tom Conti, Bob Dylan, Ashley Greene, Jon Stewart, Paul Simon, Bill Murray, Hilary Duff, William Hurt, David Berkowitz, Gemma Ward, Robbie Cultrane, Katie Holmes, Stephen Cannell, and Katherine Heigl.

Personality: The 2 Gua's exhibit persistence, dependability, and a calm demeanour. They can also be nurturing and supportive to their inner circle. With their calm, relaxed demeanors, 2 Guas are dependable and tend to have developed psychic abilities. They make excellent doctors or practitioners of alternate healing arts such as chiropractry, massage therapy, and acupuncture. Since the 2 Guas have the most yin energy of the Guas, they enjoy and feel comfortable in dark spaces, but have a tendency to depression or dark moodiness. Good spelunkers, these grounded people relish activities that focus on the earth—gardening, farming, construction, and agriculture.

3 Life-Gua Personalities
Enterprising • Impatient • Self-Confident

Famous 3 Guas: **Charles Manson**, Robert De Niro, **Erik Menendez**, Sharon Gless, Christopher Walken, Lynn Redgrave, Chevy Chase, Penny Marshall, Keith Richards, Isabella Rossellini, Mick Jagger, Annie Potts, Liam Neeson, Meg Ryan, Patrick Swayze, Virginia Madsen, Michael J. Fox, Bonnie Hunt, Laurence Fishburne, Heather Locklear, Eddie Murphy, Rachel Weisz, Matt Damon, Uma Thurman, Rupert Grint, Minnie Driver, Chris O'Donnell, Tina Fey, Ralph Macchio, and Rihanna.

Personality: Three Guas are extremely enterprising and have progressive ideas. They tend to be outspoken, direct, and organized. The 3 Gua's nature is one of nervousness punctuated by lots of energy and steam. Constantly crafting new inventions, new ventures or the latest thing, they love new beginnings and 'start ups'. When in a negative energy, the 3 Guas tend to self-punish, spread their energy too thin leading to collapse, and can be abrasive. However, they are full of surprises; 3 Guas have a sense of vitality and vigor that can overwhelm people.

4 Life-Gua Personalities
Gentle • Malleable • Progressive

Famous 4 Guas: Harrison Ford, Jacqueline Bisset, **Marilyn Monroe**, Kim Basinger, Paul McCartney, Demi Moore, John Wayne Gacy, Robin Williams, Kelly Preston, Geoffrey Rush, Michelle Yeoh, Steven Segal, Felicity Huffman, Tony Danza, Zooey Deschanel, Harry Hamlin, Jordana Brewster, **Lana Clarkson**, Christina Ricci, Colin Firth, Michael Bloomberg, Queen Elizabeth II, Stanley Tucci, Sheldon Adelson, Christina Aguilera, Ice Cube, Matthew McConaughey, Ashton Kutcher and Marcia Cross.

Personality: Malleable, flexible, indecisive, the 4 Gua's may 'blow with the wind' if not grounded, finding it hard to take a stand. In general, they usually are attractive people or may have movie-star qualities. The 4 Gua's are more prone to be sexually controlled by their partners than other Guas. They have progressive ideas and can become famous in writing or rich in the publishing business. The un-evolved 4's may self-destruct by refusing good advice. The 4 Gua's can be somewhat remote and private, but they are also gentle people with an innocent purity.

6 Life-Gua Personalities
Leaders • Solitary • Creative

Famous 6 Guas: Lyle Menendez, Cher, Martin Sheen, **Michael Jackson**, Sally Field, Liza Minnelli, Chuck Norris, Candice Bergen, Richard Pryor, Dolly Parton, Brian De Palma, Suzanne Sommers, John Lennon, Susan Lucci, Ringo Star, Whoopi Goldberg, Jeff Bridges, Richard Gere, Marisa Tomei, John Belushi, Courtney Cox, Julian Fellowes, Gene Simmons, Christy Walton, Laura Liney, Kevin Bacon, Teri Hatcher, Viggo Mortensen, Prince, Melissa Gilbert, Paul Giamatti, Bridgette Wilson, Jason Statham, Anne Hathaway, Ice-T, and Kristen Dunst.

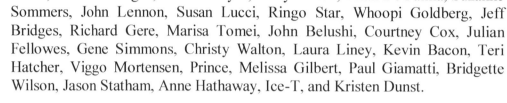

Personality: The 6 Guas can easily step into positions of power and authority as they are natural leaders that seem to be blessed by the heavens. They make excellent lawyers, judges, and CEO's as their energy commands respect. The 6 Gua's have a regal, royal air that is naturally unpretentious. Clear thinkers, lots of courage, possessing foresight, extremely creative, and they can hold their own in a debate. They need time alone as they often get caught up in over-thinking, which can lead to being sleep-deprived. Oozing with creativity, the 6 Guas are filled with ideas that involve large groups of people, a community or an organization.

7 Life-Gua Personalities
Charming • Excessive • Talkative

Famous 7 Guas: Natalie Wood, Frances Ford Coppola, **Phil Hartman**, John Clesse, Mark Zuckerberg, Glenn Close, Kim Cattrall, Mike Tyson, Carrie Fisher, Linda Hamilton, **Phil Spector,** Samuel L. Jackson, Joan Allen, Bo Derek, Billy Crystal, Kyra Sedwick, Phil Hartman, Elizabeth Hurley, Kristin Davis, Ray Romano, Brooke Shields, Bernie Mac, Eva Mendes, Adam Sadler, Cameron Crowe, Kiefer Sutherland, Connie Nielsen, Emily Blunt and Jenna Jameson.

Personality: 7 Guas tend to be youthful in behavior or appearance. They are very attracted to metaphysical studies and arts; they can be talkative, lively, and nervous. The 7 female Guas are often blessed with very good looks, and sensuous beauty. Comfortable with a lot of 'stage', the 7 Gua's are good at acting, speaking, in front of the camera or on the radio. With a strong tendency to over indulge in the pleasures of life such as food, drink, money, and sex, they must keep a balanced life. They can be a fast-talker, smooth talker, or have a razor-sharp tongue. The 7 Guas are very social, charming, and charismatic; they create stimulating, informative conversation wherever they go.

8 Life-Gua Personalities
Successful • Hoarders • Dependable

Famous 8 Guas: Jon Voight, Princess Kate Middleton, **O.J. Simpson**, Ali McGraw, Elliot Gould, Lily Tomlin, Michael Dell, Tina Turner, Kevin Kline, Goldie Hawn, James Woods, Mia

Farrow, Richard Dreyfuss, Pricilla Presley, Jaclyn Smith, Ted Danson, Deborah Harry, Stephen King, Olivia Newton-John, David Bowie, Lisa Kudrow, Paris Hilton, Vanessa Williams, Cameron Diaz, Dwight Yoakam, Halle Berry, Charlie Sheen, Julia Stiles, Cynthia Nixon, Chris Rock, Jenny McCarthy, Ryan Philippe, Drew Barrymore, Robert Downey Jr., Britney Spears, Kevin James, and Gwyneth Paltrow.

Personality: The 8 Guas have a stubborn, dependable, and steadfast nature. They tend to have a great deal of integrity and are vey attracted to all things spiritual. They can become spiritual seekers, and trek the mountains in search of 'answers' and to find themselves. Hardworking and loving things of the earth, the 8's are talented in construction, real estate, and landscaping. They also have a little of 'save the world' energy. While the 8 Guas tend to resist change, they can deftly handle trouble without falling apart. Un-evolved 8 Guas can become hoarders, self-righteous, and short-tempered. They are geared for success and often become very rich with worldly honors, recognition, and status.

9 Life-Gua Personalities
Adventurous • Rash • Brilliance

Famous 9 Guas: Anthony Hopkins, **Anna Nicole Smith**, Jack Nicholson, Meryl Streep, Warren Beatty, Sigourney Weaver, Steven Spielberg, Sissy Spacek, Alan Rickman, **Brynn Hartman**, Sharon Stone, Annette Bening, Tommy Lee Jones, Michelle Pfeiffer, John Woo, Bruce Willis, Madonna, Kelsey Krammer, Holly Hunter, Russell Crowe, Nicole Kidman, Andi MacDowell, Steve Jobs, Clive Owen, Laura Dern, Rob Lowe, Mira Sorvino, Pamela Anderson, Reese Witherspoon, Yun-Fat Chow, Keri Russell, Carey Mulligan, Lenny Kravitz, Faith Hill, Oliver Stone, Keira Knightley, Danny Glover, Brian Cox, and Bill Gates.

Personality: 9 Guas have a sharp, brilliant intellect; they can also be wise, loyal, and sentimental. Blessed with a fiery spirit and energy, these Guas have a decided adventurous streak. The female 9's are usually beautiful like a diva or goddess but can be argumentative, aggressive, and rash. With concentrated and focused effort, they can reach great height of achievements and standing in the world. The truly un-evolved 9 Guas will exhibit mental illness such as paranoia, or psychotic and unstable behavior. When grounded and evolved, the 9's can light up a room with their radiance.

Flying Stars Feng Shui

When Flying Stars was first introduced to the English-speaking world, most thought it was too mathematical and technical. However, with the passage of time Feng Shui enthusiast are now far less intimidated by the system and there is much more information available. In times past, it was not always clear as how to apply it and was presented as complicated. Nowadays, Flying Stars has garnered international interest and people are avidly looking for information on the potent formulas of *Xuan Kong Fei Xing* (Flying Stars).

While there are an impressive number of Feng Shui formulas and techniques, Flying Stars is, in fact, the most mathematical method as it deals with numbers and the computation of numbers. As a result, many compare it to numerology or astrology, while it is neither, it does have similarities. Flying Stars explains why no structure would forever enjoy good or bad Feng Shui which is why it is sometimes referred to as Time Dimension Feng Shui. The *time* aspect of Flying Stars can work in tandem with or be in conflict with the space design; everyone's Feng Shui needs regular updates.

The Chinese use two calendars, the solar *(based on the cycles of the Sun)* and lunar *(based on the cycles of the Moon)*; because the solar calendar is more accurate, this is exclusively used in Feng Shui because so much depends on accurate timing. Additionally, the New Year usually (99.9% of the time) begins on February 4th. On rare occasions, it starts on the 3rd or 5th.

This is a very interesting time in Flying Stars. It hit a major milestone in energy, worldwide, on February 4, 2004. Another capital change will occur on February 4, 2024. These milestones have a tremendous impact on the luck transformations of all homes and buildings and will affect them for twenty-year time periods. Many things will happen on the world stage during these times; the idea is to use Flying Stars to safeguard the energy of your homes and workplaces to not just survive, but thrive.

Figure 21: This home is missing the Tiger-side and may indicate an aggressive female in the house. This would also depend on which Flying Stars are in that sector.

Natal Star Charts

Contingent upon the specific compass direction that a structure faces, it will have a unique natal *Flying Star Chart;* this is like an astrological chart as it identifies strong and weak aspects.

Except in this case, it identifies the building's potential and energy map. Once you have identified or flown a Natal Star chart, you will know how to correctly activate the different sectors with auspicious energy.

In general, the practice of Feng Shui lies in how skillfully one analyzes, corrects and enhances the energies as they evolve through time; remember the *nature* of energy is change. In essence, Flying Stars is used to evaluate the invisible life forces that influence the environment/structures and the impact it may have on those who live or work there. While there have been several books on Flying Stars in recent years, most Americans have barely heard of it being more familiar with the Westernized styles of Feng Shui such as the Black Hat style. In addition, current books might leave readers a bit confused about this extraordinary and multi-layered system. While it is an advanced, compass-based method, it is not impossible even for a novice, to capture its essence and implement its precise techniques with a little effort.

You will see the *Flying Star Charts* for each of the celebrity properties in Chapters Five through Fifteen. This gives rich detail as to what went on in their lives, and in many cases how it fell apart. Even though we are examining the homes of our 10 celebrities, you may want to use the information in this chapter to find your home's *Flying Star Chart*. They are provided in Appendix IV.

What are the "Stars"?

The 'stars' are not actual stars in the constellation; rather they are simply the numbers 1 through 9 with energy being expressed in a numerical form. Their purpose is to evaluate the quality of energy in a *building*. This is quite different from other systems that focus more on the *people* aspect such as *Eight Mansions*.

Each "star" has unique qualities and energy that can influence behavior and events. For example some stars indicate wealth, sickness, romance, scholarly pursuits, writing, fame, divorce, and so forth. While the 'stars' are not actual planets located in the sky, the nine stars do however, have an earthly correlation to the seven, real stars of the Big Dipper *(aka the Northern Ladle)* with two imaginary ones. Like many ancient cultures, the Chinese were 'sky watchers' and had an extremely developed sense of *time* based on the movement of the planets.

Time Cycles of Flying Stars Feng Shui

Cycle	Period	Years	Trigram
Upper	1	1864-1884	Kan
	2	1884-1904	Kun
	3	1904-1924	Chen
Middle	4	1924-1944	Xun/Sun
	5	1944-1964	
	6	1964-1984	Qian/Chien
Lower	7	1984-2004	Dui/Tui
	8	2004-2024	Gen/Ken
	9	2024-2044	Li

As we discussed earlier, Flying Stars has a time dimension aspect. And it has several key areas regarding the cycles of time and understanding them brings it forward to modern-day Feng Shui. The Flying Star system is based on huge time cycles and planetary alignments. Basically, there are three important blocks of time in Flying Stars 1) the **180 Great Cycle**; 2) **Three 60-year cycles**; and finally 3) there are **nine 20-year increments** known as 'Periods". The last is where we will really focus on in the book, although all are important in the system.

Regarding the Great Cycle aka Mega Cycle, according to the ancient Chinese scholars, the planets in our Solar System aligns in a straight line once every 179/180 years. It is believed that the first observation of this phenomenon was around 2500 BC. The Chinese next divided this 180 year cycle into three (3) sixty-year cycles (called Upper, Middle and Lower).

The sixty year cycles were once more divided into 20-year increments which they called Periods or Ages. Each Period is assigned a number (1-9) and a trigram (except the 5, it has no trigram) that has a unique energy that it exhibits for 20 years that affects the world. Why 20-year Periods? It is interesting that they also noted that the Milky Way shifted every 20 years thus affecting the luck of a building/home and human beings. See the chart giving an example of the nine (9) 20-year Periods comprising the 180-year Great/Mega cycle of time that covers the years of 1864 to 2043.

As you can see we are currently in the Lower Cycle (which is nearing completion) and in Period 8. The next Period will start February 4th 2024; this begins Period 9. The ruling energy or influence is always the number and associated trigram of the Period. For example, in *Period 8*, the 8 Star is king; Period 8 began February 4, 2004 and will end February 3, 2024.

Locating the Right Star Chart

If you wish to locate a home's unique *Flying Star Chart* you will need the following information. There are two important factors that must be determined, 1) **the move-in date** and 2) the **house facing**. The *house facing* is how the structure receives energy from a specific direction. And the move-in date will tell us which *Period* the structure belongs to; this is where those time cycles come into consideration.

Move-In Date

The move-in date is used to determine the Period of a building. However, not all masters agree with this. Nevertheless, since we are in the lineage of Grandmaster Yap Cheng Hai, we use the move-in date as he taught and stressed. Regarding the construction date, is it reasonable to think that a home or building could have the exact same energy after 20, 30 years or more after being built? This rule seems counterintuitive to the whole idea of Flying Stars which rightly suggests that energy does not remain stagnate, it changes! The main thing that changes energy is humans moving in and out of spaces/buildings.

According to Master Yap discussions on the subject between the Asian masters are heated debates. Essentially, masters in Hong Kong prefer the construction date, while those in Malaysia, Singapore and Taiwan use the move-in date. At the end of the day, since we are in the lineage of Grandmaster Yap, we use move-in date; I find it extremely reliable and accurate in my 20+ years of practice.

Use the following information to determine what Period your home belongs to:

Your home is a **Period 7**, if you moved in between **February 4th, 1984** to **February 3rd, 2004**.
Your home is a **Period 8** if you moved in between **February 4th, 2004** to **February 3rd, 2024.**

Exceptions for Period 7 homes are if major renovations took place *after* February 4th, 2004.

What constitutes a major renovation? Removing the entire roof (*and some small percentage must be exposed to the open sky at least for a few hours),* major interior remodeling, renovating the front entrance and door, painting the entire inside and outside at the same time, remodeling kitchen or bathrooms, installing a skylight/s, changing all the floors at the same time, adding on a room or adding an attached garage. All of these things will cause a major shift in energy, and therefore your Flying Star Chart will change. So if you did any of these things or a combination of them (*after* February 4th, 2004) and you moved in Period 7, your home will now be a Period 8 chart. If you moved into your house *after* 2004, and have done or are currently doing some renovations, your home is **still** a Period 8.

How to Determine the Facing

You will need a fairly accurate compass to get the correct degree that your home faces. Or you can use your Smart/Android cell phone with a compass app. A good hiking compass also works very well as it has an actual magnet, where phones do not.

Let's see the basic rules to determine these two important factors in order to locate the correct chart. Take your compass measurement/degree from the front door if it *faces* to the road. More than 80% of homes will have the door facing the road, and be located in the center of the house. In these homes taking your compass direction will be fairly straight forward. If the door *does not* face the road, then stand in the middle of your front yard/garden to determine the facing degree. Any side doors or angled doors (*even if they seem to face the road)* cannot be used to measure from to determine the facing in *this system.*

The general rule for determining the facing is where the most yang energy (activate and vibrant) is; the truth is almost nothing competes with the energy of a street. For those who live in apartment buildings or condo complex, use the main door/entrance as the facing direction. See Appendix I on *How to Take a Compass Direction.*

Figure 22: A regular hiking compass may be used to get the facing degree or use your smart phone app.

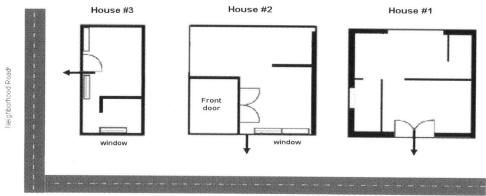

Determine the Facing Examples: House #1 is how most homes are built, take the compass direction at the door to determine the facing. In house #2, the front door cannot be used to determine the facing, even if this were angled and appeared to face the road. While this door's facing star will be extremely important to the occupants luck, it cannot be used to fly or locate the Star Chart. For house #3, use the door to determine the facing, not the window.

The 24 Mountains

In Classical Feng Shui and in Flying Stars, the 360 degrees of the compass is divided into 24 sections/directions (each comprised of 15 degrees). This famous division is referred to as the *24 Mountains.* According to this understanding, all abodes, buildings/homes can only face one of these 24 directions. The 24 Mountains are not literal mountains, just a term. These 24, 15-degree increments are also referred to as subsectors of a main direction. For example, terms such as South 1, South 2 and South 3 indicate the entire 45 degrees of South, but for Feng Shui purposes, are divided neatly into three subsectors.

The Sub-sectors

Once you have the exact compass degree, you can easily find the right sub-sector on the 24 Mountains Chart. For example, you have measured the facing direction of your property and get a compass reading of 123 degrees. You can see that by referring to the *24 Mountain Chart*, that the structure faces Southeast 1. Or your compass reading may be 110 degrees; according to the chart, this is East 3. Remember this information is needed whether you're simply *locating* the correct Natal Star Chart or if you wish to *fly* a Star Chart.

The 24 Mountains Chart: this chart indicates the general **direction** (North, South, East, etc.) and the **sub-sector** with the exact degree range (S1, E2, NW1, etc.). Once you have determined the facing degree, refer to this chart.

The 24 Mountain Chart		
General Direction	**Exact Direction**	**Compass Degrees**
SOUTH	S1	157.6-172.5
	S2	172.6-187.5
	S3	187.6—202.5
SOUTHWEST	SW1	202.6—217.5
	SW2	217.6—232.5
	SW3	232.6—247.5
WEST	W1	247.6—262.5
	W2	262.6—277.5
	W3	277.6—292.5
NORTHWEST	NW1	292.6—307.5
	NW2	307.6—322.5
	NW3	322.6—337.5
NORTH	N1	337.6—352.5
	N2	352.6—7.5
	N3	7.6—22.5
NORTHEAST	NE1	22.6—37.5
	NE2	37.6—52.5
	NE3	52.6—67.5
EAST	E1	67.6—82.5
	E2	82.6—97.5
	E3	97.6—112.5
SOUTHEAST	SE1	112.6—127.5
	SE2	127.6—142.5
	SE3	142.6—157.5

Components of a Flying Star Chart

So what does a Flying Star chart look like? A Natal Flying Star Chart is not as complex looking as say, an astrological chart. Remember, the Flying Star Chart of a property is simply an **energy map** of a building and its potential for auspicious or negative events.

Feng Shui masters use the *Flying Star Chart* to make accurate predictions on relationships, romance potential, success in a career, wealth prospects, when a promotion or marriage may take place, lawsuits—anything that may happen in the human experience. A Flying Star Chart is made up of three numbers in a nine-square grid (mimicking the Luo Shu). The chart shown here is a Period 7 house facing South (the arrow indicates the facing direction).

- **Facing Star** *(Shui Xing)*. Also known as *water stars*, these numbers are located in the upper right-hand corner in all nine palaces of the chart.

- **Mountain Star** *(Shan Xing)*. Also known as *sitting stars*, these numbers are located in the upper left-hand corner in all nine palaces of the chart.

- **Time Star** *(Ling Xing)*. Also known as the *base star*, this number indicates the period to which the chart belongs. It is the single star below the facing and mountain stars.

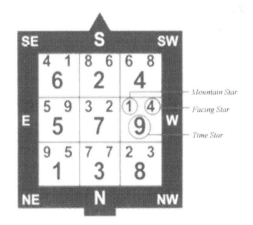

Some common terminology about the nine-celled grid is that each 'box' is referred to as a **palace, sector** or **direction**; all are correct and interchangeable. Using the *Flying Star Chart* on the previous page, we might say "notice that the North *sector* has a 7 mountain and a 7 facing star" or "the North *direction* has double 7's". To keep things simple and consistent throughout the book, we will use the terms *facing star* and *mountain star*; for purposes of activating a chart, the facing and mountain stars have the most weight and significance.

Facing Stars *(aka Water Star)*

Always located in the upper right-hand corner in each cell of a natal *Flying Star Chart*, these stars affect money, financial status, growth, business prospects, and career-luck. They symbolize wealth potential and prosperity prospects. Due to the fact that it can indicate riches, having an auspicious *facing star* in important areas (front door, desk-facing, or real water) is said to bring enormous wealth-luck. Good stars indicate wealth luck, while bad stars denote money loss.

Mountain Stars *(aka Sitting Star)*

Always located in the upper left-hand corner in each cell of a natal *Flying Star Chart*, these stars will affect health-luck, romance, people, relationships, family, authority, mental attitudes, career, fertility, and employees. It also symbolizes social status or standing in the community and the family's popularity.

Time Stars *(aka Base Star)*

The time stars are the single star located directly below the facing and mountain stars in each cell of a natal *Flying Star Chart*, they are not activated individually as the mountain and facing stars can be. Time stars are the least potent of all three stars. However, they have significance in the 'special' charts such as the Pearl and Parent Strings and the Combination of Ten charts.

Good and Bad Stars

In order to fully understand the soul of Flying Stars, you must know the meaning each star and what it portends. In this system, the good stars are the 1, 6, 8, and 9 whether they are facing or mountain stars. The 4 Star represents romance/sexual energy, travel, writing/publishing/scholarly pursuits, and fame and supports those who have a public persona. Please note that the 2, 3, 5, and 7 are very bad stars that can deliver sickness, lawsuits, bankruptcy/cancer, and robbery respectively.

Figure 23: Water features will magnify the *facing star* of its location. It will activate and enhance good facing stars. It will also stimulate bad facing stars such as a 5 or 2 if located there. Water is a very powerful activator of chi and must be placed properly according to the *Flying Star Chart.*

The 5 Star is the worst star and is considered evil and the harbinger of all types of disasters. The bad stars are only good in their period; otherwise, they are considered inauspicious. In other words, the 5 Star is only advantageous in Period 5; remember 'Periods' are those 20-year increments. Same goes for the 2, 3, and 7 stars. When a Flying Star chart is analyzed, there are several important factors—the *nature* of the star (good or bad), your immediate, external environment and the interior layout of your living space.

If the external formations (mountains, water, roads and so forth) support the energy of the chart, you will get a positive result. An auspicious formation can bring good fortune, while landforms that do not support the chart can attract misfortune. The chart can only come *alive* and bestow benevolent energy when the interior environment and external landforms support it.

The Ending of Period 7
(February 4, 1984 to February 3, 2004)

Period 7 homes instantly lost much of its vitality as soon as we entered the new Period of 8. In fact, all structures including office buildings, shopping centers, malls, and so forth, also suffered the energy waning and losing its former prestige. Our celebrity homes span from Period 5 to Period 8, most were Period 7. We left Period 7 on February 3, 2004; this marked a capital change in energy and masters believe it is always worth the effort to bring the property to the current Period.

The Nine Stars

Stars exert great influence, both good and bad, on human behavior—they represent energy and potential events/behaviors. Each of the nine stars of the *Flying Star* system has a positive and negative aspect as well.

The *Nine Stars* of Flying Star Feng Shui

Star	Fortunate Indications	Unfortunate Aspect
1 Money	Research/thinking, knowledge, intelligence, examination, scholar, good government positions, promotion and studies, distinction and abundance. It can turn you into a super star. Very smart boys, good philosopher, honest/fair, and healthy.	The wife dies early, wandering, divorce, detachment, and disconnection from people and things. Moving away, the wife can get blind, change residency, the robber, sex maniac, the thief, smuggling, stubborn and foolish; aggressive with no goals in life.
2 Sickness	Wellness and well-being, success at work, money and riches; lots of sons, military officers, women in authority, vibrant health, effectiveness, fertility and productiveness. Affluence and wealth. A calm person, wealth and children, the army general, and warm-hearted people.	Difficulty in child birth, dying young, bad illness, sickness in the stomach, and abdominal problems; abortion, miscarriages, easily affected by disease and sickness; the miser, very cheap, pessimistic people, cowardly and a scum bag.
3 Lawsuits	Power of speech, a linguistic, bright future, good reputation, good scholar, and success to the first business. Food stores and other accumulations of wealth are full. The eldest son of the family becomes the most successful and prosperous person. An excellent businessman.	Insane, asthma, hurting the wife, lawsuits, gossip, and slander. Prosecution, trails by law, legal problems, and arguments. Breathing problems and theft. The wife will get hurt, always sick, lots of gossip, lawsuits by the government, ruthless, childish people, no common sense, never completes a project, and boasts and brags.
4 Romance	Knowledge and passion/romance, and wisdom. Harmony and success in exams. Honest and good authority. Beautiful children. High Officials. Great wealth.	Suicide by hanging, madness, children display bad sexual conduct. Scandals/extra martial affairs and adultery. The family breaks up.
5 Bankruptcy	Accomplishments, prosperity, high authority and power. Good family. Honest and sincere. Good girls in the family. Superb in its Period, can be as powerful as a king and can run a Country. Very noble, women in the family are highly respected, special people, superman-like, extraordinary people, facial features are unusual, mysterious, virtuous, and lots of power.	Lawsuits by the government. Five people in the house can die. Disasters, calamity, catastrophe, lawsuits, setbacks, disease, death, grave misfortune. One parent hurts the son, five males can die in the house, rebellious, an extremist, the butcher, and eccentric, and lots of lawsuits.
6 Authority	Authority, power, government, nobility distinction, respect, fame and honors. Activity, fame and success; good money decisions, and a world-famous son. A leader, good senior officer, family produces good army-oriented children, world famous, wealth, children, beautiful in appearance, a natural deal-maker, the diplomatic and good politician.	Hurts the wife and sons, very poor and very mean. Solitary, lonely, self-centered, robberies. The father can hurt the wife and kill the sons, then he is lonely and poor. Bad complexion with pot-holes, harsh voice, cannot bear children, bachelor and poverty.
7 Robbery	Spirituality, metaphysics, good authority and control. Lots of money and many sons. Famous actors, military officers, wealth and mysticism, and productivity. Excellent at martial arts, good actor, lots of children and money, tall in stature, food socialists, revolutionist, famous author and very dignified facial features.	Robbery, theft, government lawsuits, jailed, indictment, and fires. Becomes the thief and robber and then is jailed as a result. Lots of government lawsuits, could die a loner in solitude. Very flirtatious, sexy appearance, very witty, sweet-talker but deadly, and could become psychotic or a prostitute.
8 Wealth	Riches, wealth and finance. Good reserves, investments are excellent if the person is in their Sheng Chi (+90). Gentle person. Loyal. Cultivation. The gentleman or the hermit. Very loyal to friends, country, and has much honor. The youngest son will be the most successful, steady people, patriotic, honest, very firm, very kind, very thrifty, good lawyers, high morals and virtue, and the young child could become famous and rich.	The youngest son dies at very early age. Bad diseases in the family. Hurts young children and tendon problems. Several serious diseases could affect the family emotionally, short temper, impulsive, stubborn, self-centered, hunch-back, limping, and cancer.
9 Celebration	Advancement and graduation. Reputation and emotion. Very smart people. Good scores on government exams. Middle son gets very rich. Great achievements, promotions, accomplishments, and status. Slim, tall people, very kind-hearted, a lot of charity work, high standards, and very honest.	Disease of the blood (e.g. Leukemia), blindness, and government shoots you. Fires. Litigations, paranoia, psychotic; heart and eye problems. Miscarriages, difficult child births, blood disease, very violent, fighting, cripple and the hypocrite.

The 81 Combinations

When the energies of the *facing star* and the *mountain stars* combine, they can invite certain outcomes. More importantly, the ensuing energy will influence human behavior in a household.

The combined energies of the nine stars are known as the *81 Combinations* (9 x 9). The *81 Combinations* are extracted from various distinctive Feng Shui classic works; the ancient texts are:

The Purple White Scripts *(Zi Bai Jue)*
Ode of Time and Space *(Xuan Kong Zi Mi)*
Heavenly Jade Classics *(Tien Yu Jing)*
Time Space Mysticism *(Xuan Kong Mi Zhi)*

The following Chinese-to-English translations of the *81 Combinations* are from Grandmaster Yap Cheng Hai. The English has been corrected to make them a little more 'reader friendly'; however the meaning has not been altered.

We are not including **all** *81 Combinations* only those that are part of our 10 celebrities' *Flying Star Chart*.

Keep in mind that the *81 Combinations* represent potential energy and does not mean a particular result is present, guaranteed, or even foreseeable. In order for the energy to be activated, requires daily use; doors, bed placement, stoves, fireplaces, bathrooms and desk direction. Equally important are the large environmental features such as water, mountains, driveways, and roads near the property. These features are considered 'big ticket' items in Feng Shui and can determine the quality of a home's energy. We have indentified which star combinations actually affected our celebrities (good and bad) in our in-depth examinations in Section Two. However, here you may peruse all the possibilities.

O. J. Simpson's Rockingham Home
(See Chapter Five for Feng Shui Examination)

3, 7 Combination (West)
Positive Aspects and Outcomes: This combination indicates lots of money and wealth in Period 7. It fosters good children and a very rich family. You also can succeed as government officials and military personnel. When a 1 star visits, it could produce a new son; when the 2 visits, you can get rich. *Negative Aspects and Indications:* These stars will strongly indicate robbery (especially by a family member), stealing, stubbornness, government lawsuits, thievery, and being betrayed or scammed by a trusted friend or family member. Also, the family breaks apart, feet problems, ghosts in the house, and the eldest son succumbs to alcohol and falls prey to promiscuous women. Be careful of metal-related injuries, drinking alone, and rivals at work.

8, 3 Combination (Southwest)
Positive Aspects and Outcomes: These stars indicate a very long life, wealth, creditability, status, and respectful children, especially sons. The family is always in touch with the latest trends of the time and is very shrewd. It also fosters literary talent, success in writing, and success in government exams. *Negative Aspects and Indications:* This combination signifies young sons die, the loss of all money and property, no harmony in the family, possible divorce, suicide, and being childless. The children of the house may become difficult and run into problems at school. Singles intending to get married should avoid this combination at all costs.

1, 5 Combination (South)
Positive Aspects and Outcomes: When timely, these stars indicate the scholar and a champion of exams. It also supports a good thinker and wise children. The 5 star is a king-maker in its own Period bringing power and wealth! Out of timing, it's considered the 'disaster' or trouble-making star. *Negative Aspects and Indications:* The indications here are water related danger, bankruptcy, and being bloated by water. This combination brings a host of health issues such as hearing problems, kidney problems, sex-related diseases, genital disease, boils in private parts, inability to conceive, and tubular pregnancies. The negative aspects of the 5 Yellow are highlighted here bringing cancer, toxemia, poisoned by drinking, illnesses, food poisoning, and diarrhea. Women may have a miscarriage, uremia, or womb cancer.

6, 1 Combination (Southeast)
Positive Aspects and Outcomes: This combination indicates wealth, good career, being accomplished in literary pursuits, good government relations, money, strong athletes, good in all sports, and physical activities. These stars support accomplishing high ranks in the military, or anyone in positions of power or in senior management, including judges and lawyers. This energy is a peach blossom combination, so expect lots of romance in the air. *Negative Aspects and Indications:* These stars support lawsuits by the government, fighting over property and land, a revolution, bleeding in the brain, getting hurt with knives, controlling women in the family, and it weakens the father or the head of the family. Metal and water can cause one to feel too sentimental and to be excessively emotional. Metal and water are cold; indications are that men here are mean and egoistical, or even feminine.

7, 2 Combination (East)
Positive Aspects and Outcomes: This combination of stars signify good doctors, surgeons, officers, good health, very intelligent men, a supportive family, wonderful children, good for medical studies, and excellent for sports and sportsmen of all types. *Negative Aspects and Indications:* These stars support abortions, miscarriages, fire hazards, women fighting in the family, vomiting up blood, difficulties in conceiving, and a young wife prematurely becoming a widow. Mothers-in-law and daughters-in-law may also find themselves at loggerheads all the time.

2, 6 Combination (Northeast)
Positive Aspects and Outcomes: This combination, when timely, will lead to an affluent and easy life. It brings great wealth and a great family; more good luck and wealth comes in the presence of an 8 visiting star. When a 9 visits, this combination can bring world-fame. A prosperous combination that brings the occupant financial gains, most probably from real estate ventures. *Negative Aspects and Indications:* These stars can indicate lung, tongue and throat disease, hot/cold sickness, dysentery, greed, baldness, no property, a miser, and fathers and sons fighting. When a 5 visiting star comes in it could bring apparitions, spirits or ghosts; bad spirits can cause disharmony in the family. The man of the house may be sick all the time, especially if he smokes. The mother may experience breathing problems. This energy may also encourage the making of nuns and monks.

9, 4 Combination (North)
Positive Aspects and Outcomes: These stars foster prosperity, peace, good children, success in exams, a world-famous author, good-looking people, successful trade, happy occasions, and very smart girls. This energy indicates a highly respected reputation in society, the birth of a brilliant son, and a celebrated poet or mystic. In Periods 7 and 8, the 9 mountain star supports excellent health. *Negative Aspects and Indications:* This combination indicates the wife leaving (jumping over the wall), no support at work, failing exams, fire disasters, and a selfish family. These stars can lead to very abnormal and inappropriate sexual encounters, even incestuous relationships.

4, 8 Combination (Northwest)
Positive Aspects and Outcomes: This combination supports and encourages charitable deeds, the dairy industry, good secretaries, philanthropy, the forestry and farming business, land acquisition and horses. Within good periods, expect real estate deals under the influence of the 4-8 combo; excellent financial possibilities. Due to the mother's excellent nurturing of the children, it brings fortune and fame to the family. *Negative Aspects and Indications:* These stars signify no harmony among the sons in the family; brother-in-law and sister-in-law have an illicit affair, rheumatism, death from abortions, and nerve pain. This combination supports becoming a solitary nature-lover, hurting young children, and problems with small bones. Other health issues could involve gallstones, kidney diseases, emotional and mental problems.

Nicole Brown Simpson's Bundy Condo
(See Chapter Six for Feng Shui Examination)

1, 4 Combination (Northeast)
Positive Aspects and Outcomes: This combination is good for scholarly achievements, media attention, writers, irrigation, the mining business, publicity, study, and romance. It's excellent for gold, silver or diamond interests and investments. In good Periods expect promotions and other perks at work when these stars bless you. This is a very strong *Peach Blossom,* especially for women. *Negative Aspects and Indications:* Too much water may bring scandals made public (e.g. sexting), flirtations, alcoholism, misbehavior, promiscuity, and criminals. Also this energy creates a strong sexual appeal, sluttish behavior, and forgery of bonds/stocks will be apparent. When the stars are in a malignant position or there is too much water, expect affairs and bad romances.

8, 6 Combination (North)
Positive Aspects and Outcomes: This combination of stars indicates illustrious bankers, fame, notable preachers of moral ethics, wealth through real estate, good reputation, learning, success in all military arts, impressive career luck, and very profitable army books and manuals. *Negative Aspects and Indications:* These stars signify being childless, accidents, loss of wealth, no sons or descendants, mental instability, and the dislocation of the joints or bones.

3, 2 Combination (Northwest)
Positive Aspects and Outcomes: This combination indicates money, fame, a good life and those providing good service. Success in the medical field is supported by this energy; good doctors and surgeons. *Negative Aspects and Indications:* These stars represent the famous 'bull fight sha' formation and will bring lots of arguments, quarrels, civil lawsuits, bickering, disagreements, and controversy. It also fosters government lawsuits and punishment/being jailed by the government. Mothers and sons may be constantly bickering, bringing instability to the relationship. Stomach-related illnesses may result in a person feeling starved.

2, 3 Combination (West)
Positive Aspects and Outcomes: This combination will bring good charitable deeds and religious status; fosters the Sage or monk who may achieve high religious status. *Negative Aspects and Indications:* These stars represent antagonistic energy and is the famous 'bull fight sha' combination indicating gossip, arguments, lawsuits, legal entanglements, bickering, disputes, family break-ups, and bad things fall on you—literally and figuratively; a fatal landslide or getting hurt at work. It signifies greedy people, cheating people, aggressive behavior, court cases, reversal of fortune, jail time, and very bad family luck. Residents become stingy, mean, depressed, and women will likely dominate the household; the husband tortures the wife and makes her terribly unhappy.

7, 7 Combination (Southwest)
Positive Aspects and Outcomes: These stars indicate money, wealth, riches, metaphysics, great prosperity, good sons, very smart girls, famous military officers, beautiful, celebrated and famous actresses. This energy favors women over men. *Negative Aspects and Indications:* This combination of stars signify fire hazards, armed robbery, loss of the wife, accidents, death, small talk, quarrels, slander, sex scandals, unfavorable affairs for men, superficiality, risk of road accidents, surgical operations, and men in the house may be seduced by sweet-talking women.

9, 5 Combination (South)
Positive Aspects and Outcomes: These stars encourage great success in literature and writing, many children, lots of properties, and can reach high positions of power such as a President or King. It indicates a holy man, Sage or a Savant. *Negative Aspects and Indications:* This combination signifies stress, mental pressure, a religious fanatic, caner, money loss, and lawsuits. The 9 star accentuates the negative aspects of the 5. It also indicates drug overdoses, poisons, injuries, death, accidents, inflammatory situations, sex diseases, leukemia, fire disasters, eye disease, and when the annual 7 visits, suicide by drugs or poison. This is an inauspicious combination that could leave anyone in the immediate area with a fiery feeling. These stars lead a person to develop some very hard-headed and stubborn characteristics.

5, 9 Combination (Southeast)
Positive Aspects and Outcomes: These stars encourage great success in literature and writing, many children, lots of properties, and can reach high positions of power such as a President or King. It indicates a holy man, Sage or a Savant. *Negative Aspects and Indications:* In Period 8, this combination may produce a down-syndrome child or mental retardation. It supports accidents during happy events; joy turns to sorrow. An inauspicious combination that could leave anyone in the immediate area with a fiery feeling (e.g. Shingles). These stars could also lead to a person developing some very hard-headed and stubborn characteristics. It signifies religious mindfulness turning to a religious fanatic. The 9 accentuates the negative aspects of the 5, drugs/poisons, injuries, death, accidents, inflammatory situations, sex diseases, leukemia, fire disasters, lawsuits, and eye disease. When the annual 7 visits, suicide by drugs or poison is possible.

6, 8 Combination (East)
Positive Aspects and Outcomes: These stars portend great wealth and fortunes, especially through real estate. Also, great authority, fame, achievements, accomplishments, success in the military, money, distinguished careers, and excellent reputations. It also indicates sons and fathers getting rich together; a very wealthy family with children and grandchildren inheriting. *Negative Aspects and Indications:* This combination could indicate losing a spouse (widows and widowers), no children or descendants, being ignored and loneliness. It also signifies mental illness, instability, gangsters, and attaining wealth, and money by illegal means.

Anna Nicole Smith's Studio City Home
(See Chapter Seven for Feng Shui Examination)

8, 2 Combination (Southwest)
Positive Aspects and Outcomes: These stars bring rank, great success, riches and affluence in raw land, real estate transactions, property, and in the construction business. It signifies a real estate magnate; it is rife with financial opportunities and possibilities. This combination can make you rich as a country! *Negative Aspects and Indications:* This combination signifies illness with the reproductive organs, gastrointestinal issues, young males servants/employees mixing with the girls in the family, the youngest and brightest son gets hurt, and possible financial ruin. This energy is best suited for a temple or monastery.

6, 9 Combination (South)
Positive Aspects and Outcomes: These combination of stars support riches, happiness, success, world-famous authors and editors, being honored by the government (given the 'purple cloth' which means accolades, recognition, titles, and so forth), and respected authority. Living long, healthy lives are also indicated. *Negative Aspects and Indications:* This combination is the famous 'fire burning heaven's gate' and indicates sons challenging fathers and violent revolts against authority or the government, especially when there is sharp, jagged mountains in the immediate environment. It brings numerous health issues such as leukemia, breathing and lung problems, blindness, brain disease, vomiting, high fevers, and high blood pressure. This energy will hurt the father of the house; children will misbehave and be hard to control. These stars also encourage sex scandals, masochism, and accidents after a happy event or occasions.

1, 4 Combination (Southeast)
Positive Aspects and Outcomes: This combination is good for scholarly achievements, media attention, writers, irrigation, the mining business, publicity, study, and romance. It's excellent for gold, silver or diamond interests and investments. In good Periods expect promotions and other perks at work when these stars bless you. This is a very strong *Peach Blossom*, especially for women. *Negative Aspects and Indications:* Too much water may bring scandals made public (e.g. sexting), flirtations, alcoholism, misbehavior, promiscuity, and criminals. Also this energy creates a strong sexual appeal, sluttish behavior, and forgery of bonds/stocks will be apparent. When the stars are in a malignant position or there is too much water, expect affairs and bad romances.

9, 3 Combination (East)
Positive Aspects and Outcomes: This combination signifies prosperity and great fame for the occupants. They are also blessed with intelligent, extremely brilliant, and gifted children. These stars bring illustrious judges and wise advisors. *Negative Aspects and Indications:* These stars indicate very cunning and wicked people, being jailed bitten by animals, and liver disease. With the exception of lawyers, this combination should be avoided. It leads to lawsuits and other legal disputes. Practices that may be a little shady may see a person end up in jail with this energy.

5, 8 Combination (Northeast)
Positive Aspects and Outcomes: This combination supports being loyal to the government, long-time prosperity, lots of money, and produces a Sage, shaman, or holy man. *Negative Aspects and Indications:* These stars may bring betrayals, tensions, serious problems, young boys fall sick, issues with the lungs, and stomach, broken ribs or tendons, cancer of the bones or nose, and paralysis. Other indications are sweet-talking and flirting.

7, 1 Combination (North)
Positive Aspects and Outcomes: These stars signify getting rich in the hunting and fishery business, a famous sculpture, beautiful children, very good fortune for young women, glamorous lifestyles and travel, and those who are litigation experts. This combination of stars is good for anyone whose career requires them to travel. These stars are also a *Peach Blossom* and romance. They can go very well or bring scandals and affairs depending on the overall energy of the home. *Negative Aspects and Indications:* This combination of energy support abortions, brothels, flirting, lots of parties with too much wine, women and song, stammering, stuttering, kidnapping, alcoholism, and being expelled from the country. Romance is also very prevalent with this combination, however by the same token, these romances could also be affairs, so married men should be careful. Robberies are possible with the criminals being armed with guns or knives, and it could get fairly violent when these stars come together.

3, 6 Combination (Northwest)
Positive Aspects and Outcomes: These stars indicate growth; great support from government VIPs, business success, a good conductor, and good political luck. *Negative Aspects and Indications:* This combination fosters government lawsuits, fathers and sons fighting, being jailed, and a hard and poor life. Headaches are prevalent and accidental injuries, especially from sharp metal objects, which must be guarded against. Money does come in, but you may have a limp, and getting shot in the leg or the leg is cut. A person's health is compromised when these two stars combine; a fall from a horse could happen as well.

4, 7 Combination (West)
Positive Aspects and Outcomes: This combination of stars supports very smart children, who are gentle and very attractive. It indicates holding power, being honorable with money dealings, romance and honesty. *Negative Aspects and Indications:* These stars are notorious for encouraging women in the house to fight, and no harmony. It also indicates lawsuits (husband-wife court cases), being wounded by knives, lonely people, sibling rivalries among sisters, marital problems, vomiting, and broken marriages. There is also a danger of violence/death associated with sexual matters (S & M gone wrong).

Michael Jackson's N. Carolwood Home
(See Chapter Eight for Feng Shui Examination)

8, 8 Combination (West)

Positive Aspects and Outcomes: This combination of stars support being rich, noble, honor in the family, loyalty, long-term prosperity particularly for the youngest son, splendid wealth, the accumulation of assets, financial gain, illustrious children, and all holy people. *Negative Aspects and Indications:* These stars can bring nose disease, bone fractures of the arm and legs, tendon injuries, sprains, being bloated or puffed up, and young sons leave and never return.

3, 4 Combination (Southwest)

Positive Aspects and Outcomes: This combination indicates being very, very rich, as rich as a King; very famous and noble. The family will have bright and smart children who bring honor to the family. *Negative Aspects and Indications:* These stars support mental and emotional difficulties, psychological issues, thievery, and begging; men may attract crazy, mentally unstable girlfriends. This is a peach blossom for males; they may suddenly find they are the center of attraction for literally every female when this energy is activated. Older ladies must be on their guard. This combination forms a negative *Peach Blossom or Flower of Romance combo.*

1, 6 Combination (South)

Positive Aspects and Outcomes: This combination brings great intelligence and financial skills. It indicates success in the theatrical arts, literary pursuits, and writing. It supports the famous teacher or scholar, good astronomer, brilliant career, and great professor. These stars can make you very famous; rising to a high rank in the military or FBI, CIA, and the police force. Also happy occasions such as marriages or births can happen with these stars. This combination is good for cultural and artistic activity in Periods 7, 8 and 9. *Negative Aspects and Indications:* This combination may cause migraine headaches, bleeding in the brain, mental disorders, concussions, paranoia, and brain infections. Fathers and sons fight; this combination also indicates thieves, being jailed, and fear of the cold. When visited by a 5 or 2, it may trigger a nervous breakdown. Metal and water can cause one to feel too sentimental and to be excessively emotional. Metal and water are cold; indications are that men here are mean and egoistical, or even feminine. Accidents that involve knives and blood may also arise, so be careful with sharp metal objects.

5, 2 Combination (Southeast)

Positive Aspects and Outcomes: When timely, these stars indicate an abundance of wealth and great fortunes with windfall gains. It is also good for producing a large family. It fosters good judges, even a Supreme Court judge and military personnel. During good periods (Period 2) this combination favors property, real estate and the construction business (all earth stars) leading to surprising prosperity. *Negative Aspects and Indications:* This combination of stars is known as the 'weeping formation' and brings great misfortune, all types of calamites, and catastrophes. This energy is the worst possible and indicates lots of illness, death, disease, cancer, bankruptcy, unwanted abortions, appendicitis, divorce, and widow-hood. This is an extremely bad combination which harms the owners of house in every way. The house can be haunted by bad spirits; they will especially affect the middle-aged woman. During bad periods, it can cause older or middle-aged women to fall sick or die of cancerous diseases.

4, 3 Combination (East)

Positive Aspects and Outcomes: In good Periods, these stars indicate making money as smooth as a breeze. There will be good and noble sons who may become very famous; money and success to the family. *Negative Aspects and Indications:* This combination fosters unfriendly rivals; children becoming thieves or beggars, and unreasonable people. Males under the influence of this combination will find women literally hounding them. Beware though, not all may have the best of intentions. Ladies who are under the influence of these stars may face mental disorders and nervous conditions. It also indicates male aggression against females, most likely by cheating.

9, 7 Combination (Northeast)

Positive Aspects and Outcomes: This combination signifies lots of money, media publicity, promotion, being rich, and powerful. It also indicates being innovative, clever, and bright. *Negative Aspects and Indications:* These stars promote women trouble, being over-sexed, fire hazards, AIDS, bad reputation, tuberculosis, couples fight, too many parties with women, wine and song, fire-related accidents, and people with heart issues should not activate this direction and this combination.

2, 5 Combination (North)

Positive Aspects and Outcomes: When timely, these stars indicate an abundance of wealth and great fortunes with windfall gains. It is also good for producing a large family. It fosters good judges, even a Supreme Court judge and military personnel. The 5 star is a king-maker in its own Period bringing power and wealth! Out of timing, it's considered to bring catastrophic results. However, during good periods (Period 5) this combination favors property, real estate and the construction business (all earth stars) leading to surprising prosperity. *Negative Aspects and Indications:* This combination of stars is known as the 'weeping formation' and brings great misfortune and all types of calamites and catastrophes. This energy is the worst possible and indicates lots of illness, death, disease, cancer, bankruptcy, unwanted abortions, appendicitis, divorce, and widow-hood. This is an extremely bad combination which harms the owners of the house in every way. The house can be haunted by bad spirits; they will especially affect the middle-aged woman. During bad periods, it can cause older or middle-aged women to fall sick or die of cancerous diseases. This is the most dangerous combination of all, and should not be activated in any way!

7, 9 Combination (Northwest)

Positive Aspects and Outcomes: This combination of stars indicate innovation, inventors, very clever and bright people, progression, a good marriage, an activist for human rights or fighting against a corrupt government (Gandhi, Nelson Mandela, Martin Luther King), good family luck, light and playful behavior, good love and romance energy. A *Peach Blossom* combo. *Negative Aspects and Indications:* These stars support flirting, sexual abuse, venereal disease, seductions, fire hazards, heart disease, eye issues, illicit seductions, and can be very serious when combined with a visiting 5 star. When another 9 star visits, expect fires or large blazes.

Michael Jackson's Neverland Ranch Home
(See Chapter Eight for Feng Shui Examination)

7, 7 Combination (Southwest)
Positive Aspects and Outcomes: These stars indicate money, wealth, riches, metaphysics, great prosperity, good sons, very smart girls, famous military officers, beautiful, celebrated and famous actresses. This energy favors women over men. *Negative Aspects and Indications:* This combination of stars signify fire hazards, armed robbery, loss of the wife, accidents, death, small talk, quarrels, slander, sex scandals, unfavorable affairs for men, superficiality, risk of road accidents, surgical operations, and men in the house may be seduced by sweet-talking women.

5, 9 Combination (South)
Positive Aspects and Outcomes: These stars encourage great success in literature and writing, many children, lots of properties, and can reach high positions of power such as a President or King. It indicates a holy man, Sage or a Savant. *Negative Aspects and Indications:* In Period 8, this combination may produce a down-syndrome child or mental retardation. It supports accidents during happy events; joy turns to sorrow. An inauspicious combination that could leave anyone in the immediate area with a fiery feeling (e.g. Shingles). These stars could also lead to a person developing some very hard-headed and stubborn characteristics. It signifies religious mindfulness turning to a religious fanatic. The 9 accentuates the negative aspects of the 5, drugs/poisons, injuries, death, accidents, inflammatory situations, sex diseases, leukemia, fire disasters, lawsuits, and eye disease. When the annual 7 visits, suicide by drugs or poison is possible.

9, 5 Combination (Southeast)
Positive Aspects and Outcomes: These stars encourage great success in literature and writing, many children, lots of properties, and can reach high positions of power such as a President or King. It indicates a holy man, Sage or a Savant. *Negative Aspects and Indications:* This combination signifies stress, mental pressure, a religious fanatic, caner, money loss, and lawsuits. The 9 star accentuates the negative aspects of the 5. Also it indicates, drug overdoses, poisons, injuries, death, accidents, inflammatory situations, sex diseases, leukemia, fire disasters, eye disease, and when the annual 7 visits, suicide by drugs or poison. An inauspicious combination that could leave anyone in the immediate area with a fiery feeling. These stars lead a person to develop some very hard-headed and stubborn characteristics.

8, 6 Combination (East)
Positive Aspects and Outcomes: This combination of stars indicates illustrious bankers, fame, notable preachers of moral ethics, wealth through real estate, good reputation, learning, success in all military arts, impressive career luck, and very profitable army books and manuals. *Negative Aspects and Indications:* These stars signify being childless, accidents, loss of wealth, no sons or descendants, mental instability, and the dislocation of the joints or bones.

4, 1 Combination (Northeast)
Positive Aspects and Outcomes: These stars represent the famous 'literature formation' and fosters success in writing, publishing, and all scholarly pursuits. It also supports love and romance. This combination indicates the good ship captain, money, academic success, knowledge, and high grades/scores. The 4, 1 is an excellent combination for anyone still studying or academicians. This combination encourages spiritual pursuits such as prayer of meditation. This is a very strong/good *Peach Blossom*, especially for women. *Negative Aspects and Indications:* This combination signifies extra-marital affairs, a bad director, bad, useless and good-for-nothing sons that spend money and fight with each other; family separates due to fighting. With too much water, love affairs may result depending on the annual stars within the area. Young children may suddenly become frightened with this energy.

6, 8 Combination (North)
Positive Aspects and Outcomes: These stars portend great wealth and fortunes, especially through real estate. Also, great authority, fame, achievements, accomplishments, success in the military, money, distinguished careers, and excellent reputations. It also indicates sons and fathers getting rich together; a very wealthy family with children and grandchildren inheriting. *Negative Aspects and Indications:* This combination could indicate losing a spouse (widows and widowers), no children or descendants, being ignored and loneliness. It also signifies mental illness, instability, gangsters, and attaining wealth, and money by illegal means.

2, 3 Combination (Northwest)
Positive Aspects and Outcomes: This combination will bring good charitable deeds and religious status; fosters the Sage or monk who may achieve high religious status. *Negative Aspects and Indications:* These stars represent antagonistic energy and is the famous 'bull fight sha' combination indicating gossip, arguments, lawsuits, legal entanglements, bickering, disputes, family break-ups, and bad things fall on you—literally and figuratively; a fatal landslide or getting hurt at work. It signifies greedy people, cheating people, aggressive behavior, court cases, reversal of fortune, jail time, and very bad family luck. Residents become stingy, mean, depressed, and women will likely dominate the household; the husband tortures the wife and makes her terribly unhappy.

3, 2 Combination (West)
Positive Aspects and Outcomes: This combination indicates money, fame, a good life and those providing good service. Success in the medical field is supported by this energy; good doctors and surgeons. *Negative Aspects and Indications:* These stars represent the famous 'bull fight sha' formation and will bring lots of arguments, quarrels, civil lawsuits, bickering, disagreements, and controversy. It also fosters government lawsuits and punishment/being jailed by the government. Mothers and sons may be constantly bickering, bringing instability to the relationship. Stomach-related illnesses may result in a person feeling starved.

Sharon's Tate Benedict Canyon Home
(See Chapter Nine for Feng Shui Examination)

6, 6 Combination (Southeast)
Positive Aspects and Outcomes: These stars support good careers, authority, fame, plenty of government support, extremely powerful military leaders, excellent physical prowess, and good sportsmen. It also signifies lots of good sons/children, great wealth, and illustrious careers. Scholars will gain recognition and reap great rewards; unexpected windfall luck. *Negative Aspects and Indications:* This combination indicates lawsuits, rumors, foolish sons, lung disease, abusing the wife, loneliness, employee or labor problems, liver issues, family feuds, and quarrels.

5, 7 Combination (East)
Positive Aspects and Outcomes: These stars indicate being famous in the military, money, medical specialists, skilled lawyers, ambassadors, diplomats, orators, and excellent sharp speakers. *Negative Aspects and Indications:* This combination of stars support food poisoning, serious diseases of mouth, perversions, bad-mouthing, throat cancer, drug addiction, heart issues, venereal disease, prostitution, bleeding of the tongue, damaged vocal cords, problems with the mouth, speech, and communicating. Take care of being poisoned; signifies a sharp tongue with cutting and damaging language.

1, 2 Combination (Northeast)
Positive Aspects and Outcomes: During Period 2, this combination indicates being supported by the public. These stars signify a high position such as a favored and celebrated high Prime Minister. This energy also supports a King or his son who becomes a President, Prime Minister or King. These stars will empower women; they may achieve high positions of authority in the government, the health care industry or in corporations. *Negative Aspects and Indications:* This combination is very unfavorable to middle-aged men; husband gets humiliated or henpecked by the wife. It indicates no support, rebelliousness, murderers, auto accidents, disputes, divorce, and dominating females. As a mountain star and period star, it suggests feelings of tension and inner antagonism. Illness involves abdominal problems, swollen body, bleeding, and an ugly appearance; women activating this energy will suffer from water retention and look fat as a result. Males will get cheated and may develop stomach, intestinal, and digestion problems. Women may develop stomach and gynecological problems.

3, 9 Combination (North)
Positive Aspects and Outcomes: This combination signifies prosperity, glamour and great fame for the occupants. They are also blessed with intelligent, extremely brilliant and gifted children. These stars bring wisdom, happiness, cleverness, and mysticism. It signifies that the children will build the wealth for the family. *Negative Aspects and Indications:* These stars indicate very smart and cunning people. When they are untimely, fire-related injuries are likely to happen and obesity; also, success at first, then failure.

8, 4 Combination (Northwest)
Positive Aspects and Outcomes: This combination encourages literary prowess, financial intelligence, land acquisition, and estate planning. Within good periods, expect real estate deals under the influence of the 8-4 combo, and excellent financial possibilities. These stars also signify great success in industry-related businesses, honest people, textile mills, and very sharp lawyers. *Negative Aspects and Indications:* These stars indicate kidney-related diseases, gallstones, young people in the household die, and other illnesses. It encourages reclusive behavior or aspiring to be the 'hermit in the mount'. Since this combination is known to cause lots of marital discord, newlyweds and couples should avoid activating this energy or direction.

9, 3 Combination (West)
Positive Aspects and Outcomes: This combination signifies prosperity and great fame for the occupants. They are also blessed with intelligent, extremely brilliant, and gifted children. These stars bring illustrious judges and wise advisors. *Negative Aspects and Indications:* These stars indicate very cunning and wicked people, being jailed bitten by animals, and liver disease. With the exception of lawyers, this combination should be avoided. It leads to lawsuits and other legal disputes. Practices that may be a little shady may see a person end up in jail with this energy.

4, 8 Combination (Southwest)
Positive Aspects and Outcomes: This combination supports and encourages charitable deeds, the dairy industry, good secretaries, philanthropy, the forestry and farming business, land acquisition and horses. Within good periods, expect real estate deals under the influence of the 4-8 combo; excellent financial possibilities. Due to the mother's excellent nurturing of the children, it brings fortune and fame to the family. *Negative Aspects and Indications:* These stars signify no harmony among the sons in the family; brother-in-law and sister-in-law have an illicit affair, rheumatism, death from abortions, and nerve pain. This combination supports becoming a solitary nature-lover, hurting young children, and problems with small bones. Other health issues could involve gallstones, kidney diseases, emotional and mental problems.

2, 1 Combination (South)
Positive Aspects and Outcomes: This combination indicates fame and great fortunes as a real estate magnate. It fosters good children and a son who may become a military General. It signifies a good teacher, top industrialist, a Chairman, and CEO. *Negative Aspects and Indications:* These stars indicate marital disharmony, premature births, untimely deliveries, abortions, bloating, ear and hair problems, diabetics, gastric-related problems, upset bowels, and swollen bumps. Males may experience stomach, intestinal and digestive problems, impotence and other problems with their sex lives. There could be land and property loss along with a middle son who leaves and never returns. These stars (2,1 or 1,2) are a famous 'divorce' combination.

The Menendez Beverly Hills Home
(See Chapter Ten for Feng Shui Examination)

4, 1 Combination (Southwest)
Positive Aspects and Outcomes: These stars represent the famous 'literature formation' and fosters success in writing, publishing, and all scholarly pursuits. It also supports love and romance. This combination indicates the good ship captain, money, academic success, knowledge, and high grades/scores. The 4, 1 is an excellent combination for anyone still studying or academicians. This combination encourages spiritual pursuits such as prayer of meditation. This is a very strong/good *Peach Blossom*, especially for women. *Negative Aspects and Indications:* This combination signifies extra-marital affairs, a bad director, bad, useless and good-for-nothing sons that spend money and fight with each other; family separates due to fighting. With too much water, love affairs may result depending on the annual stars within the area. Young children may suddenly become frightened with this energy.

6, 8 Combination (South)
Positive Aspects and Outcomes: These stars portend great wealth and fortunes, especially through real estate. Also, great authority, fame, achievements, accomplishments, success in the military, money, distinguished careers, and excellent reputations. It also indicates sons and fathers getting rich together; a very wealthy family with children and grandchildren inheriting. *Negative Aspects and Indications:* This combination could indicate losing a spouse (widows and widowers), no children or descendants, being ignored and loneliness. It also signifies mental illness, instability, gangsters, and attaining wealth, and money by illegal means.

2, 3 Combination (Southeast)
Positive Aspects and Outcomes: This combination will bring good charitable deeds and religious status; fosters the Sage or monk who may achieve high religious status. *Negative Aspects and Indications:* These stars represent antagonistic energy and is the famous 'bull fight sha' combination indicating gossip, arguments, lawsuits, legal entanglements, bickering, disputes, family break-ups, and bad things fall on you—literally and figuratively; a fatal landslide or getting hurt at work. It signifies greedy people, cheating people, aggressive behavior, court cases, reversal of fortune, jail time, and very bad family luck. Residents become stingy, mean, depressed, and women will likely dominate the household; the husband tortures the wife and makes her terribly unhappy.

3, 2 Combination (East)
Positive Aspects and Outcomes: This combination indicates money, fame, a good life and those providing good service. Success in the medical field is supported by this energy; good doctors and surgeons. *Negative Aspects and Indications:* These stars represent the famous 'bull fight sha' formation and will bring lots of arguments, quarrels, civil lawsuits, bickering, disagreements, and controversy. It also fosters government lawsuits and punishment/being jailed by the government. Mothers and sons may be constantly bickering, bringing instability to the relationship. Stomach-related illnesses may result in a person feeling starved.

7, 7 Combination (Northeast)
Positive Aspects and Outcomes: These stars indicate money, wealth, riches, metaphysics, great prosperity, good sons, very smart girls, famous military officers, beautiful, celebrated and famous actresses. This energy favors women over men. *Negative Aspects and Indications:* This combination of stars signify fire hazards, armed robbery, loss of the wife, accidents, death, small talk, quarrels, slander, sex scandals, unfavorable affairs for men, superficiality, risk of road accidents, surgical operations, and men in the house may be seduced by sweet-talking women.

5, 9 Combination (North)
Positive Aspects and Outcomes: These stars encourage great success in literature and writing, many children, lots of properties, and can reach high positions of power such as a President or King. It indicates a holy man, Sage or a Savant. *Negative Aspects and Indications:* In Period 8, this combination may produce a down-syndrome child or mental retardation. It supports accidents during happy events; joy turns to sorrow. An inauspicious combination that could leave anyone in the immediate area with a fiery feeling (e.g. Shingles). These stars could also lead to a person developing some very hard-headed and stubborn characteristics. It signifies religious mindfulness turning to a religious fanatic. The 9 accentuates the negative aspects of the 5, drugs/poisons, injuries, death, accidents, inflammatory situations, sex diseases, leukemia, fire disasters, lawsuits, and eye disease. When the annual 7 visits, suicide by drugs or poison is possible.

9, 5 Combination (Northwest)
Positive Aspects and Outcomes: These stars encourage great success in literature and writing, many children, lots of properties, and can reach high positions of power such as a President or King. It indicates a holy man, Sage or a Savant. *Negative Aspects and Indications:* This combination signifies stress, mental pressure, a religious fanatic, caner, money loss, and lawsuits. The 9 star accentuates the negative aspects of the 5. Also, it indicates, drug overdoses, poisons, injuries, death, accidents, inflammatory situations, sex diseases, leukemia, fire disasters, eye disease, and when the annual 7 visits, suicide by drugs or poison. An inauspicious combination that could leave anyone in the immediate area with a fiery feeling. These stars lead a person to develop some very hard-headed and stubborn characteristics.

8, 6 Combination (West)
Positive Aspects and Outcomes: This combination of stars indicates illustrious bankers, fame, notable preachers of moral ethics, wealth through real estate, good reputation, learning, success in all military arts, impressive career luck, and very profitable army books and manuals. *Negative Aspects and Indications:* These stars signify being childless, accidents, loss of wealth, no sons or descendants, mental instability, and the dislocation of the joints or bones.

Phil Hartman's Encino Home
(See Chapter Eleven for Feng Shui Examination)

7, 3 Combination (East)

Positive Aspects and Outcomes: These combination of stars support making lots of money, talented business men and women, success in the military, great success in writing and literature, and making a fortune on sports books. It also indicates an unexpected gain in business. *Negative Aspects and Indications:* This combination signifies bad health, internal injuries, and bleeding requiring surgery, hot tempers, fraud, financial troubles due to lawsuits, stealing, burglaries, and eye-related injuries or illness. The 7 and 3 are both robbery stars; expect trouble in this area when they are activated.

3, 8 Combination (Northeast)

Positive Aspects and Outcomes: These stars indicate wealth, creditability and status; very good children, especially sons. The family is always in touch with the latest trends of the time and is very shrewd. It also fosters literary talent and success in writing. *Negative Aspects and Indications:* This combination suggests that brothers become enemies (two male stars), and fight due to misunderstandings; young males will have to be careful with this combination. Health issues such as miscarriages, heart disease and asthma are likely to occur; families may fall apart.

5, 1 Combination (North)

Positive Aspects and Outcomes: When timely, the 5, 1 combo indicates the scholar and a champion of exams. It also supports a good thinker and wise children. *Negative Aspects and Indications:* The indications here are water related danger, bankruptcy, and being bloated by water. This combination brings a host of health issues such as hearing problems, kidney problems, sex-related diseases, genital disease, boils in private parts, inability to conceive, and tubular pregnancies. The negative aspects of the 5 Yellow are highlighted here bringing cancer, toxemia, poison by drinking, illnesses, food poisoning, and diarrhea.

1, 6 Combination (Southwest)

Positive Aspects and Outcomes: This combination brings great intelligence and financial skills. It indicates success in the theatrical arts, literary pursuits, and writing. It supports the famous teacher or scholar, good astronomer, brilliant career, and great professor. These stars can make you very famous; rising to a high rank in the military or FBI, CIA, and the police force. Also happy occasions such as marriages or births can happen with these stars. This combination is good for cultural and artistic activity in Periods 7, 8 and 9. *Negative Aspects and Indications:* This combination may cause migraine headaches, bleeding in the brain, mental disorders, concussions, paranoia, and brain infections. Fathers and sons fight; this combination also indicates thieves, being jailed, and fear of the cold. When visited by a 5 or 2, it may trigger a nervous breakdown. Metal and water can cause one to feel too sentimental and to be excessively emotional. Metal and water are cold; indications are that men here are mean and egoistical, or even feminine. Accidents that involve knives and blood may also arise, so be careful with sharp metal objects.

2, 7 Combination (West)

Positive Aspects and Outcomes: These stars will create great judges, doctors, winning money from the lottery, finding money, good investigators or inspectors, and a very rich family with more girls than boys. This combination brings good prospects and opportunities; money will roll in but spend it wisely as it can roll out just as easily. In Period 7, this brings lots of financial prospects and gain. *Negative Aspects and Indications:* This combination indicates no sons, bad daughters, stomach illness, fire hazards, diarrhea, abortions, illicit affairs, money loss, and robberies, especially for those who became wealthy in Period 7. There could be affairs that lead to divorce; possible fire hazards when the 9 star flies in. This energy signifies difficulty in producing children, epidemics and incurable diseases, bleeding wounds, and knife injuries.

6, 2 Combination (Southwest)

Positive Aspects and Outcomes: This combination brings extreme wealth where you can be the richest in the land; great health is also indicated. A distinguished family who are powerful industrialist with lots of sons to run the business. This is a prosperous combination that brings the occupants financial gains, most probably from real estate ventures. *Negative Aspects and Indications:* These stars support mental disturbance, hot/cold sickness, one-sided love, greed, miserly, monks, nuns, and expect lots of gastrointestinal problems. With this combination, ladies should be extra cautious as they may find themselves faced with a host of problems relating to their reproductive system. When a 5 visiting star comes in it could bring apparitions, spirits or ghosts; bad spirits can cause disharmony in the family. The man of the house may be sick all the time, especially if he smokes. The mother may experience breathing problems.

4, 9 Combination (South)

Positive Aspects and Outcomes: These stars foster very special and intelligent children, women in the family run the family business, good-looking people, successful trade, happy occasions, and very smart girls. This energy indicates a highly respected reputation in society, the birth of a brilliant son, and a celebrated poet or mystic. This is an excellent direction to activate for a gifted, male child. *Negative Aspects and Indications:* This combination signifies failure in exams/testing, blood disease, fire hazards, accidental deaths, and being extradited from the country. This energy also encourages abnormal, unusual and peculiar sexual liaisons.

8, 4 Combination (Southeast)

Positive Aspects and Outcomes: This combination encourages literary prowess, financial intelligence, land acquisition, and estate planning. Within good periods, expect real estate deals under the influence of the 8-4 combo, and excellent financial possibilities. These stars also signify great success in industry-related businesses, honest people, textile mills, and very sharp lawyers. *Negative Aspects and Indications:* These stars indicate kidney-related diseases, gallstones, young people in the household die, and other illnesses. It encourages reclusive behavior or aspiring to be the 'hermit in the mount'. Since this combination is known to cause lots of marital discord, newlyweds and couples should avoid activating this energy or direction.

Phil Spector's Castle (Alhambra)
(See Chapter Twelve for Feng Shui Examination)

8, 6 Combination (South)
Positive Aspects and Outcomes: This combination of stars indicates illustrious bankers, fame, notable preachers of moral ethics, wealth through real estate, good reputation, learning, success in all military arts, impressive career luck, and very profitable army books and manuals. *Negative Aspects and Indications:* These stars signify being childless, accidents, loss of wealth, no sons or descendants, mental instability, and the dislocation of the joints or bones.

6, 8 Combination (Southwest)
Positive Aspects and Outcomes: These stars portend great wealth and fortunes, especially through real estate; great authority, fame, achievements, accomplishments, success in the military, money, distinguished careers, and excellent reputations. It also indicates sons and fathers getting rich together; a very wealthy family with children and grandchildren inheriting. *Negative Aspects and Indications:* This combination could indicate losing a spouse (widows and widowers), no children or descendants, being ignored and loneliness. It also signifies mental illness, instability, gangsters, and attaining wealth and money by illegal means. *Cure:* Water.

1, 4 Combination (West)
Positive Aspects and Outcomes: This combination is good for scholarly achievements, media attention, writers, irrigation, the mining business, publicity, study and romance. It's excellent for gold, silver or diamond interests and investments. In good Periods expect promotions and other perks at work when these stars bless you. This is a very strong *Peach Blossom*, especially for women. *Negative Aspects and Indications:* Too much water may bring scandals made public (e.g. sexting), flirtations, alcoholism, misbehavior, promiscuity and criminals. Also *"jumping over the wall"* (wives leaving their husbands); strong sexual appeal, sluttish behavior and forgery of bonds/stocks will be apparent. When the stars are in a malignant position or there is too much water, expect affairs and bad romances.

2, 3 Combination (Northwest)
Positive Aspects and Outcomes: This combination will bring good charitable deeds and religious status; fosters the Sage or monk who may achieve high religious status. *Negative Aspects and Indications:* These stars represent antagonistic energy and is the famous 'bull fight sha' combination indicating gossip, arguments, lawsuits, legal entanglements, bickering, disputes, family break-ups, and bad things fall on you—literally and figuratively; a fatal landslide or getting hurt at work. It signifies greedy people, cheating people, aggressive behavior, court cases, reversal of fortune, jail time, and very bad family luck. Residents become stingy, mean, depressed, and women will likely dominate the household; the husband tortures the wife and makes her terribly unhappy.

7, 7 Combination (North)
Positive Aspects and Outcomes: These stars indicate money, wealth, riches, metaphysics, great prosperity, good sons, very smart girls, famous military officers and beautiful, celebrated and famous actresses. This energy favors women over men. *Negative Aspects and Indications:* This combination of stars signify fire hazards, armed robbery, loss of the wife, accidents, death, small talk, quarrels, slander, sex scandals, unfavorable affairs for men, superficiality, risk of road accidents, surgical operations, and men in the house may be seduced by sweet-talking women. *Cure:* Fire or small water to deplete. No door facing this energy!

9, 5 Combination (Northeast)
Positive Aspects and Outcomes: These stars encourage great success in literature and writing, many children, lots of properties, and can reach high positions of power such as a President or King. It indicates a holy man, Sage or a Savant. *Negative Aspects and Indications:* This combination signifies stress, mental pressure, a religious fanatic, caner, money loss and lawsuits. The 9 star accentuates the negative aspects of the 5; drug overdoses, poisons, injuries, death, accidents, inflammatory situations, sex diseases, leukemia, fire disasters, eye disease and when the annual 7 visits, suicide by drugs or poison. An inauspicious combination that could leave anyone in the immediate area with a fiery feeling. These stars lead a person to develop some very hard-headed and stubborn characteristics.

5, 9 Combination (East)
Positive Aspects and Outcomes: These stars encourage great success in literature and writing, many children, lots of properties, and can reach high positions of power such as a President or King. It indicates a holy man, Sage or a Savant. *Negative Aspects and Indications:* In Period 8, this combination may produce a down-syndrome child or mental retardation. It supports accidents during happy events; joy turns to sorrow. An inauspicious combination that could leave anyone in the immediate area with a fiery feeling (e.g. Shingles). These stars could also lead to a person developing some very hard-headed and stubborn characteristics. It signifies religious mindfulness turning to a religious fanatic. The 9 accentuates the negative aspects of the 5; drugs/poisons, injuries, death, accidents, inflammatory situations, sex diseases, leukemia, fire disasters, lawsuits, eye disease and when the annual 7 visits, suicide by drugs or poison is possible.

4, 1 Combination (Southeast)
Positive Aspects and Outcomes: These stars represent the famous 'literature formation' and fosters success in writing, publishing and all scholarly pursuits. It also supports love and romance. This combination indicates the good ship captain, money, academic success, knowledge and high grades/scores. The 4, 1 is an excellent combination for anyone still studying or academicians. This combination encourages spiritual pursuits such as prayer of meditation. This is a very strong/good *Peach Blossom*, especially for women. *Negative Aspects and Indications:* This combination signifies extra-marital affairs, a bad director, bad, useless and good-for-nothing sons that spend money and fight with each other; family separates due to fighting.

Marilyn Monroe's Brentwood Hacienda
(See Chapter Thirteen for Feng Shui Examination)

5, 8 Combination (Southwest)
Positive Aspects and Outcomes: This combination supports being loyal to the government, long-time prosperity, lots of money, and produces a Sage, shaman, or holy man. *Negative Aspects and Indications:* These stars may bring betrayals, tensions, serious problems, young boys fall sick, issues with the lungs, and stomach, broken ribs or tendons, cancer of the bones or nose, and paralysis. Other indications are sweet-talking and flirting.

3, 6 Combination (South)
Positive Aspects and Outcomes: These stars indicate growth; great support from government VIPs, business success, a good conductor, success, and good political luck. *Negative Aspects and Indications:* This combination fosters government lawsuits, fathers and sons fighting, being jailed, and a hard and poor life. Headaches are prevalent and accidental injuries, especially from sharp metal objects, which must be guarded against. Money does come in, but you may have a limp, and getting shot in the leg or the leg is cut. A person's health is compromised when these two stars combine; a fall from a horse could happen as well.

7, 1 Combination (Southeast)
Positive Aspects and Outcomes: These stars signify getting rich in the hunting and fishery business, a famous sculpture, beautiful children, very good fortune for young women, glamorous lifestyles and travel, and those who are litigation experts. This combination of stars is good for anyone whose career requires them to travel. These stars are also a *Peach Blossom* and romance. They can go very well or bring scandals and affairs depending on the overall energy of the home. *Negative Aspects and Indications:* This combination of energy support abortions, brothels, flirting, lots of parties with too much wine, women and song, stammering, stuttering, kidnapping, alcoholism, and being expelled from the country. Romance is also very prevalent with this combination, however by the same token, these romances could also be affairs, so married men should be careful. Robberies are possible with the criminals being armed with guns or knives, and it could get fairly violent when these stars come together.

6, 9 Combination (East)
Positive Aspects and Outcomes: These combination of stars support riches, happiness, success, world-famous authors and editors, being honored by the government (given the 'purple cloth' which means accolades, recognition, titles, and so forth), and respected authority. Living long, healthy lives are also indicated. *Negative Aspects and Indications:* This combination is the famous 'fire burning heaven's gate' and indicates sons challenging fathers and violent revolts against authority or the government, especially when there is sharp, jagged mountains in the immediate environment. It brings numerous health issues such as leukemia, breathing and lung problems, blindness, brain disease, vomiting, high fevers, and high blood pressure. This energy will hurt the father of the house; children will misbehave and be hard to control. These stars also encourage sex scandals, masochism, and accidents after a happy event or occasions.

2, 5 Combination (Northeast)
Positive Aspects and Outcomes: When timely, these stars indicate an abundance of wealth and great fortunes with windfall gains. It is also good for producing a large family. It fosters good judges, even a Supreme Court judge and military personnel. The 5 star is a king-maker in its own Period bringing power and wealth! Out of timing, it's considered to bring catastrophic results. However, during good periods (Period 5) this combination favors property, real estate and the construction business (all earth stars) leading to surprising prosperity. *Negative Aspects and Indications:* This combination of stars is known as the 'weeping formation' and brings great misfortune and all types of calamites and catastrophes. This energy is the worst possible and indicates lots of illness, death, disease, cancer, bankruptcy, unwanted abortions, appendicitis, divorce, and widow-hood. This is an extremely bad combination which harms the owners of the house in every way. The house can be haunted by bad spirits; they will especially affect the middle-aged woman. During bad periods, it can cause older or middle-aged women to fall sick or die of cancerous diseases. This is the most dangerous combination of all, and should not be activated in any way!

4, 7 Combination (North)
Positive Aspects and Outcomes: This combination of stars supports very smart children, who are gentle and very attractive. It indicates holding power, being honorable with money dealings, romance and honesty. *Negative Aspects and Indications:* These stars are notorious for encouraging women in the house to fight, and no harmony. It also indicates lawsuits (husband-wife court cases), being wounded by knives, lonely people, sibling rivalries among sisters, marital problems, vomiting, and broken marriages. There is also a danger of violence/death associated with sexual matters (S & M gone wrong).[1]

9, 3 Combination (Northwest)
Positive Aspects and Outcomes: This combination signifies prosperity and great fame for the occupants. They are also blessed with intelligent, extremely brilliant, and gifted children. These stars bring illustrious judges and wise advisors. *Negative Aspects and Indications:* These stars indicate very cunning and wicked people, being jailed bitten by animals, and liver disease. With the exception of lawyers, this combination should be avoided. It leads to lawsuits and other legal disputes. Practices that may be a little shady may see a person end up in jail with this energy.

1, 4 Combination (West)
Positive Aspects and Outcomes: This combination is good for scholarly achievements, media attention, writers, irrigation, the mining business, publicity, study, and romance. It's excellent for gold, silver or diamond interests and investments. In good Periods expect promotions and other perks at work when these stars bless you. This is a very strong *Peach Blossom*, especially for women. *Negative Aspects and Indications:* Too much water may bring scandals made public (e.g. sexting), flirtations, alcoholism, misbehavior, promiscuity, and criminals. Also this energy creates a strong sexual appeal, sluttish behavior, and forgery of bonds/stocks will be apparent. When the stars are in a malignant position or there is too much water, expect affairs and bad romances.

Brittany Murphy's Hollywood Hills Home
(See Chapter Fourteen for Feng Shui Examination)

7, 7 Combination (South)
Positive Aspects and Outcomes: These stars indicate money, wealth, riches, metaphysics, great prosperity, good sons, very smart girls, famous military officers, beautiful, celebrated and famous actresses. This energy favors women over men. *Negative Aspects and Indications:* This combination of stars signify fire hazards, armed robbery, loss of the wife, accidents, death, small talk, quarrels, slander, sex scandals, unfavorable affairs for men, superficiality, risk of road accidents, surgical operations, and men in the house may be seduced by sweet-talking women.

2, 3 Combination (Southeast)
Positive Aspects and Outcomes: This combination will bring good charitable deeds and religious status; fosters the Sage or monk who may achieve high religious status. *Negative Aspects and Indications:* These stars represent antagonistic energy and is the famous 'bull fight sha' combination indicating gossip, arguments, lawsuits, legal entanglements, bickering, disputes, family break-ups, and bad things fall on you—literally and figuratively; a fatal landslide or getting hurt at work. It signifies greedy people, cheating people, aggressive behavior, court cases, reversal of fortune, jail time, and very bad family luck. Residents become stingy, mean, depressed, and women will likely dominate the household; the husband tortures the wife and makes her terribly unhappy.

1, 4 Combination (East)
Positive Aspects and Outcomes: This combination is good for scholarly achievements, media attention, writers, irrigation, the mining business, publicity, study, and romance. It's excellent for gold, silver or diamond interests and investments. In good Periods expect promotions and other perks at work when these stars bless you. This is a very strong *Peach Blossom*, especially for women. *Negative Aspects and Indications:* Too much water may bring scandals made public (e.g. sexting), flirtations, alcoholism, misbehavior, promiscuity, and criminals. Also this energy creates a strong sexual appeal, sluttish behavior, and forgery of bonds/stocks will be apparent. When the stars are in a malignant position or there is too much water, expect affairs and bad romances.

6, 8 Combination (Northeast)
Positive Aspects and Outcomes: These stars portend great wealth and fortunes, especially through real estate. Also, great authority, fame, achievements, accomplishments, success in the military, money, distinguished careers, and excellent reputations. It also indicates sons and fathers getting rich together; a very wealthy family with children and grandchildren inheriting. *Negative Aspects and Indications:* This combination could indicate losing a spouse (widows and widowers), no children or descendants, being ignored and loneliness. It also signifies mental illness, instability, gangsters, and attaining wealth, and money by illegal means.

8, 6 Combination (North)
Positive Aspects and Outcomes: This combination of stars indicates illustrious bankers, fame, notable preachers of moral ethics, wealth through real estate, good reputation, learning, success in all military arts, impressive career luck, and very profitable army books and manuals. *Negative Aspects and Indications:* These stars signify being childless, accidents, loss of wealth, no sons or descendants, mental instability, and the dislocation of the joints or bones.

4, 1 Combination (Northwest)
Positive Aspects and Outcomes: These stars represent the famous 'literature formation' and fosters success in writing, publishing, and all scholarly pursuits. It also supports love and romance. This combination indicates the good ship captain, money, academic success, knowledge, and high grades/scores. The 4, 1 is an excellent combination for anyone still studying or academicians. This combination encourages spiritual pursuits such as prayer of meditation. This is a very strong/good *Peach Blossom*, especially for women. *Negative Aspects and Indications:* This combination signifies extra-marital affairs, a bad director, bad, useless and good-for-nothing sons that spend money and fight with each other; family separates due to fighting. With too much water, love affairs may result depending on the annual stars within the area. Young children may suddenly become frightened with this energy.

5, 9 Combination (West)
Positive Aspects and Outcomes: These stars encourage great success in literature and writing, many children, lots of properties, and can reach high positions of power such as a President or King. It indicates a holy man, Sage or a Savant. *Negative Aspects and Indications:* In Period 8, this combination may produce a down-syndrome child or mental retardation. It supports accidents during happy events; joy turns to sorrow. An inauspicious combination that could leave anyone in the immediate area with a fiery feeling (e.g. Shingles). The 9 accentuates the negative aspects of the 5, drugs/poisons, injuries, death, accidents, inflammatory situations, sex diseases, leukemia, fire disasters, lawsuits, and eye disease. When the annual 7 visits, suicide by drugs or poison is possible.

9, 5 Combination (Southwest)
Positive Aspects and Outcomes: These stars encourage great success in literature and writing, many children, lots of properties, and can reach high positions of power such as a President or King. It indicates a holy man, Sage or a Savant. *Negative Aspects and Indications:* This combination signifies stress, mental pressure, a religious fanatic, caner, money loss, and lawsuits. The 9 star accentuates the negative aspects of the 5. Also, it indicates, drug overdoses, poisons, injuries, death, accidents, inflammatory situations, sex diseases, leukemia, fire disasters, eye disease, and when the annual 7 visits, suicide by drugs or poison. An inauspicious combination that could leave anyone in the immediate area with a fiery feeling. These stars lead a person to develop some very hard-headed and stubborn characteristics.

Annual Stars

Not only does the *Flying Stars* reveal the energy map of a home or business, it offers information on how the energy changes from year to year and even month to month. In other words, in order to ensure continual good fortune, you must be aware that this is a dynamic and changing practice that requires some attention each year. This is one of the 'time' dimension aspects of the *Flying Stars* system. While the annual stars are not a capital change or a milestone marker such as leaving one Period and going into another, they are important to consider. Annual stars should always be factored in as they can greatly impact everyday events and affect your overall luck. Several of the celebrity homes were greatly affected by the annual, visiting energy. Monthly stars are not as significant as yearly ones, but they should be noted as well. Neither, the monthly or annual stars are of the same importance as the natal *Flying Star Chart*.

The purpose of the annual and monthly stars is to alert you to dangerous or pernicious energy that may bring trouble. When you're able to identify these afflictions, you can take action to mitigate their influence. It also signals where additional prosperous energy may visit for the year.

Four Annual Afflictions: *Three Killings, Grand Duke Jupiter, Year Breaker, and 5 Yellow Star*

At its core, Feng Shui is about enhancing your luck and opportunities, so timing is an important factor, good and bad. Not all Feng Shui masters accept the validity of the 'sha' energy that we will discuss here. Sha means poisonous or killing energy. Keep in mind that it would be remise to ignore the effects of negative energy. Good Feng Shui can turn bad due to nothing more than the passage of time. The key is to be prepared. Keep the energy flow refreshed and up-to-date. This creates beautiful energy for the home and you will enjoy good fortune, secure wellness, and maintain a harmonious environment for you and your family.

There are four different types of energy that visit four sectors/directions of your property each year. They are inauspicious and these afflictions can cause negative events in your life. Depending on the type of affliction it is, and in which sector the affliction visits, these malevolent energies can cause bankruptcy, loss, illness, divorce, separations, business collapse, and in extreme cases, death.

This happened in 2008 when three of the four shas visited the South. Disturbing this area in that year could have had devastating results. Several of the afflictions/shas are based on planetary alignments and magnetic fields; these areas are taboo for deep ground digging or major renovations. The four negative energies are the Grand Duke Jupiter (*Tai Sui*), Year Breaker (*Sui Po*), Three Killings (*Sam Sart*), and the annual *5 Yellow Star*. Each year, beginning February 4th, they will migrate to a new area/direction.

Figure 24: Do not disturb the *Three Killings* position with deep digging, remodeling or demolition.

Grand Duke Jupiter and Year Breaker

The *Grand Duke Jupiter* and the *Year Breaker* are intangible stars, and are a more esoteric aspect of Feng Shui. However, it is widely respected by the Chinese and some attention is devoted to these visiting energies. The Grand Duke Jupiter always corresponds to the ruling animal year, for example 2018 is the *Year of the Dog* (location is Northwest 3). Other names for the Grand Duke are the Grand General or the Commander of the Year.

The *Year Breaker* is in the exact opposite location as the Grand Duke. While the *Grand Duke* and *Year Breaker* are not as serious as the 5 Yellow and the Three Killings, you will still want to avoid construction work or digging in these directions. For protection, you may bury some metal objects (brass, bronze, copper and so forth) near the construction site as an extra precaution. Some believe you should not face the Grand Duke Jupiter or Year Breaker directions for the year as it may 'offend' him. We don't advocate avoiding this if it has a great facing star.

The Three Killings Taboo

The *Three Killings* can be the most serious of the four negative energies. Disturbing the *Three Killings* has various levels of consequences. Some people have reported illnesses, accidents, marital problems, and money loss. Extreme bad luck is rare, but if unfavorable landforms are also present, it is possible.

Do not renovate, landscape, hang new doors, remove big trees from the roots, or install a pool or pond in this direction or location if you can avoid it. If this is not a frequented part of your home or yard, there is no need to implement a cure or countermeasure.

Basic gardening will have no affect on the *Three Killings* area of your yard because it does not displace enough dirt.

It is common for the Chinese to place three bronze Chi Lin dragons, a turtle, laughing Buddha or the God of War in the *Three Killings* location. All of these items should be made of metal; that is the real cure, not the *image* of the object. In ancient times, masters used the God of War (Guan Di) most often, as it was believed that the *Three Killings* was a gang of thieves that would rob and injure you. The powerful Guan Di could easily banish the three Bandits. However, the best cure is NOT to dig in the *Three Killing* area at all!

The *Three Killings* involves not only 45° of the afflicted direction but also 15° to the left and right for a total of 75°. For example, in 2017 (*Year of the Rooster*), the *Three Killings* was located in the East. However, it also involved the last 15° of Northeast (known as NE 3) and the first 15° of Southeast (known as SE 1). These left and right 15° areas are called the 'assistant killers'.

The 5 Yellow Star

The 5 star in the *Flying Stars* system is the worst possible energy—but rest assured, the 5 annual star will only visit one direction or sector of your house a year. If it takes up residence in the front of your home, you may experience difficulties with money, health, or relationships. By placing metal in this location, it can be countered or completely averted. However, *do not* place metal where the *5 Yellow Star* visit if you have an 8 facing star there; this will weaken the most powerful, benevolent energy. The 8 energy is more powerful than the 5 and is 'friends' with it (they are both earth energy). The 8 energy, especially if it is activated by real water, will protect you from the normal affects of the *5 Yellow Star*.

Figure 25: The *5 Yellow Star* visits one of the eight directions each year. Often it may bring disastrous events if the circumstances are ripe. Many of the celebrities' home were visited by this energy in the year they died.

Here's a recap of the annual 'sha' energies; the most serious is the *Three Killings* and then the *5 Yellow Star*. It is taboo to engage in earth-moving activities such as prepping a swimming pool, pond, lake or removing a huge tree stump. Construction or remodeling where there is extensive demolition, shaking of the house or walls may also trigger negative events in your life.

Critique of the 10 Celebrity Homes

We're excited to share what we've discovered in the 10 celebrity homes. There are actually eleven examinations as we assessed two homes for Michael Jackson, Neverland Ranch and his luxury rental in Holmby Hills. Let's do a quick review so that you may get the most from the in-depth examinations. First let's review basic landforms; support should be represented on the left and right-hand side as well as the back. This is known as the *Dragon, Tiger* and *Turtle* respectively. If these areas are exposed by a road for example, it can cause serious problems in the household.

In the *Eight Mansions* system, based on your birthday and gender, you're assigned a Life-Gua Number. The *Life-Gua Number* allots four good and four bad directions. There are two Life Groups, East and West. It is best if couples share the same Life Group. Throughout the assessments, we'll use the GMY code for the good and bad directions. Good directions will support wealth (+90), health (+80), relationships (+70), and stability (+60). Bad directions will attract divorce (-90), bad health/betrayals (-80), bad romance/lawsuits (-70), and setbacks (-60). In *Eight Mansions*, the most important features are the main door, master bedroom, kitchen/stove and toilet locations. Due to the nature of toilets, they should be located in negative areas (-60, -70, -80, or -90). The same goes for a stove location. Doors, beds and desks should activate good energy (+90, +80, +70, or +60).

In the *Flying Stars* system, the good stars are 1, 4, 6, 8, and 9. They will activate money, fame/romance, authority, wealth or promotions/accolades respectively. The bad stars are 2, 3, 5 and 7. They will usher in sickness, lawsuits, disasters and robbery in that order. The most dangerous star is the 5. We have evaluated only one Period 5 home, Marilyn's Monroe hacienda in Brentwood.

It will not surprise you that *all* the celebrity homes have some of the worst formations revealed in Chapter Three. They are the *Eight Roads of Destruction, Peach Blossom Sha, Eight Killing Mountain Forces, Robbery Mountain Sha*, extreme design, *Death and Empty Lines*, and many more. We'll start with the homes of O.J. Simpson and his former wife, Nicole Brown. This was a heart wrenching story. It was also one of the most famous and controversial trial in American history.

SECTION TWO
The Celebrities

Chapter Five
O. J. Simpson: *The Football Star*

While living at the Rockingham house, O.J. was twice divorced, lost a two-year-old daughter in a drowning accident, was charged and acquitted of a double homicide, later found guilty in a civil suit for those murders, charged with domestic violence, had numerous affairs, and ultimately lost the home to foreclosure.

Feng Shui and Facts
Address: 360 N Rockingham Ave., Los Angeles, CA
Period 7, West 2
Moved in: 1979
Facing Direction: 268°
O.J. Simpson: 8 Life-Gua
Nicole Brown: 1 Life-Gua
Children: 5
Married: February 2, 1985
Divorced: October 15, 1992
Negative Features: Two *Peach Blossoms Sha* formations, two *Four Destruction* formations, the *Tiger* is missing, extreme house design, bed placement indicates affairs, and stove placement activated bankruptcy.

Background on Celebrity and Property

Orenthal James Simpson (O.J.), a *NFL Hall of Fame* football star, moved into 360 North Rockingham Avenue in 1979 with his first wife Marguerite. They had three children; Arnelle, Jason, and Aaren. The bad luck started almost immediately. The couple's two-year old daughter Aaren, drowned in the swimming pool. While still married to Marguerite, O.J. met 18-year old Nicole Brown at The Daisy, a Beverly Hills nightclub where she was waitressing. She was the girl next door; young and full of life. Less than a year after moving into the home, O.J. and Marguerite divorced. O.J. married Nicole in 1985, she moved into the Rockingham house and they had two children.

The sweet, passionate love story between O.J. Simpson and Nicole Brown soon morphed into violence, affairs, divorce, and accusations of murder. Very much like his first marriage, this relationship too would involve a death. O. J. was charged with her

1994 murder and the details of their lives were put under the microscope. The double murder, televised court case was dubbed the 'Trial of the Century.' How could have this

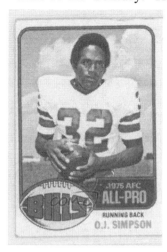

happened by a beloved football star? The case threatened to tear America apart, as it was hard to fathom that a celebrated, charismatic star could commit such a horrific crime. It also pitted blacks against whites and was, ultimately, disturbing on many levels. It was no secret that the relationship between the couple was passionate, oftentimes violent, and plagued with affairs that eventually led to divorce. Even then, they were connected through strong karmic ties. They were never quite finished with each other.

Life-Gua Numbers and Personality

O.J. is an 8 Life-Gua and Nicole was a 1 Life-Gua. When the 1 and 8 come together in a relationship, the 8 will try to dominate. In Feng Shui, this is considered a less-than-desirable match. However, it could work if the couple were evolved in consciousness. At least one person in the relationship must be evolved for it to work successfully. In Nicole's case, we believe she had more awareness than O.J. That's likely why this energetic match was unfavorable and caused conflict on a regular basis. The 1 Guas, in particular, will resist being controlled as their energy is very free-spirited. Nicole and O.J. are part of different Life Groups, he is part of the West Life Group and she belonged to the East Life Group. From the

very beginning, their relationship started off on a bad note.

The Home's Best Features

Front Door Facing Road Indicated Opportunities for Money and Career

The home was situated in a beautifully pristine, tree-lined neighborhood. Brentwood, a suburb of Los Angeles has wonderful high energy. The home's front door faced the road and was able to receive its vibrant energy. This feature alone would support excellent career luck. In this home, O.J. was able to capitalize on his career by doing commercials, movies, and sports casting.

Generous Ming Tang Indicated Money

O.J.'s home also had a generous *Ming Tang*, or *Bright Hall*, area in which energy (or chi) could accumulate. When energy can pool or accumulate in a particular area, the occupants will have wealth and numerous opportunities that lead to abundance. The *Ming Tang* can be defined simply as the open space near the entrance.

Ideally, the *Ming Tang* should be open, unobstructed and well-defined. The Rockingham house had an excellent *Ming Tang* area, inside and out. The *Ming Tang* feature can work two ways – it can support or thwart opportunities. In O.J.'s home, because of the proportion of the home's *Bright Hall*, the opportunities were endless. This was very lucky indeed!

Flying Star Chart Indicated Money and Opportunities

The Rockingham house faced 268° to the West direction. The home was occupied in 1979 but when the murders took place, the home was actually a *Period 7* (Feb 4, 1984 to Feb 3, 2004).

This means O.J. Simpson either moved in, or did extensive renovations, during *Period 7*. Since he moved in the late 70's, it would be reasonable to assume that extensive remodeling was done to bring the home into the 80's. He and Nicole married in 1985 and more

remodeling or redecorating likely took place as well. In her book, Faye Resnick speaks of Nicole putting her stamp on things. These remodeling projects would have completely changed the energy of the house. In Feng Shui terms, this is changing the *Flying Star Chart* or the energy map. While Faye's book did not give an exact year, if any major renovations were undertaken after February 4, 1984, the house was most definitely a *Period 7*.

During the *Period 7* years is when O.J. enjoyed great wealth (1984 to 2004). He had retired from professional football but was acting and doing commercials. It was also very auspicious that he found a wife and fathered two healthy children in this house. The house was obviously not 100% unlucky. No home is. The house faced O.J.'s relationship direction (+70) and a wealth star (*7 facing star*). For him, personally, the West direction indicated luck and opportunities with relationships. The media loved him and refused to believe anyone so handsome and charming could engage in evil acts or crimes. After a long, drawn out trial, O.J. was acquitted of all charges

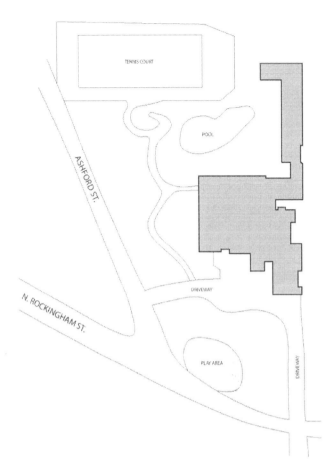

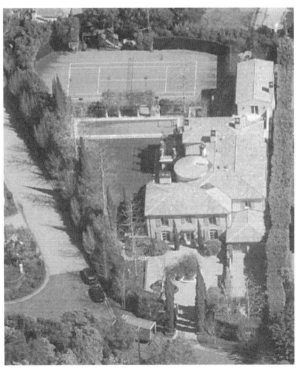

Figure 26: The house shape is extreme and similar to a gun or a weapon. These extreme home designs deliver disasters to the occupants.

against his former wife, Nicole Brown Simpson, and of her friend, Ronald Goldman.

In Faye Resnick's book, *Nicole Brown Simpson: The Private Diary of a Life Interrupted,* she mentions that wherever O.J. went, people loved him. Often chanting, "Juice! Juice! Juice!". Once, while out for the evening, Resnick recalled that O.J. was drinking heavily and began verbally abusing Nicole. When police officers noticed this, they told him to get in his car, drive home, and let Nicole leave with her friends. If this would have been anyone else, he would have been arrested with no questions asked. The front door certainly helped and supported O.J. with relationships but this wasn't the case for Nicole. The West-facing front door indicated mishaps, setbacks, and instability (-60). With her life being so public, it was obvious that this is what she experienced.

Negative Features

Extreme House Design Indicated Money Loss, Violence, and Relationship Problems

Unfortunately, the house design was extreme and its shape actually resembled an axe. In Feng Shui, extreme designs are considered highly inauspicious and rarely promote positive results. The ancient Chinese discovered that homes designed with square or rectangular shapes best support the human experience. The reason for this is that chi/energy can flow and be distributed evenly. They called this stable design the *four-point gold.*

When homes have extreme designs or shapes, they can harm the occupants in every way. There will be serious issues with relationships, money, health, reputation, and may even support violence. The shape of the Rockingham home was only one piece of

many negative features. In 1997, the house was sold to the bank due to foreclosure. This was also the same year that Simpson was ordered to pay $33 million to the Goldman family in a wrongful death civil suit.

Double Four Destructions Indicated Disharmony, Discord, and No Peace

The energy from the South-facing door, and the degree of the driveway (268°), created a formation known as the *Four Destructions.* These rare formations are seriously negative and can cause disharmony, discord, and no peace in the household. It will also create a string of unending hassles. There are only four such possible formations for any home. In order to have this negative formation, both an exterior door and a road/driveway must fall within a specific, 15-degree increment.

In her book, Faye Resnick, recounted the many times Nicole had been brutally beaten by O. J. One time was so severe that she called the police. When the media got wind of the story, Nicole tried to diffuse it by saying it was 'no big deal'. In the book, Resnick says that Nicole could not recall how many times she was beaten because it was so often. Adding insult to injury, there was a second *Four Destructions* formation created by the West-facing front door (268°), which clashed with water flowing from the North direction (pool waterfall). This is extremely unusual, but very telling. We are affected by energy and the energy created by these formations was extremely negative and, as it turns out, detrimental.

Double Peach Blossom Sha Indicated Affairs, Divorce, Scandals, and Illicit Behavior

The South-facing door and the water (in this case, the swimming pool) located in the East created another highly negative formation known as a *Peach Blossom Sha.* These formations are notorious for causing salacious scandals, affairs, sexual improprieties, and adultery. Resnick's book gave a detailed chronicling of both of their sexual escapades. There are four different types of sexual energy generated by *Peach Blossoms*. This particular *Peach Blossom Sha* indicated exile, bankruptcy, sexual problems (or obsession with sex), disloyalty, scandals, and turning the family upside-down. These things certainly did happen to this family with all the media frenzy around the abuse, the murder and the murder charge itself. Who could ever forget O.J. being chased down the freeway in his white Bronco for the entire world to see, his life and family's never to be the same.

There was a second *Peach Blossom Sha* formation in this house with the back East-facing door and the water from the North direction (pool waterfall). This particular formation indicated bankruptcy and soiling the reputation of the household. Not only did the murder trial soil his reputation with its numerous unflattering revelations but, later, the same thing happened with the armed robbery conviction. These events fully decimated his good standing in the world's eyes.

For a home to have two *Peach Blossom Shas* is an extremely rare occurrence. The circumstances brought on by these formations support everything that happened in this home. So far, we have identified four seriously negative Feng Shui formations and we haven't even entered the home yet!

Missing Tiger Side Indicates Unsupported Females

The basics of Feng Shui state that a home should be supported on the left-side, right-side, and at the back. This "support" could be your neighbor's home, a small hill, or even a tall, solid fence. In other words, it's best if homes are surrounded or 'embraced' in the back and on the sides. When there is no support on the right-hand side *(as you are looking out your front door)* this indicates the 'female' or woman of the house will suffer. Abuse could also be involved, but this alone would not indicate abuse. There would have to be other negative energy to support that suspicion. The Rockingham house was situated on a corner lot. The female *(Tiger)* side was not represented because a road (a virtual river) was there in its place (see Figure 26).

After Nicole divorced O.J., she often told friends that he molded her into the woman that she became. She said she hardly knew who she was after so many years with him. When the *Tiger* isn't represented properly, or its support is missing, females of the household may exhibit aggression. In some cases, it can indicate spousal abuse. A good portion of the incessant fighting between O.J. and Nicole revolved around O.J.'s sexual improprieties, which Nicole often brought up. She refused to back down and would show passive-aggressive behavior in public places in order to embarrass her husband.

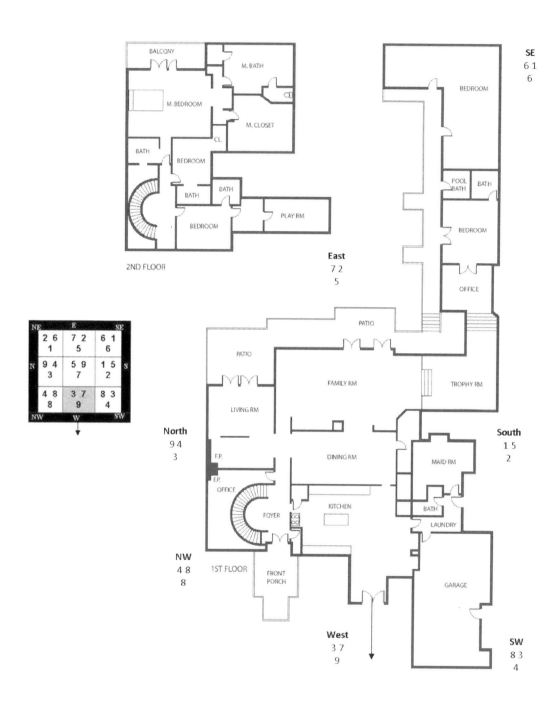

Figure 27: 360 N. Rockingham floor plan with the Period 7, West 2 *Flying Star Chart*. There are doors that face to the West, South, North, and East. The shape of the house is extreme and the worst feature of the property in Feng Shui terms.

The Kitchen Indicated Issues with Relationships and Money

In Feng Shui, the kitchen plays a vital role in the overall energy of a home. It's an opportunity to create wealth, enhance relationships, and improve health. If the kitchen isn't placed well, it can bring unwanted events and circumstances. The Simpson's home presented additional challenges because O.J. and Nicole were in different Life Groups in the *Eight Mansions* system. So, what was good for him, was bad for her. However, since he was the breadwinner and she was a housewife, important rooms and features, such as the kitchen and stove, should be placed in his favor to support the family.

The kitchen was located in the West and this 'burned up' his relationship luck (+70). While the front door supported his relationships, the kitchen's location worked against them. This is why he got mixed results/signals concerning his spousal relationship. It played out in other areas of his life as well. However, while the kitchen did not support good relationships, the stove location did. The stove burned up his -70, which would have assisted him in finding a wife and fathering children.

Additionally, in the *Flying Star* system, the stove activated the 9 wealth star and would have brought excellent money luck and opportunities. The worst aspect of the kitchen/stove scenario was that the stove's knobs/controls stimulated eventual loss of wealth, bankruptcy, widowhood, and possibly cancer. In this house, that activated the South direction with the deadly, evil *5 facing star*. When this star/energy is activated, it brings calamity in all forms. Again, O.J. predictably got mixed results—having money but losing large sums. This actually played out in his life over and over again.

The kitchen/stove brought mixed results for Nicole as well. It would indicate disturbing her stability (+60). However, the South-facing controls activated good relationship luck. While the South was one of her best directions, the *5 facing star* canceled out most of the benefits. By using the *Eight Mansions* and *Flying Stars* systems together, we get a very accurate picture of what really went on in the house. As you can see, both partners were affected differently.

Bathroom Locations Indicated Money Loss and Contentious Relationships

The home had bathrooms located in the Southwest, Southeast, Northwest, West, and North sectors of the house. Feng Shui proposes that toilets (a negative feature) should be located in your bad sectors *only* (your -90, -80, -70, and -60). This will be different for each person depending on their *Life-Gua Number.*

For O.J., the bathrooms/toilets were located in his +90, -90, +80, +70, and -70, respectively. In general, these factors would indicate that his money and relationships would have ups and downs. His health could have been adversely affected as well, depending on which of these bathrooms he used the most. Eventually, his money luck was adversely affected because his home was foreclosed on.

For Nicole, the bathrooms were located in her -90, +90, -80, -60, and +60, respectively. This would indicate mixed money luck with a few setbacks and mishaps.

Master Bedroom Location/Bed Direction Indicated Affairs

The master bedroom is yet another room in the house that has an enormous impact on the fate, opportunities, health, relationships, and wealth of its occupants. Since humans spend about one-third of their lives in the sleep state, the bed direction has a tremendous weight in Feng Shui. Great care should be taken to ensure that the couple is well-placed, especially if they are different Life Groups, like Nicole and O.J.

Looking at the floor plan, we assumed that they would have the bed placed on the North wall. This seemed reasonable as this was the only solid wall in the room. In this case, this would mean that they activated the 9, 4 star combination that could bring fame. It would suggest prosperity, peace, and good sons to the family. Without a doubt, O.J. attained fame and, sleeping toward this combination of energy would ensure that it continued. When did fame turn to infamous? If the

overall Feng Shui is negative – and it was – their bed direction would have contributed to more negative events. Activating this energy would indicate the wife leaving, no support at work, selfish family, and abnormal affairs (even incestuous relationships). Also, ladies under this influence are highly susceptible to lesbianism *(see the negative aspects of the 9,4 stars on page 56).*

According to Faye Resnick, O.J. had numerous affairs and sexual conquests with women. O.J. and his friends (Al Cowlings, aka A.C., and Marcus Allen) would take bets on who could land a woman first and then share her among themselves. These little escapades and cavalier skirt-chasing were brought up during the famous murder trial. Much of this information was confirmed in Nicole's famous undated letter that was entered into evidence. O.J. was known to be a selfish man, oftentimes not paying attention to his children and relying on Nicole to do everything.

Resnick also confessed in the book that she and Nicole had an isolated, intimate encounter. It was brief, rash, and they both agreed that they were not really lesbians and resumed a normal friendship. This happened when Nicole was living in the Bundy condo. However, she was still on-and-off with O.J. and at her old home often. The book also mentioned Nicole's voracious sexual appetite. Faye said this was the reason she always went back to O.J. She confessed that no one quite fulfilled her sexually as her former husband. O.J. and Nicole were exceptionally passionate people and the home completely

supported their energy – the good, the bad, and the ugly. The bedroom energy indicated the wife leaving, and this was a prophecy that became a reality.

Feng Shui Restoration

In order for O.J. and Nicole to both benefit from Feng Shui, their home would have needed special attention. However, even the most skilled Feng Shui master in the world can't override a person's free will and natural inclinations. In other words, people still have a choice. If the energy was extracted differently in both homes, it may have still ended in divorce, but not murder. If the Simpsons had been our clients, we would've recommended the following changes to Rockingham.

The Home's Extreme Shape
The shape of the house would have to have been corrected in order to get rid of its odd axe-shaped design. The shape of the house also excluded the 'heart of the house,' which is typically located at the exact center of the home. If the center of the house is missing, it will adversely affect its occupants. In the Simpson's home, it was missing because of the strange shape. We would've recommended that the house design be expanded to create a more rectangular shape. While a big undertaking, this could've been accomplished by adding some rooms on the North side of the house.

The Front Door
The front door worked best for O.J. if it was used by Nicole at all, it would not have brought her any luck at all. Changing the front door to face between 277.6° to 292.5° would've served them both. The same could be said for the interior garage door. It also should've been tilted, or re-angled. The whole family would have benefited by shifting these two doors just a few degrees.

These doors then would've supported both Life Groups. This would be accomplished through a door tilt, which is hugely popular in Southeast Asia but rarely heard of in America. See Appendix III for door tilts photos.

The Missing Tiger
Creating proper support on the female side *(Tiger)* could've been easily accomplished by installing a 6-12-foot wall of brick/stucco or huge landscape mounds, as seen on golf courses. Another structure, such as a guest house, would've also fulfilled the criteria. Either of these cures could've been augmented with dense landscaping to fully represent this side of the property.

Figure 28: After the murders, police and the press converged on the Rockingham house.

The Pool Location
Even with changing the degree of the door, the pool was ill-placed and it brought premature aging and illness/disease to the householders. Relocating the pool would have been a huge undertaking but would have been money well-spent. The pool should have been located in the Southeast corner of the property. Relocating the pool there would have brought stable wealth-luck and opportunities to the couple. Additionally, this would've allowed construction of the room additions that would've corrected the overall shape of the house.

Two Peach Blossom Sha Formations

Because *Peach Blossoms* are based on specific 15-degree increments, if the angle of the doors had been changed and the water relocated, both *Peach Blossom* formations would've been automatically eliminated as a result.

Two Four Destructions Formations

Like the *Peach Blossoms* mentioned previously, the *Four Destructions* are based on specific 15-degree increments. Changing the angle of the doors and relocating the water would've cancelled out these formations.

The Stove/Kitchen

We would have recommended relocating the stove to the East wall. The knobs/controls should have faced to the West. In *Period 7*, this would've been great for money and would've eliminated activating the most dangerous energy in their *Flying Star Chart* (*5 facing star*).

The Master Bedroom

The bed should've been moved and situated in the Northwest corner. The combination of stars there were a 4, 8 and this energy was good for money luck and fame. More specifically, the bed should have been situated between 292.5°-307.5°. This way, it would've had a positive effect on Nicole's relationships. This placement would've been good for O.J.'s health and wealth.

360 North Rockingham Today

It may not be a surprise to you to learn that 360 North Rockingham Avenue is now gone! In 1998, the Simpson's home was sold and demolished completely, down to the dirt. When Jennifer went to assess the 'new'

property, she determined that the facing of the home is somewhere between 262.5° degrees to 277.5°.

The new owners of the property opted to build a new Italian-style villa. Simpson lived in the luxurious estate for 20 years, basking in the successes of his pro football career. He paid $650k for it in 1977. The 6,200-square-foot mansion, with its waterfalls, tennis court, swimming pool and guest quarters, was bought by Kenneth Abdalla, an investment banker and president of the Jerry's Famous Deli chain, for nearly $4 million.

Many people intuitively know when a property isn't good and this was a brilliant call on the new owners' part. After all, who wants to buy someone else's bad luck? From the Google Earth maps aerial view, it looks as if the pool has been covered over, which would remove the negative formations; hence eliminating the negative energy that O.J. and Nicole experienced during their time there. All of the changes the new owners made, of course, completely changed the energy of the property. Also, according to the aerial view, the house is a normal square-shaped house, versus the odd axe design of the Simpson's house.

Figure 29: 360 N. Rockingham was torn down in 1998. A new Italian-style villa was constructed.

Chapter Six
Nicole Brown Simpson: *The Girl Next-Door*

While living at 875 S. Bundy Drive for only five months, Nicole experienced money loss, debt, strained relationships, illness, and the brutal murder of herself and Ron Goldman.

Feng Shui and Facts

Address: 875 S. Bundy Drive, Los Angeles, CA
Period, Northeast 1
Facing Direction: 31°
Divorced: October 15, 1992
Moved in: 1994
Nicole: 1 Life-Gua
Died: 1994
Negative Features: *Eight Roads of Destruction, Robbery Mountain Sha,* detrimental bed placement, badly located toilets, and very bad doors.

Background on Celebrity and Property

Nicole Brown Simpson moved into the Bundy condo on January 15, 1994, just two days before the Northridge earthquake. This is actually where she and Ron Goldman were murdered. The condo was part of her divorce settlement from O.J. and she paid cash for it. However, she had another residence in Brentwood on Gretna Green Street. She lived there before she eventually moved into the Bundy condo. Family and friends were aware that Nicole continued to have an on-again, off-again relationship with her ex-husband. Feng Shui Grandmaster Yap was very fond of saying, *"Good Feng Shui takes time, while bad Feng Shui can happen immediately."* In Nicole's situation, this seemed exceptionally true. She was murdered on June 13, 1994, just five months after living in the Bundy condo.

This case was particularly intriguing to Jennifer because she and Nicole both attended Dana Hills High School in Dana Point, California. It was at this school that

Nicole was crowned homecoming queen in the late seventies. While Jennifer was nearing her own graduation in 1994, she heard the news of Nicole's murder. Nicole and Jennifer also had the same Government teacher. He was very moved by her death and told the class that Nicole was a beautiful person, inside and out. Even 24 years later, many of us are still haunted by her tragic story.

Life-Gua Number and Personality

Nicole Brown was a 1 Life-Gua and part of the East Life Group. The 1 Guas love their freedom, have secrets, or may even lead a secret life. She was born in the *Year of the Pig*, which is a water sign in Feng Shui. The 1 Guas tend to be emotional but Nicole was double water and that gave her a propensity for very deep feelings. Her husband's Earth energy was constantly trying to control her more mercurial, water energy.

The Home's Best Features

Like her former Rockingham home, Nicole's new condo on South Bundy was also located in the exclusive neighborhood of Brentwood. This area is very affluent and the homes reflect the overall vibrant energy of Brentwood. A very fortunate feature was her front patio because this area had a door facing the road. While this was not the 'front' door, it is still considered a prosperous feature.

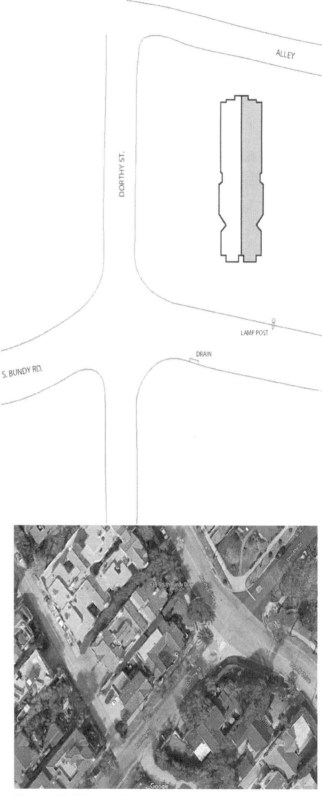

Figure 30: The condo was very narrow as shown above (the gray shaded area). In Feng Shui, this design is known as squeezed chi.

The Kitchen and Stove Indicated Money Luck and Opportunities

The kitchen and stove were located in the Northwest (-80). This would suppress bad health and betrayals. However, on the flip side, it may also have indicated fighting, gossiping, arguments, and lawsuits because the stove activated the *3 mountain star*. Faye's book revealed that Nicole experienced all of those things, except lawsuits. The best part of the stove was the knob direction. Nicole's stove knobs faced to the Southeast (+90) and activated the 9 wealth star. This would've been excellent for attracting wealth, prosperity, and abundance in general.

Negative Home Features

The Facing Direction Indicated Difficult Relationships

Nicole's Bundy home faced the Northeast direction at 31°. The 4 facing star would have supported romance, writing, publishing, travelling, and fame. However, because Northeast is not one of her good directions (-70), it has implications for discord, lawsuits, and bad romance. In her case, this would indicate issues with romance. When these two energies are paired up, it indicates attracting romance but ending badly. According to Resnick's book, this was most certainly what she experienced during her time in the Bundy condo. There was no question she would attract men because she was a gorgeous

woman. However, for one reason or another, these liaisons never lasted. She would always gravitate back to her ex-husband.

Extremely Narrow House Shape Indicated Debt and Money Loss

Unfortunately, the condo was not lucky for consistent prosperity. The shape of the condo is extremely narrow, a feature that causes money loss and debt. Known as *squeezed chi*, this design restricts the flow of energy. If energy is restricted, so is money. Faye's book confirms some of Nicole's financial woes and difficulties. At one point, O.J. threatened to report her to the IRS for tax fraud. Evidently, she filed that she was still living at the Rockingham home.

This was to avoid paying a capital gains tax on a condo she sold in San Francisco. Nicole was also entertaining the idea of getting back together with her ex-husband. The plan was to keep the Bundy condo as an investment but when things turned sour again, she took up residence there. During this time, Faye said Nicole had only $90k in her bank account. An IRS payout could have wiped out her finances. With her funds dwindling, Nicole planned to sell her Bundy condo and move on. In fact, days before her death, she put the property up for lease. While she had no problem getting money, she had difficulty retaining it. Less-than-ideal Feng Shui didn't help matters.

Figure 31: The outside and street view of the S. Bundy condo.

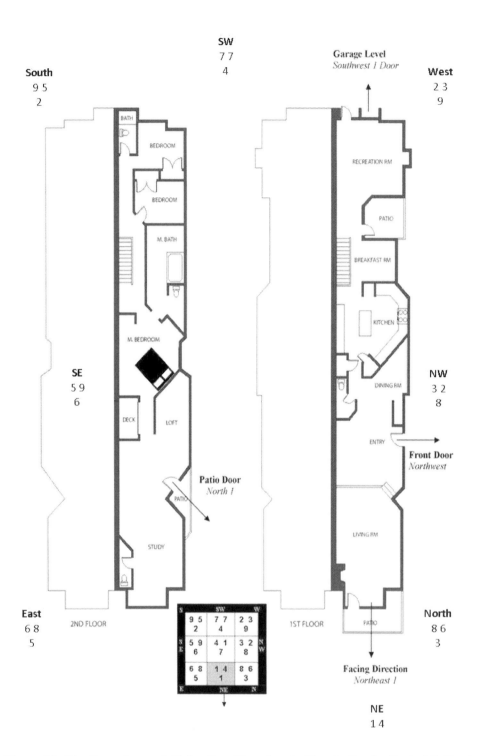

Figure 32: The floor plan and *Flying Star Chart* for the Bundy Condo; Period 7, Northeast 1. The worst feature is the extreme narrow design which indicates debt. Notice the bed is now placed on the North wall which is excellent.

Eight Roads of Destruction Indicated Disastrous Events

When water (virtual or real) exits at a site in a particular way, it can indicate disastrous events for the occupants. One of these rare formations is called *Eight Roads of Destruction*. In the Bundy condo, this is formed by the upstairs North-facing patio door and a very prominent drain (water exit) in the Northeast (approximately 39°). These formations are known to cause great disharmony in the home including divorce, bankruptcy, affairs, bad health, and even death. The drain or water exit must be visible from an exterior door/house to constitute a bona fide *Eight Roads of Destruction*. At the time Nicole owned the property, the huge drain was present and visible. Also back then, the house had a wrought iron fence in the front. This made the home easily visible from the street. The *Eight Roads of Destruction* alone can destroy people's lives, however, there were even more negative features that would play a part in Nicole's fate.

Kitchen in Center of the House

While the kitchen and stove worked overall, the location in the center of the house could have caused panic attacks, high blood pressure, anxiety, and heart attacks. This likely would have not manifested for at least another six months.

Robbery Mountain Sha Indicated Violence with Knives

The Bundy house had another negative formation known as a *Robbery Mountain Sha*. This feature 'robs' energy from the home. It indicates getting hurt by knives, or the whole family contracting an unusual disease. This formation is more common than the deadly *Eight Roads of Destruction*. In the Bundy house, it was created by the large lamppost (considered sha/negative energy in Feng Shui) located in the North between 7° and 22° degrees. This played out with Nicole and Ron because the weapon used to murder them was a knife.

Figure 33: The lamppost outside Nicole's home was in the *Robbery Mountain* position. Not all lampposts bring harm to the occupants.

The Northwest Front Door Indicated Romance, Money Issues, and Illness

The 'front door', or intended front entrance, of the Bundy condo was actually located on the side of the house. This door faced the Northwest. Front doors located on the side of the house indicate struggles with money and relationships. Further, the star combination (2, 3) at the door is famous for activating incessant arguments. It's known as the *bull-fight sha*.

Additionally, Northwest is a negative direction for Nicole (-80) and can portend bad health, betrayals, and illness leading to a very unfortunate accident. It may also have attracted women being harmed, ghosts, abortions, and issues with the reproductive organs.

It was no secret that Nicole's relationship with O.J. was extremely volatile. Up until her last day, the pattern of abuse and violence continued. The day of their daughter's dance recital, she resolved to be done with him for good. This was not the first time she told him this and, unfortunately, she would always go back. This conflict is very typical of the *bullfight sha* energy that was evident in her home. Her Northwest door also indicated illness (2 facing star). During her brief time at the condo, sometime in mid-May, she contracted double pneumonia. This was highly unusual as Nicole was very healthy and health-conscious. She was in amazing shape, worked out regularly and ran nine miles a day. It's very strange for someone this healthy to come down with something as serious as double pneumonia. No doubt the stress of being in a perilous relationship didn't help. However, the energy in the home wasn't supportive of great health.

The Back/Interior Garage Indicated Good Money Luck

The Southwest-facing garage door and interior garage door activated the prosperous energy at the time (7, 7). This would have brought Nicole good money luck and resources. However, the Southwest was not one of her good personal directions (-90). In fact, using this door daily would have activated divorce, bankruptcy, and failures in general. Again, she got mixed luck with the energy of this very important door! At the end of the day, it would look like having money, losing money, meeting men, and failing to cultivate a lasting relationship with them.

Bathrooms and Toilet Locations Indicated Mixed Luck

Regarding the nature of toilets, they should be located in the negative areas of our homes. For Nicole, all toilets, except one, were located in her good sectors. The one located in the Southeast (+90) would harm her wealth, the East toilet (+80) would cause health issues, the South toilet (+70) would harm relationships, and the toilet in the Southwest (-90) would assist in good money luck. If she frequented the one located in the Southeast, her troubles with money would have been fully activated. If she used the one in the master bedroom more, this would have counterbalanced it. Regular use of the toilet located upstairs in the study, would have caused issues with health.

Master Bedroom Indicated Disastrous Events

The narrow width of the master bedroom space would only allow the bed to be placed on the Southeast, North or the Northwest walls. It is highly probable that Nicole's bed was situated on the Southeast. This arrangement would allow for nightstands on either side of the bed, while the Northwest and North would not. The Southeast was her personal best direction (+90), but the star combination was detrimental (5, 9). While both *Eight Mansions* and *Flying Stars* are factored in, the stars are more powerful for interior Feng Shui. In this case, the bad stars overrode her great direction. If you recall, the *5 Yellow Star* is the calamity star that can deliver disasters. Sadly, her bed placement was one of the most detrimental features of the house. Furthermore, the annual *5 Yellow Star* visited the Southeast in 1994, creating the perfect storm.

Figure 34: Nicole was sleeping to the Southeast (5, 9). In 1994, the evil *5 Yellow Star* visited that direction. The 5, 9 is a very negative combination, but when paired with the 5 annual, it can bring devastating results.

This home was enormously unlucky because of the exterior formations that were present, specifically the *Eight Roads of Destruction* and *Robbery Mountain Sha*. In many cases, death does not occur, but in more extreme cases, it is a possibility. Basically, when exterior features are exceptionally pernicious, such as in Nicole's case, everything interior can turn bad, too. The energy of the external environment can affect the home's internal chi. In the Bundy home, the energy and formations were so dominant, they turned 'fairly good' into 'really bad'.

Feng Shui Restoration

Nicole's home would have needed some drastic alterations. In order for her to realize her dreams of a happy life and a good husband, the energy would have to have been extracted differently. It's important to note that the *Eight Roads of Destruction* and *Robbery Mountain Sha* would have affected anyone occupying the home. These features will impact the property no matter what the *Flying Star Chart* is or your Life-Gua Number. Having said that, the home is better suited for the West Life Group (2, 6, 7 or 8 Guas). The following would have been our recommendations to improve her experience in the house.

Eight Roads of Destruction
There are two ways in which this formation can be eliminated. The first is to re-angle the North-facing door located on the upstairs patio. Or secondly, install a stucco wall, a barrier of trees or plants to block the drain from view of the house.

Robbery Mountain Sha
In order to remove the *Robbery Mountain Sha* formation, the lamppost would have to be blocked off from view of the house, making it essentially disappear. It could have been blocked off by a stucco wall, a large tree, or some creative landscaping.

Extremely Narrow Shape
There is no remedial measure for the very narrow-shaped house design. It will continue to cause issues for anyone who occupies this house, namely the retention of their wealth.

The Doors
The front door, located on the side of the house, should have been cured with metal. This would have calmed the sickness energy down. This door could have also been closed off altogether, making the door in the Northeast the new front door. In Feng Shui, it is more desirable to have the front door facing the road. The back door (interior garage door) would have been the best door to use, and likely was. This Southwest-facing door would have brought Nicole money luck. A water feature should have been installed near this door, either inside or out, to fully capture the good *Period 7* luck of the time.

Bed Direction
Nicole's bed should have been located on the North slanted wall of the master bedroom (see Figure 32). The combination of stars had superior energy (8,6). This would have been excellent in both *Flying Stars* and *Eight Mansions* for her even in

Period 7. The North indicated stability for Nicole (+60).

Toilet Usage

Unfortunately, the only toilet that would not have harmed Nicole's good luck was the one located in the master bathroom. Not using the other toilets would've greatly benefitted her relationships, health, and money.

875 South Bundy Drive Today

Just like the Rockingham address, 875 South Bundy no longer exists. When the condo went up for sale, it's not surprising that it stayed on the market for over two years. When it did sell, it was at a bargain basement price. The new owners have made several changes that will insulate them from the more serious negative features. They started by changing the numbers of the address. Who could blame them? The old address had too much horror attached to it. The new address is 879 South Bundy. Right from the start, the new owners shored up the property with tall retaining walls and thick landscaping. This essentially made the drain and lamppost disappear. At the time that Nicole lived in the home, it was completely exposed to the street, having only a wrought iron fence as a barricade. Thus, the property was vulnerable to the negative formations caused by the lamppost and the drain across the street.

When the wrought iron fence was removed and replaced with an eight-foot stucco wall, large trees and thick landscaping, so was the *Eight Roads of Destruction* and *Robbery Mountain Sha* formations. While many of these changes were most likely initiated to deflect unwanted spectators of the now infamous property, it did improve the Feng Shui a great deal. Additionally, the sidewalk where Nicole's body was found was torn up and relocated.

The energy on the inside of the home would have shifted if major renovations were done after 2004, making it a Period 8 home. This would have changed the energy completely and the new occupants would have a totally different experience living in the home. Also, if the new owners are West Life Group, they will have an advantage with the facing that Nicole did not. The home has had two owners since Nicole's death. Public records reveal that it was last sold in 2006 for $1.72 million.

Final Thoughts

The homes owned and lived in by O. J. and Nicole, are text-book examples of how the negative energy such as the *Eight Roads of Destruction, Peach Blossom Sha, Four Destructions* and *Robbery Mountain Sha* formations can destroy people's lives. Without a doubt, our case studies are very extreme indeed. This does not mean however, that regular, non-famous people can't experience these formations, because they can. It may not end up in death but it can still wreak havoc and cause devastating losses of money, health, and relationships.

There is much that can be learned by examining a home's history. For example, the South Bundy condo was built in 1990 with only one previous owner. It was sold to Nicole a couple of years after that. What would have caused the previous homeowners to move so quickly? Perhaps they, too, were suffering devastating and crippling losses. Even though their situation didn't end in a death, a lot can take place in a two-year time frame that would make it extremely difficult and force a homeowner to move. It's always wise to inquire as to why owners are selling and the history before leaping into a purchase.

Chapter Seven
Anna Nicole Smith: *The Billionaire's Wife*

While living at 3646 Avenida Del Sol for less than 2 years, Anna Nicole experienced lawsuits, the loss of a child, drug abuse, loss of money, bad relationships, health issues, and loss of reputation.

Feng Shui and Facts
Address: 3646 Avenida Del Sol, Studio City, CA
Period 8, Southwest 2
Facing Direction: 221°
Moved in: April 11, 2005
Anna Nicole: 9 Life-Gua
Died: February 8, 2007
Children: 2
Negative Features: *Eight Roads of Destruction*, severe sloping land at the rear, cutting-feet formation, unsupported *Tiger* side, and a malevolent mountain.

Background on Celebrity and Property

Anna Nicole Smith was born in Houston, Texas on November 28, 1967 as Vickie Lynn Hogan. From humble beginnings in the small Texas town of Mexia, Anna Nicole clawed her way to the top. She first became a centerfold in *Playboy* magazine and later modeled for Guess Jeans. However, she gained spectacular, worldwide fame when she married a Texas billionaire. In 1994, the 26-year-old bombshell married 89-year-old oilman, J. Howard Marshall II.

However, there was no fairy tale ending for Anna Nicole. Her life was tainted with drama, larger-than-life aspirations, excessive partying, and heartbreaking loss. To many, she was an icon who resembled the classic beauty of Marilyn Monroe and Jane Mansfield. Her life, even to the bitter end, was plagued with controversy. On February 8, 2007, Anna Nicole Smith died of an accidental drug overdose in Hollywood, Florida. She was only 39 years old. Her son, Daniel Smith, died in a similar fashion the year before, just three days after his baby sister, Dannielynn, was born.

Anna Nicole purchased 3646 Avenida Del Sol on April 11, 2005. It had been built in 2002. Several homes were on the same property that date back to 1992, but our assessment is based on the floor plan of 2002. While Anna Nicole did not die in this home, it still accurately reflected her state of mind and life events. It was not accidental or by coincidence that Anna chose a house with disastrous Feng Shui.

Her life was a series of extreme highs and lows. A good portion of her energy, resources and time were spent engaged in lawsuits. These involved her late husband's $1.6 billion dollar estate, her partnership with TrimSpa, a lawsuit over the Bahamas' residence with ex-lover, G. Ben Thompson, and finally, the high-profile debate surrounding her daughter's lawful paternity with Larry Birkhead.

The home is situated in the hills of Studio City, California. The winding road leading up to the property is a very steep climb from

the flats below. When Jennifer drove up to see Anna Nicole's house, it was a frightening experience. The hillside home is situated on a narrow road that is so tight and constricted that when two cars are on the road at the same time, one car has to wait for the other to pass. Homes built in that area are situated on small lots. Large parcels of land are very rare in Los Angeles. Only the super rich can afford them. Consequently, builders tend to take advantage of every square foot of land, even the impractical and treacherous parts.

Life-Gua Number and Personality

Anna Nicole Smith was a 9 Life-Gua. They are known for being fiery, beautiful diva-like goddesses, which she certainly exhibited. The darker side of their nature is to be impatient, argumentative, rash, impulsive, mentally unstable, and paranoid. These are traits and tendencies she struggled with. As a child abandoned by her father, she craved attention. Anna basked in the spotlight, regardless of how it came. She was often quoted as saying, *"Bad publicity is good publicity...as long as they're still talking about me, I'm alive."* When these individuals are highly evolved, they demonstrate the fine qualities of wisdom, high intellect, loyalty and sentimentality. This was a side of Anna that very few people were privy to, but that she absolutely possessed.

The Home's Best Features

Parent String Formation

3646 Avenida Del Sol is a Period 8, Southwest *2* property with the prestigious and rare energy *Flying Star Chart* known as a *Parent String Formation*. These special homes are purported to deliver dazzling luck in regards to relationships and money. However, they must be properly activated with a mountain in the front and water at the back. This house had both of these features, a real mountain in the front, and a swimming pool in the back. Evidently, the home's energy was fortunate enough to have conceived Dannielynn and film select episodes of *The Anna Nicole Show*. Coincidentally, the home faced the same direction as Marilyn Monroe's house in Brentwood, where she passed away. Anna Nicole idolized Marilyn Monroe and was an ardent collector of her memorabilia. She was often quoted as saying that she wanted to be just like her. Eerily, the cause of death was very similar–a drug overdose. Unfortunately, Anna Nicole's lifelong wish to be like her idol seemed to be a self-fulfilling prophecy, down to the tragic and unexpected passing at a young age.

Main Entrance Interior Garage Door

It is highly likely that everyone entered the house via the interior garage door. This Northwest-facing door activated good energy (6 facing star). While not as prosperous as the Northeast-facing back door, it would have brought some benevolent opportunities.

Figure 35: It is very probable that everyone entered the house via the side of the house and garage door shown here. There is a small road sloping to the right which creates the missing *Tiger*. However, the Northwest-facing door activated good energy.

Northeast-Facing Back Door Indicated Wealth Luck

The Northeast-facing back door activated the current prosperous energy *(8 facing star)*. If this door was used a great deal, it would have delivered money luck and opportunities. However, the Northeast was not one of Anna Nicole's good directions and (-60) indicated mishaps.

Bathroom Locations Indicated Money and Health Luck

Toilets should be placed in our negative sectors due to their nature. Anna Nicole's toilets were located in the Northwest (-90), which was great for wealth luck, and the Southwest (-80) supporting good health. There were two bathrooms on the third floor and one on the first floor, both located in the Southeast (+80), which was not ideal and, over time, could have deteriorated her health. In general, the bathrooms indicated mixed luck with health. However, if she was only using the well-placed bathrooms, it would not have negatively impacted her health.

Stove Location Indicated Romance, Wealth and Health Luck

The location of her stove suppressed the divorce and failures direction (-90). However, it did activate an energy that could ignite lawsuits *(3 mountain star)* and she certainly had lots of those. The stove knobs/controls activated the romance star (4 facing star) and her health direction. This would bring many lovers and give her good health. Anna's sister wrote a tell-all autobiography of her life. In the book, she said that Anna Nicole never had a shortage of men and had an insatiable sexual appetite. This is common when this energy is activated. While the indications of her kitchen and stove would have brought mixed luck, it was largely supportive.

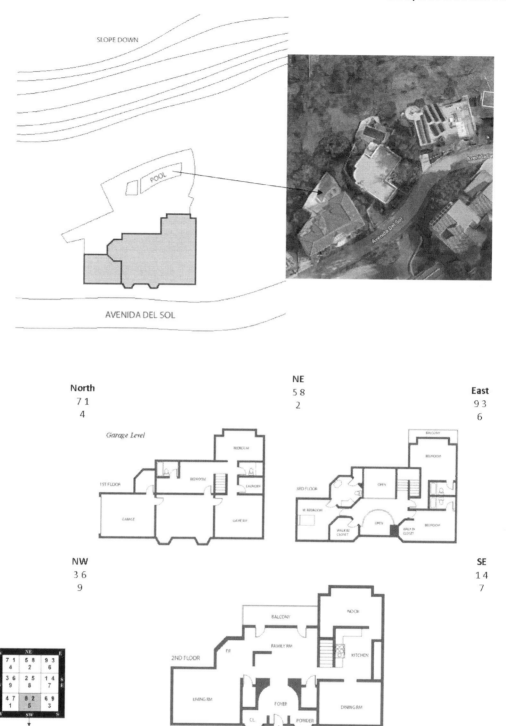

Figure 36: The floor plan and *Flying Star Chart* **for the Studio City home; Period 8, Southwest 2. This home's worst feature was the severe slope at the back. The pool did activate some wealth luck. The back patio was odd shaped as was the pool design.**

Negative Home Features

Road Too Close to the Home Indicated Instability and Money Loss

The first negative feature is that the road is dangerously close to the home. In fact, it is less than six feet from the front door. *Six feet!* This phenomenon is known as *cutting feet* and the stability of the occupants will be greatly compromised. It also indicates that the homeowners will struggle with attaining wealth and that it will sweep away opportunities for advancement.

Steep Drop-off Indicated Money Loss and Disasters

The back of the home is situated on a very steep cliff, sloping down dramatically into a canyon. The grade is approximately 45°, perhaps a bit more. There is no retaining wall or any type of fence to secure the back of the property. Extreme slopping land, particularly at the back of the home, always indicates the loss of wealth, business take-overs, loss of reputation, no support in the world, depression, and relationship issues. This is, without question, the single most detrimental feature of the home! See Figure 37 for this incredible image.

Southwest Facing Front Door Indicated Sickness and Bad Health

While it is good for a door to face the road, this door activated illness (2 facing star). However, the natural mountain in front of her property activated benevolent energy (8 mountain star).

Swimming Pool Indicated Wealth and Lawsuits

The pool is placed at an extreme angle and covers half of the Northeast, activating wealth energy (8 facing star). However, it also touches half of the East (3 facing star). This would have supported lots of legal hassles and lawsuits.

Figure 37: This steep drop-off at the back of the house was the single most detrimental feature of Anna Nicole's home. It indicates trouble with money, health, and relationships. Money gets hit the hardest!

Land Slopes on Right Side of House Which Indicated Unsupported Females

The road in front of the home slopes downward on the right (as you're looking out the front door). This suggests that females would be unsupported while living there. Women may be unable to commit in a relationship or feel misunderstood. Married or single men may also struggle keeping a wife, lover or girlfriend in this home. She may stray in affairs or leave altogether. This feature cannot be remedied as it is a public road. In order to enjoy the best Feng Shui, homes should be well-supported at the back, right and left sides. This will ensure that chi is retained. Properties set in dynamic environments such as winding roads and mountainous neighborhoods, require special attention. A serious budget should be designated for retaining walls to secure abundant and harmonious living.

Eight Roads of Destruction Indicated Money Loss and Death

This home has an *Eight Roads of Destruction* formation. It's created by the Southwest-facing front door in relationship to the neighbor's driveway coming from West 2 (see Figure 38). This formation is one of the most destructive formations there is in Classical Feng Shui, thus its ominous sounding name. The first way it may affect the homeowner is their money; a loss of wealth that can lead to bankruptcy. There could be health issues such as cancer, or even relationship woes akin to divorce. Even though it's extremely rare and unusual to have an *Eight Roads of Destruction*, so were these celebrities' lives. It points to precisely what they experienced while owning and living in these fatal homes.

Figure 38: This photo shows how the 'road' of the neighbor's steep driveway forms the *Eight Roads of Destruction* to Anna's house. The photo also shows how close the house is to the street creating the *Cutting-Feet* formation.

The *Eight Roads of Destruction* would have also delivered relentless struggles. Anna Nicole's partnership with TrimSpa proved to be an unsuccessful one, which ended in a lawsuit. Even though the bankruptcy court awarded her a share of her billionaire husband's estate, it was later rescinded. Taking the matter all the way to the Supreme Court, she fought, to the end, for the money Marshall had verbally promised. Many more court battles followed and, in the end, no money was awarded to her only living child, Dannielynn. Moreover, her short-lived achievements catapulted her into infamy due to her sporadic and outlandish behavior. After her success with Guess Jeans, *Playboy*, and movie appearances, she struggled to recapture the fame that seemed imminent. What kept Anna Nicole in the media's limelight were the high-profile court battles over her billionaire husband's money. Her potential to make money was there but it was always just out of reach. Anna Nicole's life became arduous. She struggled at every turn with money, health, relationships, and fame. She hung by a tenuous thread.

Northeast Mountain Indicated Loneliness, Lawsuits, and Short-Lived Success

In Classical Feng Shui, a lot of weight and importance are assigned to mountains. Principle things to consider are mountain's size, shape, proximity to the home, color, and location. A real, actual mountain will also activate the mountain star located there. The large, prominent mountain at the back of Anna Nicole's property is located in the Northeast. To be exact, the highest peak is between 37° to 42°. Using the *72 Piercing Dragons'* method, the description in the *72 Dragons Secret Verses* for these degrees is "loneliness, unending lawsuits from the government, brothers fighting nonstop, and short-lived success".

It continues to state that this malevolent mountain will 'release its chi' in the *Year of the Pig, Rabbit* or *Goat*. In 2007, the year of her death, was the *Year of the Pig*. The home was already incredibly unlucky but this particular release of energy didn't help matters. This could be a possible explanation as to why she passed away that year. Unfortunately, the mountain also activated the 5 mountain star, supporting more horrific luck.

Front Door Indicated Health Issues and Betrayals

Anna Nicole's front door faced the Southwest direction. This was not a good direction for her as it indicated bad health and betrayals (-80). Her front door, in the *Flying Stars* system, was also bad for health (2 facing star) and indicated illness; 'illness causing financial ruin, youngest and smartest son gets hurt and gastrointestinal problems' (read the negative aspect of the 8, 2 star combination on page 58). Anna Nicole did have some health issues, particularly with her breast implants. They caused her a great deal of pain. This may have been the beginning of the prescription drug abuse that eventually caused her demise. Sometime before her passing, she was very ill with a fever of 105° due to a blood infection. This was evidently from multiple injections of "longevity" shots in her buttocks. Even while pregnant with Dannielynn, Anna Nicole continued her prescription drugs, according to her sister, Donna Hogan, in *Train Wreck*.

Kitchen Location Indicated Health Issues

The overall location of the kitchen negatively affected her health because in the *Eight Mansions* system it was located in a good sector (+80). This was extremely unfavorable because kitchens should be located in negative sectors. Anna's delicate health played a vital role in her passing.

Bed Direction Indicated Divorce, Failures, and Lawsuits

According to the floor plan, the master bedroom is located on the third floor. The natural way to place the bed would have been on the Northwest wall. Viewing *YouTube* footage of *The Anna Nicole Show*,

it appears that the bed was placed there. This was her worst direction (-90) and would've activated disasters, bankruptcy and divorce. The stars (3, 6) would have supported disharmony, fighting, arguments, lawsuits, gossiping, and headaches. The bed placement in Feng Shui is considered a major feature. The location of the room (Northwest) and direction (Northwest) of the bed worked completely against her.

Feng Shui Restoration

Anna Nicole's home would have needed some drastic changes to extract the best energy. It's important to note that the severe slope at the back, the *Eight Roads of Destruction* and *Cutting Feet* formation, would've affected anyone occupying the home. These features will impact the property no matter what the *Flying Star Chart* or your *Life-Gua Number* is. Having said that, the home is better suited for the West Life Group (2, 6, 7 or 8 Life-Guas) because it faces Southwest. The following would have been our recommendations to improve her experience in the house.

Shore Up the Property

We would have encouraged Anna Nicole to spare no expense installing substantial retaining walls all along the back of the property. It should've been solid and composed of brick, concrete, stucco, or blocks. The back of the home is literally 'hanging' off a mountain (see Figure 37). This would have offered great stability and shown up as opportunities with money, better health and stable relationships. With this being shored-up, she might've won in court and received money from her late husband's estate (the amount of money at stake was somewhere between $88 to $445 million). While there are some huge columns holding up the extension, which is the back patio and swimming pool area, the rest of the land needs retaining walls.

Front Door Needs Metal and Insulation from Road

The front door needs metal to cure the 2 facing star and some protection from the road. A curved stucco wall between 6 to 7 feet would mimic the curved balcony above. Installing metal gates would've cured the 2 facing star. While the metal could be stainless steel, copper, brass or bronze, with its European design, bronze was the best match. The front door itself could have been a combination of glass and bronze. However, the door is already vulnerable to the road/ cars, so the stucco walls would have served to create a courtyard effect and protected it. Having steps leading up to the front door did help insulate it from the road. The courtyard walls would've also blocked

off the *Eight Roads of Destruction* created by the neighbor's driveway at *West 1* from her front door.

The Master Bedroom

Her bed should have been moved to the North wall (angled). This was her personal relationship direction (+70). The stars (6,9) were also excellent, indicating fame and money. Paired together, this would suggest her attracting an older man who also had a public persona. This bed arrangement could have led to a marriage. Another good choice would have been the Southeast wall (+80). This would have improved her health and money situation. The star combination (1,4) is a very strong romance and fame combination. She could have extended that wall a little for more room. That would have increased the closet (always a good thing).

The Toilets

We would have advised Anna to use the following bathrooms: the one by the front door, her master bathroom, and the bathroom in the Northwest sector on the first floor. The other bathrooms would have been "off-limits" and reserved for special occasions or when she had guests.

3646 Avenida Del Sol Today

Little is known about the previous tenants of this home. What is known is that Larry Birkhead lived there with his daughter, Dannielynn, shortly after Anna Nicole's death in 2007. Since that time, Larry has purchased a 10,000 square foot, six-bedroom house in his hometown of Louisville, Kentucky. In 2010, he appeared on a famous entertainment news channel that showed him selling a lot of Anna Nicole's belongings. He was auctioning off memorabilia, which included her Mercedes Benz. In the interview, he emphasized that he was not in financial distress but that he wanted to ensure that his daughter's future, including education, was taken care of and provided for. The house was finally sold in 2013 for $1.3 million.

Final Thoughts

Anna Nicole was truly blessed with good *Heaven Luck*. She lived a textbook rags-to-riches story. She had extreme beauty and used her sex appeal advantageously. Her ambition compelled her to find a way to the big city and the 'land of dreams'. Hollywood found her movie-star good looks irresistible, so reminiscent of the blonde bombshells of old.

As much as Hollywood loves a comeback, it also despises a 'train wreck.' Unfortunately, Anna was never able to move past the harsh public opinions. The constant media scrutiny must have weighed heavy on her daily life. Certainly, this would have affected her ability to select a home that would support her life-aspirations and money that was due

her as a billionaire's wife. While there were several negative features of Anna Nicole's home, the most detrimental was the land itself. The exterior energy of her home was far more instrumental in contributing to the demise of her life than the interior. In Feng Shui terms, building a home that 'hangs off a mountain', is living out of harmony with the natural environment. The ancients discovered that this scenario would always lead to disaster. It's no coincidence that Anna Nicole's tragic death and her son's early departure happened while owning this home. Had someone else lived in this house, their experiences would likely have manifested as money, relationship, and health issues, instead of death and never-ending litigations.

In the end, regardless of how much success, beauty and fame she possessed, her inner despair was apparent. It's sad that someone who had so much to give and live for, her life was reduced to a disreputable and abrupt conclusion.

Chapter Eight
Michael Jackson: *The King of Pop*

While living in this 17,000 sq. ft. French château in the prestigious Holmby Hills Estates for less than six months, Michael Jackson experienced lawsuits, bad relationships, money loss, illness, and drug abuse that led to his death.

Feng Shui and Facts

Address: 100 N. Carolwood,
Los Angeles, CA
Period 8, West 2
Moved in: December 2008
Facing Direction: 272°
Michael: 6 Life-Gua
Children: 3
Died: June 25, 2009
Negative Features: *Peach Blossom Sha, Four Destructions, Six Harms*, Olympic-size pool activated lawsuits, and too many roads surrounding the property.

Background on Celebrity and Property

Michael Jackson was an international superstar and hailed by the world as The King of Pop! He became one of the most successful entertainers of all time. His first public appearance was in the mid 1960's with his brothers, called The Jackson 5. In the 70's, he went solo and began building his music empire. However, Michael Jackson's fame and success was riddled with controversy. His ever-changing physical appearance, personal relationships, and the sexual allegations involving children marred his extraordinary talent and accomplishments. Under constant scrutiny by the media, his bizarre and erratic behavior eventually earned him the nickname of 'Wacko Jacko'.

The child sexual abuse charges began in 1993 while living at Neverland Ranch in Los Olivos, CA. The case was settled and no formal charges were made. While still living at the ranch in 2005, new charges surfaced. After a lengthy trial, he was acquitted of these charges as well. Shortly after the trial ended, he moved out of Neverland Ranch, *never* to return. He claimed there were too many painful memories and that the police had contaminated his beloved home.

In December 2008, Michael Jackson leased a home in Holmby Hills, an affluent neighborhood bordered by Beverly Hills, while preparing for his last and final concert series, *This Is It*. Michael died in this home on June 25, 2009, after suffering from cardiac arrest. This was spawned by an overdose of prescription drugs (Propofol and Lorazepam), administered by his personal physician, who was later charged with involuntary manslaughter. Michael Jackson's death triggered shockwaves across the globe. Billions of people around the world watched in grief as the news reported his untimely and shocking death. In this chapter, we will analyze the home he died in (100 North Carolwood), as well as Neverland Ranch (Los Olivos, CA) due to the numerous scandals that home attracted.

100 North Carolwood, located in Holmby Hills Estates, was built in 2002 with a history of three owners. Michael Jackson was renting the house for $100k per month from owner Hubert Guez, the former CEO of Ed Hardy. In 2013, Guez himself was involved in a sexual abuse lawsuit. The home was built by mega-mansion developer Mohamed Hadid, and designed by architect Richard Landry.

There are three prominent roads that surround the home. The land slopes down in the rear with a retaining wall at the back. Directly to the South is the extremely busy, world-famous Sunset Boulevard. Even though Jennifer was unable to enter the property, she was able to determine the facing degree. Tour buses swarm the area filled with those who yearn to see the place where the King of Pop lived and died.

Michael Jackson's Life-Gua Number

Michael Jackson was a 6 Life-Gua. These Guas tend to be noble, lofty, and in positions of authority. He was a natural-born leader, paving the way for future pop stars. His innovativeness with music and in business catapulted his success to an unparalleled level. These Life-Guas tend towards protectiveness with fatherly energy. On the negative side of their nature, they may be self-absorbed and over-thinkers.

The 6 Life-Guas are often sleep-deprived and crave time alone. It has been reported that Michael needed prescription medications to fall asleep. As the inventor of several unique dances, such as the moonwalk and robot, he fully exhibited the creativeness known by the 6 Life-Guas.

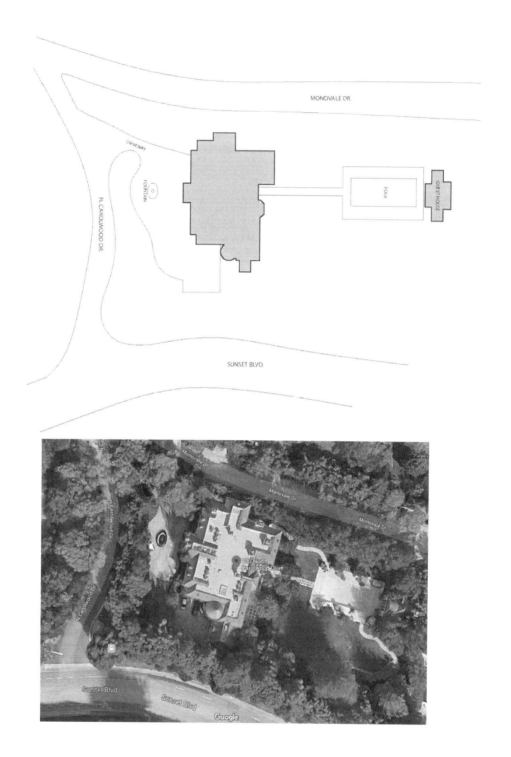

The Home's Best Features

House Facing Direction Indicated Wealth Luck

The Holmby Hills estate faces West at 272°. This was an excellent direction for Michael Jackson, being one of his best directions for wealth (+90). Also, the home facing had the current prosperous energy at the facing (8,8).

Good Ming Tang Indicated Good Opportunities, and Money

The home also had a generous open space in the front; both interior and exterior. This would have been excellent for business opportunities and money. He was able to harness this good luck because of the upcoming tour dates for the *This is It* concert. Originally, ten dates were scheduled and when those tickets sold out almost immediately, forty more concert dates were added to the schedule.

The Bathroom Locations Indicated Good Relationships, Money, and Health

All the bathrooms, with the exception of two, were located well for Michael. These were very good odds considering there were at least seven (7) bathrooms in the home. The bathrooms located in the East, South, Southeast, and North on all three levels were well-placed for him. The bathrooms/toilets located in the West (on the main level and upstairs) should not have been frequented by him. They had the potential to adversely affect his money, as they were located in his wealth direction (+90). However, if these bathrooms were rarely used, it would be a non-issue.

Water Feature Indicated Wealth Luck

The water fountain located in the front of the home was excellent because it activates the current period's prosperity energy, which is the *8 facing star*.

Negative Home Features

Too Many Roads Surrounding the Home Indicated Misfortunes

The Holmby Hills 1.26-acre estate is surrounded by three roads. This causes great instability and can indicate money loss, bankruptcy, illness, and misfortune for the residents. One of the roads that surround the property is Sunset Boulevard. The famous boulevard is known for the iconic glamour of Hollywood, aka 'Tinseltown'. Sunset Boulevard is a major thoroughfare and spans approximately twenty-four (24) miles. The road is treacherous due to the numerous winding, hairpin curves and blind crests. Car accidents are very commonplace. Most sections of the road don't have a center divider, which also makes driving precarious. With the increasing issue of over-population in Los Angeles, Sunset Boulevard is frequently congested with traffic that far exceeds its capacity. Living next to Sunset Boulevard would be equivalent to living next to a major highway in other parts of the country. The home is perpetually in a sea of energy, too overwhelming to create stable relationships, health or wealth.

Y-Juncture Road Indicated Issues with Money, Health, and Relationships

A *Y-juncture* is a formation that occurs when a road coming towards the home is forked with two roads that form a noose around the home. Such formations can be destructive because it creates a crushing intensity. Energy is good but too much can become toxic. The overabundance of energy subjects the residents to discord, money loss, divorce, accidents, and other mishaps.

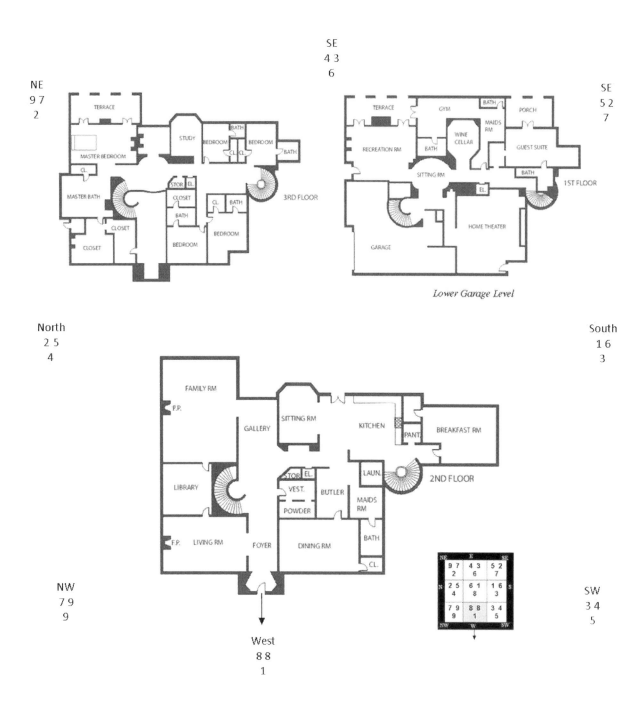

Figure 39: The floor plan and Period 8, West 2 *Flying Star Chart*. This home is surrounded on three sides with busy roads. The huge pool also activates lawsuits. Some changes are needed to mitigate the misfortunate energies.

Pool Location Indicated Gossip, Fighting, Arguments, and Lawsuits

The huge, almost Olympic-sized swimming pool activates the *3 facing star* and lawsuits. In June 2009, Michael Jackson was sued for $40 million. Allgood Entertainment claimed that the singer agreed to a single record and a $30 million reunion concert with The Jackson 5. Michael's sister, Janet, was also going to be included in the reunion. The alleged contractual agreement prevented the singer from performing elsewhere before the reunion concert, as well as for three months afterwards. Thus, when Michael agreed to a 50-date tour at The O2 Arena, he was in breach of contract with Allgood Entertainment. The unfortunate pool placement reared its ugly head!

Figure 40: The huge pool at 100 N. Carolwood activated lawsuits.

The Four Destructions Indicated Disharmony, Discord, and No Peace

A *Four Destructions* formation is created by the location of the road on the North side of the house, which is Monovale Drive, and the West-facing front door. This formation can cause disharmony, destruction, discord, and no peace. In Michael's case, 'destruction' was evident when he died of a cocktail of drugs. In the article, *Jacko's Deadly Cocktail of Drugs*, it described the dangerous mix of drugs that Michael was ingesting several times a day. Most of these

drugs were powerful narcotic pain relievers and it was his custom to take several at the same time. More than one is deemed potentially fatal by most doctors. Those close to Jackson said he was injected with Demerol, a potent pain killer often used after surgery, three times a day. Soon afterwards, he collapsed in his home in Los Angeles. Michael had also suffered a heart attack and was taking another painkiller, Dilaudid. Other sources revealed that he was prescribed yet another narcotic pain reliever, Vicodin. In addition to these, the drug cocktail taken daily included a muscle relaxant Soma, a sedative called Xanax, the anti-depressant Zoloft, Paxil for anxiety, and Prilosec for heartburn. Considering the potent mix of prescription medication he was consuming, the home's negative features such as the *Four Destructions* did not help him in the least.

Peach Blossom Sha Indicated Romance, Affairs, Divorce, and Illicit Behavior

A *Peach Blossom Sha* was created by the South-facing side door and the pool, which was located in the East. This particular formation indicates exile, bankruptcy, sexual problems, sex maniac, disloyalty, scandals, and turns the family upside down. It was rumored that the reason why Michael Jackson was doing the *This is It* tour was because he was on the verge of bankruptcy. On May 12, 2008, a foreclosure auction for the ranch was canceled after an investment company, Colony Capital LLC, purchased the defaulted loan. In a press release, Jackson stated, "I am pleased with recent developments involving Neverland Ranch and I am in discussions with Colony and Tom Barrack with regard to the Ranch and other matters that would allow me to focus on the future." There was another possible *Peach Blossom Sha* created by the West-facing front door and Sunset Boulevard (located South).

Six Harms Indicated Hassles and No Peace
The *Six Harms* formation was created by the West-facing front door and Carolwood Drive (a section in the Northwest at 299°). This formation is known to create a great deal of discord and disharmony to residents.

The East-Facing Back Door Indicated Gossip, Fighting, Arguments, and Lawsuits
The East-facing back door, just like the pool, would activate lawsuits, gossip, and discord. This energy would also hurt his relationships (-70). It had daily use and, therefore, contributed to more legal hassles.

The South-Facing Side Doors Indicated Bankruptcy and Divorce
The South-facing side door on the first floor was Michael Jackson's worst direction (-90). This energy attracts the very worst things, such as bankruptcy, fatality, divorce, business failure, family break-ups, and accidents. The two North-facing doors located on the first and third floors activated the *worst of the worst* and activated the 2,5 stars.

The Stove Direction Indicated Lawsuits and Grave Misfortune
The stove location was excellent for Michael Jackson, burning up his bad luck (-90). However, this was negated by the knobs/controls activating the North (2,5).

The Master Bed Direction Indicated Calamities, Death, and Money Loss
According to the floor plan, the natural place to locate the bed was on the North wall. This direction has some of the worst energy in the house, the detrimental 2,5 combination. To add insult to injury, the annual *5 Yellow Star* visited the North in 2009 when he died. The North was also his -80 direction and activating it could harm the body and health. Considering how Michael Jackson passed away, these are not shocking revelations.

Feng Shui Restoration

It's obvious that this stunning home is another example of a home that is out-of-harmony. It may not have been as detrimental if the roads weren't there or as close. However, presently these busy roads, especially Sunset Boulevard, create a river of energy harming the occupants of the house in every way.

Block off the Roads
The house needs solid, extremely high walls that insulate it from the three roads. This requires more than trees and lush landscaping. Since we did not actually see the property, it is uncertain if the roads could be seen from the home. From photos, it appears that there are some walls and that the roads may be seen from certain areas of the property. The roads also create some of the most negative energy features such as the *Peach Blossom Sha, Six Harms,* and *Four Destructions.*

Figure 41: The entire estate property should be surrounded by tall stone or brick walls.

Change the Flying Star Chart
We would have recommended changing the *Flying Star Chart* of this house from West 2 to West 1. The front door at 272° should have been re-angled (tilted) to 258.5°. Several problems would've been solved. The *8 facing star* is now located in the East on the huge pool and it would activate the

most benevolent wealth energy. The *Peach Blossom Sha, Four Destructions,* and *Six Harms* are not formed with the new facing direction. The exact degree of the door is on a *Precious Jewel Line* degree and will bring exceptional good luck to the residents. The front door would need a huge, bronze metal statue. This should be at least 8 to 10 feet tall. The fountains should be removed altogether. While there would be some adjustments to the kitchen and other areas, they're less expensive than removing the pool.

Side Doors
The exterior, South-facing side door in the home theater room would need a metal cure as it now has the *5 facing star*.

The Stove
The stove would need to be relocated within the kitchen as it now sits on a *2 mountain star*. Depending on who lives there, a good scenario would be to place the stove on the North (1 mountain star) with the knobs facing East (8 facing star). The kitchen remodel would be well worth the effort. This would have been good for money and health.

The Bedroom Direction
After the door tilt to West 1, Michael Jackson should have placed his bed on the East wall. The stars are excellent (8, 8) and works very well in Advanced Eight Mansions (+60).

The Bathrooms
We would've recommended that the two bathrooms on the main level and upstairs located in the West sector would be off-limits to everyone. By not using these two bathrooms, particularly the toilets, this would have remedied the bathrooms being located improperly, indicating money loss (+90).

100 North Carolwood Today

It might have all started in 2007 when the former owner, Hubert Guez, was named as a defendant in the Unzipped Apparel verses Sweet Sportswear lawsuit. The wronged company was awarded $45 million in damages. Perhaps this prompted the sale of the estate in 2008 for $38 million. Unable to sell the home, it was rented to Michael Jackson until his death. In 2011, while the home was listed, Guez sued map seller, Linda Welton, for scaring off potential buyers. In 2013, he was sued by his female masseuse for sexual misconduct. After much ado, the Holmby Hills château finally sold for $18 million on November 2, 2012 to Steven Mayer, a banker with Cerberus Capital Management.

Final Thoughts

This home has a tragic history due to all the negative formations and its unstable setting in the environment. Hubert Guez experienced money loss and several lawsuits while owning the property. Michael Jackson's luck was so bad that he used all the unfortunate Feng Shui and passed away. While much was his karma, it still indicates serious issues with the home. It will be interesting to see if the new owners thrive in the home. If so, many changes would need to be made in order to do so.

While living at **Neverland Valley Ranch** for almost 20 years, Michael Jackson was divorced twice, sued twice for sexual misconduct toward a child, had bad health, acquired heavy debts, lost money and reputation and, finally, lost majority ownership of the property.

Feng Shui and Facts

Address: 5225 Figueroa Mountain Road, Los Olivos, CA
Period 7, Southwest 1
Moved in: 1988
Facing Direction: 202°.6-217.5°
Michael: 6 Life-Gua
Children: 3
Lawsuits: 6 or more
Negative Features: *Eight Roads of Destruction*, two *Peach Blossom Sha* formations, *Goat Blade* formation, *Six Harms,* and the stove supported money loss.

Background on Celebrity and Property

Neverland Valley Ranch, almost 3,000 acres, was once known as Sycamore Valley Ranch. It's located in Santa Ynez Valley, about a two-hour drive from Los Angeles. Real estate developer, William Bone, bought the ranch in 1977. He built a home and moved in with his family in 1982. The main house was a sprawling 13,000 square feet in a traditional Tudor-style design. Robert Altevers, the architect, also designed formal gardens, a stone bridge, and a five-acre lake with a five-foot waterfall.

Once Michael Jackson purchased the ranch in 1988, he made numerous changes to the land. However, the home was kept as it was originally built and he renamed it Neverland Valley Ranch. This was Jackson's home as well as his private amusement park, which contained a petting zoo complete with chimpanzees, elephants and giraffes. It also boasted two railroads named Neverland Valley Railroad. The steam locomotive was named Katherine after his mother. Michael Jackson was also an avid art collector.

On February 25, 2008, Michael received word from Financial Title Company to pay $24,525,906.61 by March 19th. If not, a public auction would be held to sell the land, home, buildings, amusement park rides, trains, and art. However, on March 13, 2008, a private agreement was reached with Fortress Investment to save Michael's ownership of the ranch.

On November 10, 2008, Jackson transferred the title and neighbors reported immediate activity on the property, including the amusement rides being trucked along the highway. Jackson still owned an unknown stake in the property, since the Ranch was a joint venture between Jackson and an affiliate of Colony Capital, LLC (an investment company run by billionaire Tom Barrack). The Santa Barbara County Assessor's Office stated Jackson sold an unknown portion of his property rights for $35 million.

Jennifer was unable to view the property due to security. However, she was able to examine public records at the County of Santa Barbara. She determined the facing was Southwest between 202.6° and 217.5° degrees. Even without 'eyes' on it, the facing, floor plan and site plan revealed some fascinating information about Michael Jackson's life there.

The Home's Best Features

The Property Surrounded by Mountains Indicated Wealth and Support

The ranch is set in a beautiful, natural environment in a valley, surrounded by gorgeous mountains on all sides. The Chinese refer to this as a 'rice bowl'. Since chi collects in the rice bowl, it delivers great wealth and support for the occupants.

Good Ming Tang Indicated Good Opportunities for Money

The main residence at Neverland had a generous, open space in the front of the home. This space is known as the *Ming Tang* (Bright Hall) and it, too, is where energy can collect.

Water Feature in the Front of the Main Residence Indicated Wealth Luck

The huge lake and spewing fountain can be seen from the entrance and front door of the home. At the time (Period 7), this feature was perfectly placed, which activated wealth luck. The house was in Period 7 the majority of Michael's time at the ranch. This would explain why he was able to make large amounts of money while living there. However, after 2004 when we entered into Period 8, the water began working against him. This enormous water feature would have attracted robbery, thievery, a sense of hopelessness, and "things being taken away". This was the ultimate ending for him.

The Facing Direction of the Home Indicated Wealth and Good Relationships

The main residence faced Southwest. This was Michael's personal relationship direction (+70). This energy would have allowed him to cultivate new relationships, attract romance, solidify existing friendships, cement familial ties, and successfully network. The stars in the Southwest indicated fame, tremendous wealth, good sons, very smart girls in the family and famous actors/actresses (7, 7). He married twice while living in this home. First to Lisa Marie Presley, and later to Debbie Rowe, the mother of his two eldest children. It was apparent that loyal relationships and money came his way, however, with his extravagant lifestyle, money was sure to slip away.

The grounds showing the amusement park, railroad and zoo.

The grounds near the home showing the 5-acre lake, pool and tennis court.

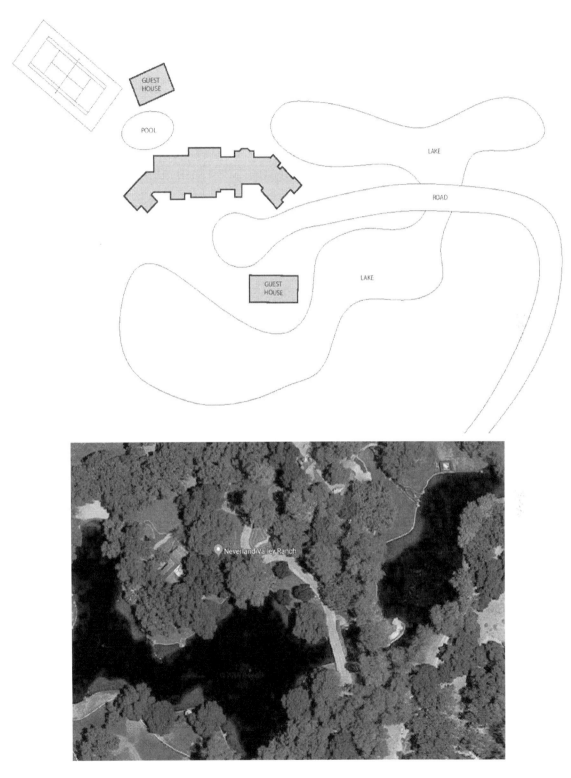

Figure 42: The huge man-made lake covers all eight directions except North. The site has too much water and can activate sexual misconduct.

In 1984, Michael Jackson had in his portfolio one of the most sought-after assets in the music industry, with a song catalog that included the works of the Beatles. Michael took out more than $270 million in loans to finance his opulent lifestyle. This included the construction of the Neverland playground and zoo. This money was acquired by putting up as collateral his 50% stake in the song catalog, Sony/ATV Music Publishing, and other assets. However, when faced with insolvency in 2006, he struck a deal. This is when he sold 50% of his stake in the song catalogue. Most likely to the Sony Corporation, the catalog's co-owner, as part of a complex refinancing transaction.

Without a doubt, Michael generated incredible wealth from his albums, concert tours, and other investments. However, after 2004, a significant amount of money was being lost, as evidenced by the loans he took on. To compound things, he was getting into serious debt and had the child sexual misconduct lawsuits to contend with. By 2006, the negative influence of the *7 stars* were starting to show their effects.

Negative Features

The Shape of the Home Indicated Disharmony
The overall shape of the house, while not totally extreme, is considered very negative in Feng Shui terms. The design was disjointed and indicated disharmony. The floor plan was angled at both ends, creating a robotic arm effect. Odd shapes and designs are considered inauspicious in Feng Shui and rarely deliver good results for the occupants.

Too Much Water Indicated Money Loss and Illicit Behavior
The main residence at Neverland was practically inundated with water. It had a huge lake, a winding stream behind the house, and a massive swimming pool. All of these water features were in very close proximity to the house. Water is a powerful activator of energy and in order to get good results, it must be placed properly. Too much water can create money loss, alcoholism, detachment, illicit behavior (such as affairs), salacious scandals, and sexual misconduct, in general. In Feng Shui, water and money are closely connected to one another. Hence, we can ascertain that the water located at the back of the house would have created incredible instability. The lake encompasses the Northwest, West, Southwest, South, Southeast, East, and Northeast. The North is the only area without water.

The Lake in the Northwest Activated Conflict and Lawsuits
The five-acre lake activated a variety of energies. The section of the property in the Northwest activated conflict and lawsuits. The star combination (2, 3) in the Northwest is known as the *bull-fight sha* and it supports disputes, arguments, bickering, gossiping, and lawsuits. This type of energy is extremely unfavorable and famous for producing discord of all types but, particularly, lawsuits. Robbery is also indicated by the *3 facing star*.

In Christopher Andersen's book, *Michael Jackson: Unauthorized*, he described the numerous lawsuits Michael had to contend with. L.A. Gear sued him for $10 million stating fraud and breach of contract. It was alleged that Unstoppable footwear flopped because Michael didn't deliver the promised album in time to promote the product. The Cleveland Orchestra sued him for $7 million stating that he lifted 67 seconds from Beethoven's *Symphony No. 9*. This was incorporated in the song *Will You Be There?* (*Dangerous* album). Songwriter Crystal Cartier filed a $40 million lawsuit against Jackson, claiming he had stolen her song. In addition to all the aforementioned lawsuits, there were the two sexual allegation suits. At any rate, lawsuits topped the list of 'conflicts' brought on by the 2, 3 energy. These numerous lawsuits were no doubt key in depleting his finances.

More unfortunate events happened due to this energy being activated by water. It supported several negative events in Michael's life – sexual misconduct and divorces. 1993 is when the first child molestation charges were made public. On May 26, 1994, Lisa Marie Presley and Michael Jackson wed in a private ceremony in the Dominican Republic. On January 18, 1996, Lisa Marie filed for divorce, citing irreconcilable differences.

On November 14, 1996, Michael wed Debbie Rowe in Sydney, Australia. Three months after Rowe and Jackson's marriage, she gave birth to Michael Joseph Jackson, Jr. (born on February 13, 1997), later nicknamed Prince. The next year, she gave birth to daughter, Paris-Michael Katherine Jackson (born April 3, 1998). Michael took full responsibility for raising the children after divorcing Rowe on October 8, 1999. She received an $8 million settlement and a house in Beverly Hills, California. In 2001, she signed over all parental rights to Michael Jackson. Having been married twice for two years or less each time, the

negative energy prevalent in the home caused by the *Eight Roads of Destruction* would support such events.

Goat Blade Formation Indicated Divorce, Alcoholism, Drugs, Affairs, and Gambling

The house had a *Goat Blade Formation* created by an East-facing door and water in the East (the lake and pool). The door is located in the upstairs part of the master suite. This formation portends divorce, alcoholism, affairs, sexual addiction, substance abuse problems, and gambling. It has been reported that Michael's dependency on prescription drugs came after he sustained skin burns while doing the Pepsi video, as well as all the plastic surgeries he underwent.

Six Harms Formation Indicated Hassles and Disharmony

The four Northeast-facing doors on the first level create a *Six Harms* in relationship to the water in the South (the lake and road). These formations ignite great disharmony in the household.

Peach Blossom Sha Indicated Illicit Sexual Behavior, Affairs, and Women Leaving

The four Northeast-facing doors also create a *Peach Blossom Sha* in relationship to the water located in the South (the lake and road). Due to the fact that the enormous lake encompasses so many directions makes it possible to activate many negative formations. The classic text, for this particular *Peach Blossom Sha*, describes it as 'your millions run away; females of the house run away with another man'. Considering that he had two divorces while residing at Neverland Ranch, this is not surprising.

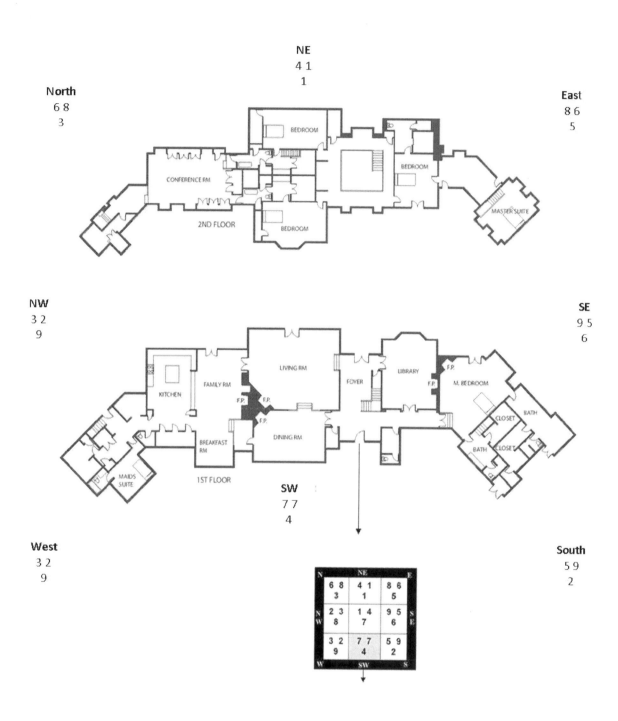

Figure 43: The Neverland Valley Ranch floor plan and Period 7, Southwest 1 *Flying Star Chart*. **The house has an extreme design which rarely delivers good results.**

Northeast-Facing Doors Indicated Strong Sexual Energy, Romance, and Family Separates

The daily use of the four Northeast-facing doors would have fully activated the 4, 1 stars. The swimming pool and lake would further charge up this energy. This set of stars has numerous implications. First and foremost, it indicates strong sexual energy. The 4, 1 is referred to as a Peach Blossom combination, not to be confused with the infamous *Peach Blossom Sha* formations. On the positive side, the 4, 1 combination can deliver good romance, travel, academic success, scholarly pursuits, and fame. The negative aspect can support affairs, sex maniacs, illicit sexual or sleazy behavior, and the family separates from fighting. Whether this set of stars is interrupted as positive or negative depends on the home's energy. If the overall Feng Shui is not good it will support the negative aspects, or you may get a mix of good and bad.

The first time that Michael Jackson was accused of child sexual abuse was with 13-year old Evan Chandler in 1993. That year the 1 star visited the Northeast. This would have made the strong sexual energy of the Northeast (4, 1) even more so. At any rate, things came to a head and a lawsuit ensued. In 2005, he was again accused of improper sexual conduct with a child; Gavin Arvizo, a 13-year-old boy. That year, the 7 annual star visited the Northeast. This pairing of energy (1, 7) created a very negative *Peach Blossom* indicating lawsuits, lots of trouble, too much sexual energy and thievery.

However, the 4, 1 energy did attract two wives for Michael. In 1994 when he and Lisa Marie married, the 9 annual star visited the Northeast. This was a favorable pairing (1, 9) and would support a steamy and passionate love affair. In 1996, the annual energy that visited was the 7 star. Still in Period 7 that year, the 7 was considered the best energy. That may explain why he married Debbie Rowe during this year.

The Bathroom Locations Indicated Good and Bad Luck

In Feng Shui, toilets should be located in our negative sectors (-90, -80, -70 or -60). Michael had three bathrooms that were well placed and five that were not. The best toilets were located in the South, Southeast, and East. These locations would have indicated support in relationships and romance. The other five located in the Northeast, Northwest, West, and Southwest would have caused issues with his health.

The Fireplace Location Indicated Health Issues

There were several fireplaces at the Neverland home. The two Northwest-facing ones located in the family room and library would have activated lawsuits if used (3 facing star). The two South-facing ones located in the dining room and master bedroom would have activated great energy (9 facing star). The East-facing one in the living room would have hurt the father of the house (6 facing star). There are three fireplaces clustered in the center of the house, this would have indicated issues with the heart, high blood-pressure or heart disease.

The Staircase Location Indicated Health Issues

Whenever a large staircase is located in the center of the home, it can lead to serious health issues over time. It would compromise the spine, joints, bones, and skeletal system.

The Kitchen and Stove Indicated Bankruptcy

The stove was sitting on a *2 mountain star* (NW) and the knobs activated the *5 facing star* (SE). In Feng Shui terms, it really doesn't get worse than this for a stove placement. This would have activated a host of misfortunate and calamitous events such as cancer, death, disease, and bankruptcy. In *Michael Jackson: Unauthorized,* Christopher Andersen describes how Michael Jackson would lavish the children and their families with gifts when they visited Neverland. This included trips to Toys R Us and $100k shopping sprees. At times, he would even gift the parents with a new Mercedes each. These kids were also invited on expensive vacations. On a high note, Michael donated millions of dollars for children's charities. However, debt and bankruptcy was looming with his extravagant spending and lawsuit settlements. When he died he left over $400 million dollars in debt.

The Master Bed Placement Indicated Disasters

According to the floor plan and viewing online photos, we believe the bed was placed on the South wall. Unfortunately, this was Michael's worst direction (-90). To make matters worse, the *5 mountain star* would have been activated supporting devastation, stress, mental pressure, lawsuits, fire disaster, sexual diseases, and calamity.

Feng Shui Restoration

The home was much luckier for the Bone family who only lived at the ranch for four years. In order to fully extract the best energy for Michael Jackson, we would have recommended some drastic changes. This would have included calming down the sexual, lawsuit, and money-loss energy.

Correcting the House Shape

The shape of the home could have been remedied by re-designing or removing the odd shaped ends. With a 'four point gold' design, the home would have provided Michael with some much-needed stability. Remember, the four point gold is primarily square or rectangular allowing a harmonious flow of energy to support the occupants.

Too Much Water Surrounding the Property

The lake, which covered all directions except North, should have been re-configured. Since Michael was living in the house in Period 8 (began on Feb 4, 2004), preparations should have been made to extract the best energy after this capital change.

The Pool

In order to place the pool where it can activate the best energy and do no harm, a decision would have needed to have been made as to whether keep the house Period 7 or change to Period 8. Once that was decided, the pool could be properly placed and where it would do 'no harm'.

Eight Roads of Destruction, Goat Blade, Six Harms, and Peach Blossom Sha

Since the *Peach Blossom Sha*, the *Eight Roads of Destruction* and *Goat Blade* all hinged on specific 15-degree increments, great care would have needed to taken so that the water would not activate these detrimental formations.

The Bathrooms/Toilets

The bathroom located in the Southwest (+70), West (+90), Northwest (+60), Northeast (+80) and in the middle of the home would be off limits to everyone living in the home. Another option would be to remove the bathrooms in those sectors and add bathrooms in the North (-80), East (-70), South (-90) and in the Southeast (-60) to suppress the negative energy in those sectors.

The Fireplaces and Staircases

Removing and relocating fireplaces and staircases are cost prohibitive. However, making sure that the big-ticket energetic items (the lake and pool) were better placed, these features would have less weight and not harm the householders.

The Stove

The stove should have been moved to the North corner (6 mountain star) with front-facing knobs (South and 9 facing star).

Health, money, and relationships would have improved tremendously.

The Bed Placement

If Michael had been willing to remodel, the best placement for the bed, in Period 7, would have been to the Southwest (7, 7). With no remodeling, the bed could have been placed East in the little angled area. Either direction would have improved his life events, particularly the Southwest. The bed would have to be repositioned if the house was brought to a Period 8.

Neverland Valley Ranch Today

Following the death of Michael Jackson in 2009, the neglected Neverland Valley Ranch fell into disrepair. As of May 2016, the 2,698 acre ranch, jointly owned by the Jackson estate and Colony NorthStar was listed with Sotheby's International Realty with an asking price of $100 million. Due to lack of interest, the asking price of the ranch had fallen to $67 million by February 2017. As of early 2018, the property is listed with Coldwell Banker for the same price.

Over the years, several ideas for the ranch were put forward. One was creating a state park that would attract millions of Jackson fans. However, the local residents opposed the idea due to the traffic congestion it would create in their rural and pristine area.

Final Thoughts

The Chinese believe that we are afforded three types of luck that will drive the trajectory of our lives. No doubt Michael Jackson was destined for greatness and tragedy. *Heaven Luck* would ensure he attained wealth, fame, triumphs, and sensational achievements. *Earth Luck* would deliver homes that would support his deep insecurities and abandonment issues. *Man Luck* supported the incredible hard-working man he was.

Michael Jackson was a hugely talented man who had a difficult upbringing. For the most part, he turned his hardships into triumphs. Unfortunately, his childhood experiences were not easily reconciled. These unresolved issues guided his choices in life. His massive fame guaranteed that he would be under constant scrutiny and openly criticized. Had he been supported by good Feng Shui, his life could have been improved and been less dramatic.

How was it possible that the previous owners did not have the same experience as Michael Jackson? Their lives, as far as we can tell, did not involve lawsuits, sexual misconduct, and huge money losses. It was not their karma perhaps. Michael extracted the energy quite differently and sadly, the worst of it. Towards the end of his life, it was hard to recognize the 'man in the mirror'. He was greatly loved, still appreciated, and sorely missed. Hopefully, for generations to come, the best of him will be remembered.

Chapter Nine
Sharon Tate: *The Movie Star*

While living at 10050 Cielo Drive for only a few months, Sharon suffered her husband's numerous infidelities, marital discord, had disturbing prophetic dreams about her death, and was brutally murdered along with four friends.

Feng Shui and Facts

Address: 10050 Cielo Drive, Los Angeles, CA
Period 6, Southeast 1
Moved in: 1969
Facing Direction: 123°
Sharon Tate: 2 Life-Gua
Roman Polanski: 4 Life-Gua
Died: August 9, 1969
Negative formations: *Peach Blossom Sha, Eight Killing Mountain Forces, Dragon* and *Tiger* side missing, severe drop-off in the front (canyon), and back door indicated young people dying.

Background on Celebrity and Property

Many considered Sharon Tate to be the most beautiful woman of her generation. She remains a fascinating pop icon and a poster child for the 1960s. The model-actress was only two weeks away from giving birth to her first child, a son. Sharon was murdered in her home on Cielo Drive in Benedict Canyon, an upscale neighborhood in Beverly Hills. Ironically, *Cielo*, in Spanish, means 'heaven'.

On that ill-fated night in 1969, Sharon Tate, along with Abigail Folger, the coffee heiress, celebrity hairstylist Jay Sebring, photographer Voy Frykoski, writer Wojciech Frykowski, and Steven Parent, a friend of the Tate gardener who happened to be in the wrong place at the wrong time, were butchered by the Manson Family. When the five bodies were discovered on the morning of Saturday, August 9, 1969, the scene was worse than anything anyone could have imagined, including Polanski, who had directed *Rosemary's Baby*. The head of the Manson Family, Charles, was not present but ordered the murders. A journalist once asked Sharon if she believed in fate. She said, *"Certainly. My whole life has been decided by fate. I think something more powerful than we are decides our fates for us. I know one thing — I've never planned anything that ever happened to me."*

Built in 1944 by French actress Michèle Morgan, 10050 Cielo Drive was a three-acre property high above Los Angeles, California. The home had panoramic views of Sunset Boulevard and the Pacific Ocean. Michèle chose a French Farmhouse style for the home. The property also included a large swimming pool and guest house. After three years of trying to become a successful Hollywood actress, Michèle packed up and went back to France.

Figure 44: The Tate house showing the pool and the Southwest-facing side door.

The home's history of famous residents included, Lillian Gish, Henry Fonda, Terry Melcher, and Candice Bergen. Cary Grant and Dyan Cannon honeymooned there in 1965. In 1969, the house was leased by director Roman Polanski and his wife, Sharon Tate, from Terry Melcher and Candice Bergen. After a short stay on Cielo Drive, Terry Melcher and Candice Bergen moved to Doris Day's (Terry Melcher's mother) house in Malibu. From the 1960s until the 1990s, the owner of Cielo Drive, Rudi Altobelli, lived in the guest house. It became infamous following the murders. In

later years, rock stars Nine Inch Nails and Marilyn Manson recorded albums there.

Sharon Tate and Roman Polanski's Life-Gua Numbers

Sharon was a 2 Life-Gua. They're known for their calm and relaxed demeanors, tend to exhibit intuitive abilities, and have a propensity to nurture people. The 2 Life-Guas are family-oriented and maintain old fashioned values. Sharon loved to entertain in her home  and often cooked home-prepared meals for friends. She expressed a desire to settle down, have children and leave the glitter of Hollywood behind. This aspiration was expressed in Greg King's book, *Sharon and the Manson Murders.*

King also reveals that Sharon Tate had a prophetic dream of her brutal murder two years before it actually took place. One night, while staying alone at her friend Jay Sebring's house, there was a 'creepy little man' outside her bedroom door. He was not quite solid, like a ghost or apparition. She got up and went downstairs. *"I saw something or someone tied to the staircase,"* she said. *"Whoever it was – and I couldn't tell if it was a man or a woman, but knew somehow that it was either Jay Sebring or me – he or she was cut open at the throat."* Call this her intuition, psychic abilities kicking in, or just a random experience. Either way, it's eerily similar to what happened to her when her life was abruptly ended.

Roman is a 4 Life-Gua. 4 Gua's tend to be malleable, flexible, highly sexual, and indecisive. They're usually attractive people with movie star qualities. Roman Polanski was a notorious playboy, even after he married Sharon Tate. The energy dynamic of these two is one of conflict and control. According to their Life-Gua numbers, Roman had the dominate energy in the relationship. In King's book, he mentions how Sharon convinced herself that an open relationship was good. Roman told her right from the start that he disliked being tied down. Reluctantly, and because she loved him, she agreed to the arrangement. However, they often argued over Roman's philandering lifestyle but he was quick to remind her of their initial understanding.

The Home's Best Features

The home was situated in the mountainous region of Beverly Hills, called Benedict Canyon. Benedict Canyon is a ravine that drops in a North-to-South direction from its high point at the crest line in the Santa Monica Mountains. Directly behind the home was a large, prominent mountain. This home was considered a Period 6 (1964-1984). Sharon Tate and Roman Polanski moved in February of 1969. Even living near the glorious Santa Monica Mountains, six months later, Sharon and her friends would be murdered.

Benevolent Mountain at the Back Indicated Great Support
In Feng Shui, a superlative situation for a home is having a good mountain behind it. This offers the occupants incredible support 'out in the world'. Sharon Tate was well-loved in Hollywood and Roman Polanski had no problem funding his various film projects.

The Assistant Star Water Method Indicated Wealth
The house had a wealth formula already in place. The *Assistant Star Water Method* was very serendipitously formed by the Northwest-facing backdoor and the big pool/water in the Southwest. This would have brought wealth-luck to any of the occupants who lived there. See the *Glossary of Terms* for more information about this wealth formula.

The Stove Indicated Money
The stove was located on the Northeast (1 mountain star) and faced the Southwest (8 facing star). Since the Northeast is a negative sector for Roman (-90), this would bring him money and wealth. However, the location would harm money luck for Sharon. The stove was used often, so this would have brought good and bad to this mixed Life Group couple.

Southwest-Facing Side Door Indicated Wealth Luck
The Southwest-facing side door was located in Sharon and Roman's bedroom. The double French doors led out to the pool and activated future money luck (4, 8). The annual 1 star visited the Southwest that year and created more money-luck. In the Eight Mansions system, the door was good luck for Sharon, indicating stability (+60). However, it was quite negative for Roman which harmed his relationships, activated affairs, and attracted lawsuits (-70). In this house, two out of the three doors indicated prosperity energy, which was excellent.

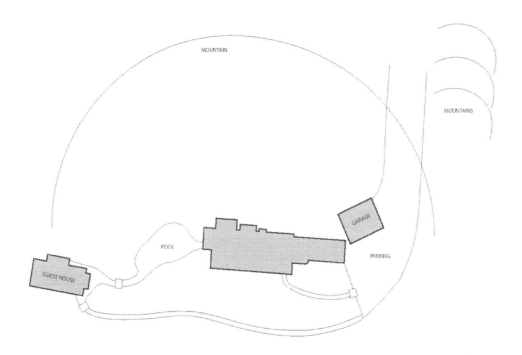

West
9 3
8

NW
8 4
7

North
3 9
2

SW
4 8
3

NE
1 2
9

South
2 1
1

East
5 7
4

SE
6 6
5

Figure 45: The driveway leading up the house.

Figure 46: A front view of the house.

Figure 47: Ariel view of the house after the police arrived to find the five bodies at Cielo Drive.

Negative Features

Missing Tiger and Dragon Sides Indicated No Support

There was no support either on the left side (male side and the *Dragon*) or the right side (female side and the *Tiger*) of the house. This is easily resolved if neighboring homes flank the left and right. On larger estate homes this can be represented with a solid stucco or brick wall, or landscape mounds. Missing the *Tiger* and *Dragon* would have made the couple feel insecure with each other. Such homes often denote affairs and divorce.

Eight Killing Mountain Forces Denoted Murder and Disasters

The home had the disastrous *Eight Killings* formed by the Southeast-facing front door (112°-127°) and the mountain located in the North (352°-7°). This formation is famous for delivering divorce, bankruptcy, diseases, danger, calamity, and in extreme cases, death. The *Eight Killings* is more lethal than the *Eight Roads of Destruction* as it has a 'timing' factor. In this case, Sharon was murdered in the *Month of the Monkey* (August). This had a direct correlation to the *Rat,* which is where the mountain was located.

Evidently, while stepping out of the house one day, her beloved Yorkshire terrier, Dr. Saperstein, was accidentally killed. Voyteck ran over him while backing out of the driveway. Roman knew this would break his wife's heart so he bought her another Yorkshire puppy which she named Prudence. She was told that Dr. Saperstein could not be found and likely ran away.

While Sharon's dog doesn't compare to the human carnage that took place at the home, it is another example of the destructive energy of the *Eight Killings*. The death of her beloved pet happened the same year and place where Sharon was murdered.

2 Peach Blossom Shas Indicated Romance, Affairs, Divorce, and Illicit Behavior

The home had two *Peach Blossom Sha* formations that cause disharmony for couples, as well as public scandals. The first one was created by the Northwest-facing back door and the East road/driveway leading to the home. This formation suggests exile, bankruptcy, sexual problems (or a sex maniac), disloyalty, scandals, and turning the family upside down. The second one was created by the Southeast-facing front door and the same road/driveway. This formation signifies incestuous relationships and sexual issues.

In Sharon's case, the entire duration of her marriage and courtship was riddled with Roman's infidelities. It was widely known that he was a ladies' man and that Sharon knew and somewhat tolerated his adulterous ways. However, she was shocked to find a sex tape of Roman making love to another woman in their bed. This hurt her so much that she confronted him. He gave his usual, flippant response about how she knew he didn't like being tied down. The two *Peach Blossom Shas* certainly supported his multiple, illicit affairs which bordered on a sexual problem. Many years later, in 1977, Roman was arrested and charged with five offenses (rape by use of drugs, perversion, sodomy, lewd, and lascivious acts) against Samantha Geimer, a 13-year-old girl. Shortly thereafter, he fled the country.

Front Door Indicated Wealth and Divorce

The house had the double 6 stars at the front door and facing. This was extremely lucky for money and accumulating wealth. However, the chi/energy was not captured either by water, nor was it retained with low walls. The front garden area had a severe drop-off into the canyon. No matter the period, this feature would cause problems for anyone who resided there, including the French actress who built it. On a personal level, the Southeast was very negative for Sharon (-70) and hurt her relationships. Many in the Tate clan were aware that Sharon was becoming increasingly resistant towards Polanski's lifestyle. Once she became pregnant, she hoped he would change. She told family that, if he didn't, she planned to divorce him.

The Bathrooms/Toilets Indicated Mixed Luck

Since Sharon and Roman were mixed Life Groups, some of the toilets would be better for her and some better for him. The master bedroom toilet was located in a good area for Sharon (+80), but would support Roman (-80). The North toilet located on the opposite side of the master bedroom would have been the best for her.

Two Bedrooms Indicated Divorce Energy

It's interesting that in this house there were two areas/bedrooms that had the famous divorce energy. This is the 2,1 or 1,2 combination located in the Northeast bedroom and South bedroom. It goes without saying that newlyweds and couples should avoid such energy. It will cause a great deal of marital discord and disharmony. The Tate-Polanski marriage was constantly in a fragile state. According to King's book, he wrote, *"On the last day before her murder, Sharon seemed disillusioned and worn out. She complained that 'Roman was a bastard' for leaving her alone with Frykowski (Abigail Folgers' boyfriend)"*. Sharon continued to maintain a close relationship with former boyfriend, Jay, and said without him, *"she would have gone out of her mind"*. Roman's apparent disinterest in their baby hurt her deeply. Above all, she felt that he was deliberately avoiding her. He seemed unwilling to put aside his own schedule to accommodate her needs and feelings. *"That's probably why the little rat is still in London,"* she added sadly. Roman had assigned Frykowski to take care of Sharon while he was away for work.

The Master Bed Direction and Back Door Indicated Young People Dying

Two important features, the back door and the master bed, were activated by the Northwest. This area had the 8,4 combination of stars. In Period 6, this was not a good energy. It indicated young people dying in the house. Five young people died in the Cielo home on the same night. Also, the *5 Yellow Star* visited the Northwest the year of the deaths (1969). This star is the disaster star and when combined with the *4 facing star* in the Northwest, it had serious implications. The 4,5 combination suggests gang-related incidents. The Manson Family was an organized gang bent on creating 'helter skelter'. On the night of the murders, three of the Manson 'gang' members carried out the killings while one of them was on lookout.

The annual *5 Yellow Star* is so pernicious that it can cause serious issues and wreak havoc as standalone energy. This would only happen if there were other very negative features at a property. This home had those things, including the detrimental *Eight Killing Mountain Forces.* It was rumored that Charles Manson said that Tate and her friends were heavy in the drug scene and that they swindled people for drugs. Sharon and Roman were known to have a lot of parties at the home on Cielo Drive. At their parties, people unknown to them would often come and go as they pleased. With the *5 Yellow Star* energy comes trouble, including troublemakers.

Feng Shui Restoration

The Canyon Front Yard Drop-off
The sharp drop-off in the front yard/garden area would have needed shoring up with solid retaining walls. This was the most negative feature on the property which would have adversely affected anyone living there. It appears the new home built there many years later had very significant walls where the property dropped off into the canyon below.

The Eight Killings
So that the *Eight Killings* formation would not bring harm to the occupants, it should have been blocked off from view with tall landscaping or a tall wall. With this installation, the Southeast-facing door could not receive the energy.

Peach Blossom Sha
Since the incoming/outgoing driveway from the East was the cause of both *Peach Blossom Shas,* the solution would be to re-do this feature. The driveway should have been designed to come from East 1 or East 3. Neither direction would create a Peach Blossom Sha formation with the Northwest-facing back door.

10050 Cielo Drive Today

In 1994, Hollywood producer Jeff Franklin bought the property. He demolished the old house, pool and guest house and erected a 16,000 square foot, Italian Mediterranean villa. The new address is 10066 Cielo Drive. It was designed by architect Richard Landry. Landry also designed 100 N. Carolwood, the estate home where Michael Jackson died in Holmby Hills. Franklin's villa is estimated to be worth $22 million in today's market. From Google maps, the front of the home appears to be East-facing. This facing would not have the *Peach Blossom Sha* or *Eight Killings* formations. It also appears to have retaining walls protecting the property from the severe drop into the canyon.

However, the site does have a horrific history. There are rumors that Sharon's ghost haunts the area of Benedict Canyon. A 2014 article in the *LA Weekly* by Nina Giovannitti entitled, *The Ghosts of the Manson Murders, Next Door to Where Sharon Tate Was Killed* interviewed a neighbor. In 2002, David Oman moved to a new home about 150 feet from Sharon's famous house. The house was torn down in 1994 and replaced with another one. Five years after the home was razed, Oman's father purchased a nearby plot for $40k, and together they built a house on it. Oman told Giovannitti that a construction worker heard voices and footsteps from the upper floor. When he looked, no one was there. Other workers also claimed to hear voices and footsteps, and feeling a cold breeze on the backs of their necks.

In July 2004, at 2:00 A.M., Oman woke from a deep sleep. Giovannitti said he saw "a full body apparition at the bottom of his bed pointing towards the driveway which leads to the murder site." Oman said the 'apparition' made no sound, but gestured three times and then disappeared. Oman was curious if any DNA or artifacts were left on the property that would serve as a connection to present day. So, he told his story to the police. It was there at the police station that he saw a photo of Jay Sebring, Sharon Tate's ex-boyfriend and hairdresser. The figure he saw at his bedside bore an eerie resemblance to Jay.

Final Thoughts

It is very curious that people will select or build a home in a negative setting that may cause havoc in their lives. Clearly, the soul has an agenda and must carry it out. This home offered the possibility of death. The property supported destruction, affairs and conflict. Sharon and Roman experienced the best and worst it had to offer. In 1968, Doris Day's son, Terry Melcher, was introduced to ex-con and aspiring musician, Charles Manson, by Beach Boy Dennis Wilson. At the time, the Manson Family was living with Wilson at 14400 Sunset Boulevard. Wilson expressed interest in Manson's music and recorded two of his songs with the Beach Boys.

For a time, Terry Melcher was interested in recording Manson's music. He was also interested in making a movie about the Manson Family and their hippie commune. Manson met Melcher at 10050 Cielo Drive, a home he shared with his girlfriend and actress, Candice Bergen. Manson eventually auditioned for Melcher but Melcher declined to sign him. There was still talk of a documentary being made about Manson's music. However, Melcher abandoned the project after witnessing Charles getting into a fight with a drunken stuntman at Spahn Ranch. Both Wilson and Melcher ended their connection with Manson, a move that angered Manson.

Not long after ending ties with Manson, Melcher and Bergen moved out of the Cielo Drive home. The house's owner, Rudi Altobelli, then leased it Roman Polanski and Sharon Tate. Manson visited the house looking for Melcher, but was turned away as Melcher had moved. Some authors and law enforcement personnel have theorized that 10050 Cielo Drive was targeted by Manson as revenge for Melcher's rejection. They thought that Manson didn't believe Melcher and Bergen had moved out.

Sharon Tate, the movie star and gentle spirit with a perfect face, remains firmly affixed in our hearts. Her life and her friends' lives were cut short by a mad man. Now she's among other Hollywood legends whose brief presence profoundly touched us.

Chapter Eleven
Lyle and Erik Menendez: *The Bad Boys*

While living in this house for less than 2 years, José and Kitty Menendez were in serious debt, had marital discord, she was deeply depressed, he had affairs, and their sons were involved in criminal behavior.

Feng Shui and Facts

Address: 722 N. Elm Drive, Los Angeles, CA
Period 7, Southwest 2
Moved in: 1987
Facing Direction: 227°
José: 2 Life-Gua
Kitty: 1 Life-Gua
Lyle: 6 Life-Gua
Erik: 3 Life-Gua
Died: August 20, 1989
Negative Features: *Eight Roads of Destruction,* gun-shaped house design, bull-fight sha activated by pool, and the kitchen 'burned up' the father of the house.

Background on Celebrities and Property

The Menendez home, where the murders of José and Kitty took place, was located in the exclusive neighborhood of Beverly Hills. The family lived at 722 North Elm Drive while extensive renovations were in-progress on their family home on Mulholland Drive in Calabasas, California.

The Beverly Hills estate was a two-story Mediterranean style house sitting on a half-acre with over 9,000 square feet of living space. The house was originally built in 1927 and redesigned in 1984 by businessman Mark Slotkin. The property had a pool, private tennis court, two-story guesthouse, and two-car garage. It's surrounded by mansions equal to and/or exceeding its size and grandeur. Beverly Hills is the address of an elite and privileged class of people who value privacy and anonymity. The atrocious murders rocked the neighborhood to its core and shocked the world.

Figure 48: Highway to Calabasas, California and the other family home.

Born to a prosperous family in Cuba, 16-year old immigrant, José Menendez, came to America in 1960. He was escaping the dictatorship of Fidel Castro who had overtaken Cuba. Castro was seizing properties from its middle- and upper-class citizens. José's father stayed in Cuba until all of his property was confiscated. While attending Southern Illinois University in Carbondale, José Menendez met his future wife, Kitty. They married in 1964 and had two sons, Lyle, born in 1968, and Erik, born in 1971. The boys grew up to be handsome and athletic. However, being born to wealth and privilege was accompanied by impossibly high expectations from their father.

José Menendez was a larger-than-life character who possessed great charm and intense drive. He was in command of every situation, often the smartest guy in the room, arrived first at every conclusion, and out-hustled every competitor. He also exercised great power over his household and hammered into his sons the ethic of success and achievement. He seemed to have a need for extreme control in every situation and this included his wife and sons.

On the night of August 20, 1989, while watching the movie *The Spy Who Loved Me*, José and Kitty were murdered. The boys, Lyle, 21, and Erik, 18, were out for the night. Kitty, just returning from the kitchen, saw her husband asleep on the sofa with his feet propped up on the coffee table. Someone with a shotgun came into the house from the side terrace and fired at the back of José's head, killing him instantly. While attempting to flee, Kitty was fired upon several times by the shooter, hitting her left leg, right arm, left hip, and chest. With the gun now spent of bullets, the shooter reloaded. This time, the shooter placed the gun directly on Kitty's cheek and fired. The autopsy report on José explained that one blast caused "explosive decapitation with evisceration of the brain" and "deformity of the face." The medical examiner wrote of Kitty, "gunshot caused multiple lacerations of the brain" leaving her face an unrecognizable pulp. Later that night on TV, a retired police detective, Dan Stewart, said: *"I've seen a lot of homicides, but nothing quite that brutal. Blood, flesh, skulls. It would be hard to describe, especially José, as resembling a human that you would recognize. That's how bad it was."*

José had a reputation of being ruthless in business and, at first, the police were looking for persons of interest in that sphere. The boys declared that it must've been a Mob hit. As a Hollywood executive and 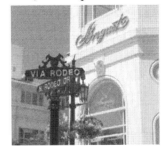 self-made millionaire, José had amassed an estate worth $14 million, so the boys were not above suspicion. In the six months following the murder, Lyle and Erik reportedly blew $1 million on parties, travel, and shopping.

Once it was clear that the boys were the perpetrators of their parents' murder, more shock ensued. On the surface, they seemed far removed from such a sordid crime. The fact is, no one wanted to believe it. Shortly before their first trial, which would end in a hung jury, they admitted to killing their parents but claimed they did so after years of sexual abuse. In a second trial, they were found guilty of first-degree murder and sentenced to life in prison without parole. No one was buying the abuse excuse.

It would later be revealed that the Menendez brothers had a troubled past and were rebellious bad boys. Shortly before the murders, they decided to go on a burglary spree, robbing homes just for the fun of it. They reportedly stole more than $100k in jewelry and cash from houses in Beverly Hills. Lyle Menendez committed the illegal act first with a group of friends, inspiring Erik to do the same. The boys were arrested but, when their father found out, he convinced authorities not to file charges after he paid off the families whose homes were ransacked. Other poor behavior included Lyle being expelled from Princeton for plagiarism in his first term. Erik wrote a disturbing and bloody screenplay in which the protagonist kills five people, starting with his own parents.

José, Kitty, Lyle, and Erik's Life-Gua Numbers

José was the patriarch of the family and was a 2 Life-Gua. Kitty was a 1 Life-Gua. His energy (Earth) would give the upper-hand over hers (water). He liked to be in control of his wife and children. According to the book *Blood Brothers* by Ron Soble and John Johnson, José ran a traditional Latin household where the man was in charge. Kitty's standing in the family fell below that of Lyle's. José made sure that Lyle, as his oldest son, had plenty of money on-hand. While Lyle had a thousand dollars lying around in his bedroom, Kitty would worry if she could afford to buy a $100 coat.

Lyle, the older brother, is a 6 Life-Gua and his younger brother, Erik, is a 3 Life-Gua. Lyle (metal) would completely control his brother (wood). It was common knowledge that Erik looked up to Lyle in everything. Lyle was the one that fired the shots killing both of his parents. José's relationship with his sons differed greatly. As the eldest son, Lyle would have been expected to take over the family enterprises and manage the wealth. The 2 Life-Gua (José) and 6 Life-Gua (Lyle) are very compatible. However, the dichotomy of the relationship was one that Lyle could never resolve. On one hand, he wanted to be just like his father but, on the other, he deeply resented José's harsh disciplinary style. The energy of the father and younger son would have been strained with both of them being disappointed. Even during family dinners, José would engage the boys in intellectual sparring to develop mental skills.

The boys had a very different relationship with their mother. She was likely very close to both of them as their energy (metal and wood) would be compatible with hers (water). According to the *Blood Brothers* book, in July of 1987, Lyle wrote a letter to his mother from Madrid: *"Hi Mom. How are you? Hope you're alright and hanging in there. I often worry about you. You're the only mother I have and would want."* While Lyle did shoot his mother, he was conflicted. Erik was known to comfort his mother whenever he overheard her crying over José's philandering. Kitty often did the boys' homework for them. Her focus in life was to be a good mother and wife, and to keep the family together.

The Home's Best Features

Perfect Land Embrace

The home was perfectly embraced. It was surrounded by a home on either side and homes in the back of the property, behind the alley. In Feng Shui, homes that are supported on both sides and in the back by another home, edifice, wall, or thick landscaping is extremely ideal. This allows for the chi to come to the site and find a place to collect. It is this energy that brings opportunities for money to residents.

Front Door Faced the Road

The front door of the home faced the road. The home was able to receive the vibrant chi, or energy, from the road, which is extremely important for residents wanting to advance in their careers and make more money. This would have served the breadwinner very well.

Good Ming Tang Indicated Good Opportunities for Money

The North Elm Drive home had a generous, open space in the front of the home by the front door, both on the exterior and interior. This is excellent and good for business opportunities and money.

Great Back Door

The Northeast-facing back door featured not only the most prosperous energy at the time (7 facing star), but it was José's very best direction (+90). The tennis court was located in the backyard. The whole family enjoyed playing tennis, so this door was used daily. At one time, both boys considered playing tennis professionally and José was not pleased. While the back door supported José as the breadwinner, for Kitty, it indicated bad relationships, particularly romantic ones.

Great Stove Placement

The stove sat on the Southwest (4 mountain star) and the knobs activated the Northeast (7 facing star). This lucky placement would have indicated success in finances and business opportunities.

Negative Home Features

The Shape of the House Indicated Money Loss and Relationship Problems

The unfortunate L-shape of the house somewhat resembled a small hand gun. This shape is taboo in Feng Shui and generally portends bad events. This negative-shape house design affects health, relationships, and money luck.

Pool Location Indicated Arguing and Fighting

The large swimming pool was located in the East sector of the property. This feature activated the 'bullfight sha' energy (3, 2). This energy is very indicative of arguing, fighting, lawsuits, and overall disharmony. In the summer of 1988, Erik graduated from Beverly Hills High School. It was during this time that the brothers began robbing their friends' parents. While their father was able to ameliorate the situation and avoid the felony offense of grand theft burglary, tensions were high. In an effort to share some time together as a family, and perhaps lessen some of the strain that everyone was feeling, José and Kitty chartered a boat to go shark fishing with the boys.

On Saturday, August 19, 1989, the day before the murders, the Menendez family travelled to Marina del Rey, a nearby seaside community. The boat's crew later reported that the Menendez family seemed miserable and non-communicative. While José was fishing from the back of the boat, the boys kept to themselves in the front. Kitty was below deck dealing with sea sickness. This was not a harmonious family outing by any means, and this is very common behavior when the bullfight sha energy is activated.

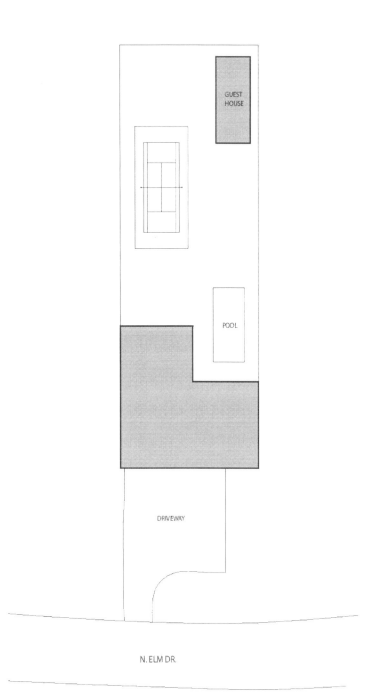

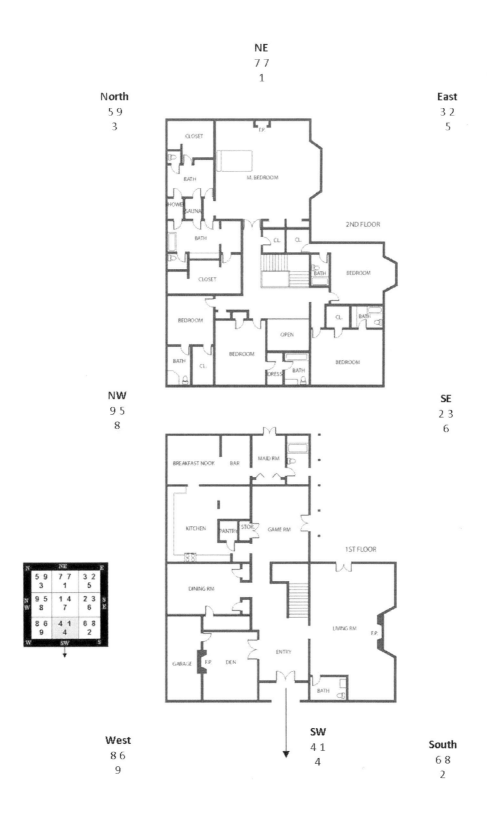

Figure 49: The floor plan and Period 7, Southwest 2 *Flying Star Chart* for the Menendez's home in Beverly Hills. The design is extreme and looks like a gun or weapon.

Eight Roads of Destruction Indicated Disastrous Events

The home had the detrimental *Eight Roads of Destruction* formation. It was created by the Southwest-facing front door in relationship to the driveway entering/exiting from South (187° - 202°). The entire family would've been influenced by this energy. In addition to attracting extremely tragic events, including murder, the *Eight Roads of Destruction* denotes massive money loss and looming bankruptcy.

According to the book *Blood Brothers* by Ron Soble and John Johnson, José Menendez was up to his ears in debt. With two hefty mortgages on million-dollar properties, he was delinquent in paying $1 million in back-taxes. The Menendez estate totaled almost $14 million in assets. However, with loans, taxes and mortgages, the net worth was closer to $2 million. After their parents died, the boys went on several wasteful shopping sprees and invested in businesses that failed. One of these businesses was a restaurant in Princeton, New Jersey that Lyle grossly mismanaged. Trying to emulate their father's business acumen and success, both boys failed miserably.

Kitty responded to the home's energy by displaying erratic mood swings and deep depression. Her condition was serious enough that she sought counsel. She was prescribed large doses of anti-depressants and tranquilizers. She told Lyle that her despair was so extreme that she needed thirteen pills each day to survive. Kitty also wrote a series of sad, suicide notes that recounted her long history and love for José. Her letters expressed her inability to live through another one of his affairs. José had no plans of running off with any of his mistresses and keeping Kitty around fed his ego. Her devotion to her husband was one of co-dependency and the boys felt that she couldn't live without him.

The Front Door Indicated Affairs

The Southwest-facing front door had energy that supported affairs and sexual energy (4, 1). This combination of stars has both a good and bad connotation, depending on the rest of the home's energy. In the Menendez residence, due to the other negative features, it would give a bad result. In the *81 Combinations*, it describes the negative aspects of the 4,1 stars as 'extramarital affairs, bad sons, bad director, family separates from fighting, useless, good-for-nothing sons spending money and clashing with each other.' That description fit all the male members of the family. José flaunted his affairs in front of his wife and the boys were reckless in their behavior and spending habits. That year (1989), the *3 annual star* visited the Southwest and, when paired with the *1 facing star*, signified gossiping, fighting, arguments, and lawsuits.

Side Door Ignited the Bullfight Sha Energy

The large swimming pool already triggered the bullfight-sha energy (2,3), however, it was further activated by the Southeast-facing side door. This energy indicates lots of arguments, disputes, bickering, gossiping, lawsuits, greedy people, cheating, and bad things falling on you – literally and figuratively. According to the *Blood Brothers* book, that accurately described their experience. There was José's questionable business dealings, his affairs, the boys stealing from their friend's parents and, finally, the dinner table laden with heated sparring sessions.

Bathroom Locations Indicated Mixed Luck

Due to the nature of toilets, they should be located in negative sectors (-90, -80, -70, or -60). The Menendez house had eight bathrooms; three of those would have supported José (East, SE, and N). Four locations were good for Kitty (NW, two in the W and SW). The bathroom located in the middle of the house indicated issues with the kidneys, bladder, and fluids in the body. The toilet/powder room near the front entrance is considered taboo in Feng Shui.

Master Bed Direction Indicated Stress, Mental Pressure, and Fire Disasters

It would be safe to assume that the master bed was placed on the Northwest wall in the room. The Southeast had a large bay window, and the Northeast had a fireplace. The Northwest had very dangerous energy (9,5). Activating this energy would denote stress, mental pressure, sex diseases, lawsuits, a religious fanatic, fire disasters, cancer, money loss, and leukemia.

While the Northwest is one of José's good directions, it was negated by the pernicious star combination. For Kitty, the Northwest was one of her worst directions known as the *Six Killings* (-80). The traditional description for the *Six Killings* states "utilizing this direction can attract 'six types of disasters' such as injury, loss of wealth, backstabbing, affairs, harm to you and the family, betrayals in business, accidents of all sorts, and serious illness such as cancer. This direction can render you *unrecognized* in the world." It's fascinating because, in fact, she was betrayed by her husband through his infidelities and, in the end, by both of her sons. Her mental health was an issue. While much stemmed from José's infidelities, she was heavily medicated to cope with the situation. Until her death, she was largely unrecognized by the world.

Kitchen Location Indicated Father-Son Conflict

Fire located in the Northwest of homes is called 'fire burning heaven's gate' which means fathers and son fight. In the Menendez home, the foremost dissention in the family was the boys' resentment and hatred of their father. In *Blood Brothers,* the authors tell, while plotting José's murder, how the boys were conflicted with regards to Kitty. In the end, they decided that she couldn't live without her husband. Basically, she was a casualty to the boys' desire to get rid of their father.

The stove was sitting Southwest on the romance star (4 mountain) and the knobs activated wealth (7 facing star) in the Northeast. The Northeast was José's best direction for accumulating wealth (+90). However, his household was filled with unhappy, desperate people. While this home had some destructive energy, not everyone who lived there would have experienced tragedy. In most cases, homes with the 'fire burning heaven's gate' energy would not have ended in death. Every home offers a variety of possibilities. It depends on the souls involved as to whether they will use it or not. Even so, this is an extreme case if you consider all the other negative energies prevalent and it's not surprising that the gruesome murders took place there.

Centrally Located Staircase Indicated Health Issues

The Menendez family lived in the house for two years. This was time enough for health issues to manifest. Stairs located in the exact center of the house indicate issues with bones, the skeletal system, and the spine.

Feng Shui Restoration

The House Shape

While the house is odd-shaped, it is not detrimental like some of the other celebrity homes mentioned in this book. With that said, we would have still recommended that an addition take place in the East-Southeast sector of the house. This would have allowed the chi, or the energy, to flow uniformly and bring more harmony and good luck to the family.

Changing the Flying Star Chart

Our main recommendation for this home would have been to tilt the front door from Southwest 2 to Southwest 1. Changing the *Flying Star* chart would have solved several problems. It would have eliminated the *Eight Roads of Destruction* and would've kept the pool from activating the bullfight-sha energy. The side door would still be very bad and needed to be replaced with large windows. Perhaps the Menendez's would have been willing to relocate the kitchen via significant remodeling. While the bathrooms couldn't be relocated, we would have given recommendations to use specific ones in the house, and avoid using others. The master bed would have needed to be relocated to the Northeast wall. The fireplace should have been closed off or re-located. These drastic changes would have offered superior living and more harmony for the family.

722 North Elm Drive Today

Understandably, the home was difficult to sell after the murders. It was put back on the market as a rental after being bought by a Saudi Prince who leased the property for $50,000 a month. Mystery writer, William Link, purchased the property in 1993, living there for eight years before putting it back up for sale. 722 Elm Drive was last sold in November 2001 to telecommunications executive Sam Delug for $3.7 million. The new owners filled in and relocated the pool which can be viewed on *Google Maps*. To create privacy, gorgeous wrought-iron gates have been installed, and the driveway completely redone. By reconfiguring the driveway, the *Eight Roads of Destruction* was eliminated. The new pool location no longer activates the *bullfight sha*. The genteel home has a long history as a residence for well-to-do celebrities and entertainment industry execs. The residence played host over the years to renters such as Prince and Elton John. The home's address was changed to 721 North Elm Drive after so much sensational publicity.

A Final Word

No one wanted to believe that the seemingly picture-perfect family could end so egregiously. At the time, the energy of this home was so malevolent that it served as a gateway in which negative experiences could manifest. The Menendez family was long-headed for tragedy and, on a subconscious level, selected a place to live it out. It's never a coincidence when something this atrocious happens. Classical Feng Shui, like any other predictive science, is a gauge of what *could* happen. When someone acts out violently or heinously, it is their own free will. The bad boys of the Menendez family left a sad and disturbing legacy. Occasionally, they appear in television interviews, looking unrepentant and displaying sociopathic tendencies. The energy we're describing in these homes is unseen, yet powerful. It will influence and support good and bad behavior. We are pleased to see that the new owners of the gorgeous home have moved the energy significantly enough for a harmonious life.

Chapter Twelve
Phil Hartman: *The Funny Man*

While living in this home for several years, Phil had two children, his wife was in drug rehab several times, he had a successful career, and finally was shot by his wife while sleeping who then committed suicide.

Feng Shui and Facts

Address: 5065 Encino Ave, Encino, CA
Period 7, East 1
Moved in: Period 7
Facing Direction: 77°
Phil: 7 Life-Gua
Brynn: 9 Life-Gua
Married: November, 1987
Children: 2
Died: May 28, 1998
Negative Features: Goat Blade formation, *Eight Killing Mountain Forces*, odd-shaped house design, *Eight Roads of Destruction*, diving driveway, extreme yin environment, the pool activated depression/sickness and the house was built over a vortex.

Background on Celebrity and Property

Phil Hartman was a Canadian-born American actor, comedian, screenwriter and graphic artist. Born in Brantford, Ontario, Hartman and his family immigrated to the United States. Phil was best known for his work on *Saturday Night Live* in the late 80's. He gained fame and notoriety with his humorous impression of President Bill Clinton. He continued to work on the show for eight seasons. In the mid 90's, he moved on to star in the hit NBC sitcom *NewsRadio*. He also had frequent roles on *The Simpsons* and appeared in the films *Houseguest*, *Sgt. Bilko*, *Jingle All the Way*, and *Small Soldiers*.

Phil had two brief marriages and remained close friends with his second wife, Lisa. He married a third time to former model and aspiring actress, Brynn Omdahl, (born Vicki Jo Omdahl) in November 1987. He met her on a blind date in 1986. Together they had two children, Sean and Birgen Hartman, and were married for 11 years. Right from the start, reports of a strained marriage circulated among family and friends. Brynn often felt intimidated by her husband's success and was frustrated as an aspiring actress. However, neither party wanted a divorce. Phil even considered retiring to save his marriage. Apparently, he tried to get Brynn some acting roles on many occasions, however, she was often in and out of rehab for drug and alcohol abuse. Brynn's narcotic and alcohol abuse was the crux of most of their disagreements.

Their family home was built in 1980 by famed architect Robert Byrd who was known for his popular California Ranch-style homes. Donald Bellisario, a famous Hollywood producer *(Mangum P.I., Quantum Leap, & JAG)*, occupied the home at one time. Soon after Bellisario sold it, the Hartmans moved in. It is located in Encino, an upper-class neighborhood located in Los Angeles' San Fernando Valley, where many famous celebrities call home.

On the eve of the murders, Brynn started a heated argument with her husband. Phil threatened to leave her if she started using drugs again. Exhausted over another confrontation with his wife, Hartman retired for bed. While he slept, Brynn entered the bedroom at around 3:00 in the morning of May 28, 1998, and fatally shot her husband. He was shot with a .38 caliber handgun twice in the head and once in his side. His daughter was asleep but his son, who was playing with his robot, heard the gunshots.

Brynn left the house and drove to a friend's house, confessing to the murder. Initially, her friend, Ron Douglas, didn't believe her and the pair drove back to the house in separate cars. Upon seeing Hartman's body, Ron called the police and the children were removed from the home. Brynn locked herself in the bedroom and, at 6:20 AM, shot herself in the head. It was later revealed in the autopsy that Brynn had consumed alcohol and the anti-depressant, Zoloft.

Phil and Brynn's Life-Gua Numbers

Phil Hartman was a 7 Life-Gua and they're known for their youthful nature and jovial attitude. They can be talkative, lively and nervous. His high-energy performances and impersonations mirrored these very traits. The 7 Life-Guas are often very attractive and become movie stars or celebrated people. The *Saturday Night Live* set considered Phil the glue because he supported and held everyone together. The 7 Life-Guas are often interested in metaphysical studies and arts; hence, Phil dropped an 'n' from his last name so that it would be more auspicious per the I Ching. However, the 7's must be careful with overindulgences in the pleasures of life, such as food, drinking, money, and sex.

Brynn Hartman was a 9 Life-Gua and these women often have incredible beauty, like a diva or goddess. They are drawn to acting, public speaking, and the entertainment business where they can showcase their considerable allure. When exhibiting the darker side of their nature, they can be rash, argumentative, exhibit a hot temper, or act impulsively. However, they tend to be highly intellectual individuals. A friend recalled that Brynn "…had trouble controlling her anger. She got attention by losing her temper." On the darkest end of the spectrum, the un-evolved 9 Life-Guas can exhibit mental illness, psychotic behavior, or may be bipolar. Brynn demonstrated these traits when she murdered her husband, Phil Hartman, and then took her own life, too.

The 7 Life-Gua (metal) paired with a 9 Life-Gua (fire) is considered inauspicious unless the couple has evolved past the darker side of their nature. The 9 will try to control the 7 and it looks like Brynn did this in every way. It appears that Phil Hartman tried everything he could to see his wife's acting career take-off but she was her own worst enemy with her dependence on drugs and alcohol. Phil simply wanted to have a happy, sober wife and mother. This was seemingly unattainable to the point that he was reluctantly considering divorce. While the 7/9 combination is usually considered undesirable, with different personalities it could have been a lasting and healthy relationship. Unfortunately, this was not Phil and Brynn's fate. Ironically, on the day she killed him, she was found wearing a Gap t-shirt with the number 9 on it. We're sure this is coincidental but it's an interesting detail.

The Home's Best Features

5065 Encino Ave was situated in a prominent neighborhood in 'The Valley'. 'The Valley' is a common term used for homes located in the San Fernando Valley area of Los Angeles. It's a typical residential neighborhood with nearby shopping and restaurants. The home was on flatland with mountains situated on the outskirts. However, as you approached the house, you would see statues of whimsical creatures everywhere. Greeting you at the front gate was a bear (see Figure 50). There were snake replicas wrapped around trees, and other creatures scattered throughout the front garden. The creatures were made of wood or plaster and had a glossy finish. The landscaping appeared menacing and was overly yin. Overall, the house appeared very foreboding, had an eerie vibe, and looked like a whimsical nightmare. It was reminiscent of a *Grimms' Fairy Tale* – very dark, brooding and inappropriate for small children. We were unable to locate a floor plan and/or site plan for this home, however, there's still a wealth of information available that would explain why a murder-suicide occurred there.

Front Door Indicated Wealth

The front door faced the main road and was Northeast 2 (37°- 52°). However, the *Flying Star Chart* is based on the facing, which was East 1. Even though the front door was angled, it was still able to receive the vibrant energy from the road. This was excellent for residents wanting to have good career luck and outstanding support, in general. Phil Hartman was beloved by all who worked with him. The Northeast-facing front door activated prosperity (8 facing star) and was Phil's personal relationship direction (+70). The front door also supported Brynn in Advanced Eight Mansions.

The Pool Supported Wealth and Opportunities

Part of the pool was located in the West, indicating money luck and fame (7 facing star). It's easy to see why Phil was a successful, gainfully employed, sought-out actor and entertainer.

Figure 50: Notice the large carved bear and other animals on the left-side of the gate.

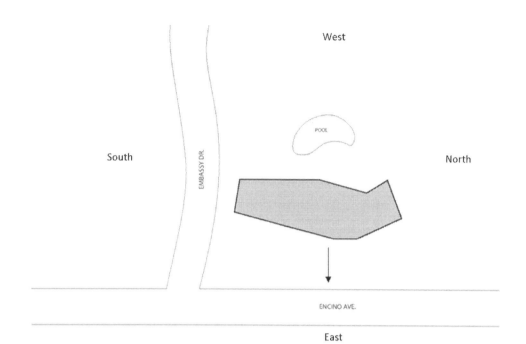

Negative Features

Annual 5 Yellow Star Visited the Front Door Indicating Disasters, Calamities, and Death

In 1998, the annual *5 Yellow Star* visited the Northeast. This star can deliver disasters, all types of calamites, and even death. Much depends on the rest of the home's energy. This home had some negative features that would have made the murder-suicide possible that year. The *5 Yellow Star's* energy is pernicious and, when it visits the front or back of a property, is considered a significant event.

House Shape/Design Hurt Money-Luck and Harmed Relationships

The shape and design of the home is considered very unfortunate in Feng Shui. Odd shapes and designs rarely bring good results. Extreme and odd-designed homes will hurt all three categories of Feng Shui; money, health, and relationships. While this is not the main reason the tragedy took place, the negative features combined altogether, does. In other words, it's not just one thing but a culmination of energetic deficiencies that can cause serious misfortune to take place.

Partial Location of Pool Indicated Illness and Mental Disturbances

Jennifer was unable to walk to the back of the property were the pool was located. However, the aerial view on *Google Maps* clearly shows its location to be in the Southwest. In Period 7, when the Hartmans lived there, the *2 facing star* would have been activated by the pool. The 2 is the 'sickness' star. Activating this energy would have been very unlucky, indicating depression, stomach, reproductive issues, widowhood, mental disturbance, miserly and greedy people, one-sided love, and cold/hot sickness. Brynn suffered with serious bouts of depression and was taking Zoloft, a strong anti-depressant. She really wanted to be a famous actress, not just a stay-at-home mom. She battled with other dark emotions as well. Not only was she jealous of her husband's success, but was also jealous of the close relationship he had with his second ex-wife, Lisa Strain. When Brynn asked Phil if Lisa was his 'soul mate', he said that she was. Brynn then angrily lashed out and sent Lisa a threatening letter saying she would 'rip her eyes out'. The 2 star activates depression as well as sickness and disease.

Diving Driveway Indicated Divorce

The driveway leading towards the garage slopes at a 15° angle. Driveways that virtually "dive" into the garage, or toward an important door, indicate relationship problems. If the couple is married, it could cause divorce. The energy from the slope of the driveway essentially "slams" into the home. This causes the chi to flow destructively and can manifest into serious relationship issues.

Goat Blade Formation Indicated Affairs, Divorce, Drug, and Alcohol Abuse

The home has several oddly angled doors and they're visible from the road. Even the backyard gate and a door on side of the house are angled. The negative and positive formulas in Feng Shui are based on important, exterior doors. Their relationship to roads, water and mountains will determine the quality of energy. Even with all the odd angles of the doors, we have an accurate point of reference – the front door degree. A *Goat Blade* formation was created by a combination of the West-facing back door and the water that was located in the West (pool). This formation indicates divorce, overindulgence in sex, affairs, alcohol abuse, gambling, and family breaks apart.

Eight Killing Mountain Forces

The home also had an *Eight Killings* formation created by the West-facing back door (262°-277°) and by the 'mountain' located in the Southeast (127°-142°) corner front yard area. The Southeast 'mountain' was created by simple landscaping mounds. In Feng Shui terms, mounds or boulders that are three feet or higher, qualify as a mountain. This formation is famous for delivering divorce, bankruptcy, diseases, danger, all types of calamitous misfortune, and, in extreme cases, death. The *Eight Killings* will ignite crimes of passion between lovers, partners or spouses. Brynn had a history of drug and alcohol abuse. This was a particularly bad mix with her insecure nature. As we mentioned previously, people will naturally gravitate to homes that support their subconscious desires. Since Phil was threatening divorce, this was no doubt the catalyst that pushed Brynn over the edge.

Missing Tiger Side Indicated Females Becoming Aggressive

The female *Tiger* side of this house is missing. Instead there's a road there. Not only will the females of the house not be supported, it will awaken aggression. Brynn was known for being argumentative and starting fights with Phil. Oftentimes, she was under the influence but, nonetheless, the energy supported her behavior.

Dr. Ann Blake Tracy, Executive Director of the *International Coalition for Drug Awareness,* comments on a 2005 article entitled, *Zoloft-Induced Suicide: A Battle for Woody.*

"As the leading expert in Phil Hartman's case, I would like to make it very clear that the evidence showed his wife had consumed cocaine AFTER she shot her husband and not before. Brynn was not in her right mind when she took the cocaine. It was a drug she was deathly afraid of and fought hard to stay away from for many, many years after a problem with it early on in her life.

It is clear that Brynn Hartman was suffering from Serotonin Syndrome and an REM Sleep Behavior Disorder at the time Phil was shot. She was so completely unaware of what was real when this happened that she went to get friends to come with her to tell her if Phil had been shot or if it was a nightmare she was having. And when they confirmed he had been shot she became hysterical, laid down next to Phil and then shot herself. And the most important piece of information this article left out is that Pfizer has settled the wrongful death case filed by the Hartman children. For anyone born just yesterday let me point out that these drug companies do not settle cases because they are benevolent."

Eight Roads of Destruction

The home has the detrimental *Eight Roads of Destruction* created by the Northeast facing front door (37°-52°) and the small alley road in the East (67°-82°). This alley is shared by the neighboring home (see Figure 51). As the ominous-sounding name implies, it indicates all types of disastrous events.

Figure 51: This is the alley/road that forms the *Eight Roads of Destruction* **in relationship to the Northeast-facing door.**

Possible Water Main Underneath the House Indicated Instability

While Jennifer perused the front of property, she noticed a water main lid on the sidewalk. This usually implies that the water main is running underneath the house. If true, this would destabilize the energy. It can cause many issues such as alcoholism, relationships issues, money loss, and ill health. It's highly inauspicious to have water flowing underneath a home.

Energy Vortexes Indicating Disorientation, Drugs, and Alcoholism

Figure 52: The twisted trees on the property indicate they are growing over an energy vortex.

The Hartman home had an energy vortex running straight through the middle of the property. While lei lines and vortexes are naturally-occurring phenomena, it's ill-advised to build a home over them. In ancient times, these special areas were used for sacred ceremonies, as they were too intense for everyday living. There are several ways to determine where these vortexes are located on a property. One clue is to observe large growing trees. The trees may coil up and change directions, which will look unusual or abnormal. Homes built over a vortex can cause dizziness, alcoholism, drug addiction, marital problems, paranoia, psychosis, health issues, and money problems. Due to the occupants feeling unstable, they may turn to drugs or alcohol as a coping mechanism.

Feng Shui Restoration

The House Shape

It would have been best if the home had been remodeled to 'fill in' the missing areas, and to have a more rectangular shape. This would have offered the much-needed stability for its occupants.

Missing Tiger Side

Since the right-hand side of the property was missing the usual support, such as a neighboring home, it needed to be shored up. This could have easily been accomplished with a solid fence (at least six feet tall) comprised of stucco, brick, wood, or any combination, thereof. Also, tall landscaping would have further helped insulate it from the road and offered great representation for the female, the *Tiger* side.

The Pool Location

The part of the pool that was located in the Southwest would have needed to be remodeled so that the pool was entirely in the West. This would have eliminated the sickness energy, which indicated depression. If this was too cost-prohibitive, a large, bronze statue (shown below) could have been placed in the Southwest.

The Goat Blade Formation

The back door would have had to be re-angled within 262.5° - 277.5° to the West. This would have taken the pool out of the *Goat Blade* formation. Tilting this door would have also eliminated the *Eight Killings* formation.

The Water Main

If this feature existed, it would have been out of the control of the homeowners since it's controlled and owned by the city.

Diving Driveway

The driveway would have needed to be reconfigured so that it was level with the road.

The Energy Vortex

These are difficult to cure, although burying metal in the ground could help. Taking care to correct all the other negative features of the home would have helped a great deal.

Eight Roads of Destruction

Tilting, or re-angling, the front door from Northeast 2 to either Northeast 1 or 3 would eliminate this deadly formation. This would not have changed the *Flying Star Chart*, which is East 1.

5065 Encino Ave Today

After the traumatic murder of Phil Hartman and the suicide of Brynn Hartman, the home was sold the following year. The current homeowners have lived there since 1999. The estimated value, in today's market, is $2,879,000.

Final Thoughts

The Hartman family thrived and suffered in this house. Phil's career was gaining serious traction, and he fathered two healthy children while living there. Even though Brynn dealt with anger and depression, they still enjoyed good relationships with family and friends in their circle. Unwittingly, this couple moved into a home that made disastrous events a possibility. However, choosing a home on a subconscious level will ensure that our karma is lived out.

Phil Hartman is still a much-loved celebrity figure. He left us a wonderful legacy, and even new generations are discovering his comedic genius.

Hollywood and the world mourned his passing. *NBC* executive, Don Ohlmeyer, stated that Hartman *"was blessed with a tremendous gift for creating characters that made people laugh. Everyone who had the pleasure of working with Phil knows that he was a man of tremendous warmth, a true professional and a loyal friend".*

In June 2013, it was announced that Hartman would receive a star on the Hollywood Walk of Fame, which was unveiled on August 26, 2014. In 2015, *Rolling Stone* magazine ranked Hartman as one of the top-ten greatest *Saturday Night Live* cast members throughout the show's 40-year history.

Chapter Thirteen
Phil Spector: *The Music Man*

While living in the 'castle', Phil Spector became reclusive, experienced bad health, feared being alone, was charged with murder, married, convicted of murder, and sentenced to 19 years in prison.

Feng Shui and Facts

Address: 1700 Grandview Drive, Alhambra, CA
Period 7, South 2
Moved in: May 22, 1998
Facing Direction: 180°
Phil: 7 Life-Gua
Lana: 4 Life-Gua
Died: February 3, 2003
Negative Formations: A major *Death and Emptiness Line* (180°), odd-shaped house design, property surrounded by too many roads, water reservoir in front of house, triangular-shaped lot, haunted by ghosts and built on top of a hill.

Background on Celebrity and Property

On February 3, 2003, actress Lana Clarkson was found dead in Phil Spector's mansion (Pyrenees Castle) in Alhambra, California. Her body was found slumped in a chair with a single gunshot wound to her mouth. Like shrapnel, her broken teeth were scattered over the carpet. Spector told *Esquire Magazine* in July 2003 that Clarkson's death was an "accidental suicide" and that she "kissed the gun". The emergency call from Spector's home was made by his chauffer, Adriano de Souza. He told the police that he saw Spector come out the back door of the house with a gun in his hand.

Most of us know Phil's early story—he was the petite musical genius from New York, produced his first pop hit at 17, and was a millionaire by 22. He is the legendary music man who produced over 25 Top 40 hits between 1961 and 1966. Phil Spector worked with artists including Ike and Tina Turner, John Lennon, George Harrison, and in 1979 he produced his last album for the punk rock group, the Ramones. He was the creator of the Wall of Sound (aka Spector Sound) which is a music production formula for pop and rock music recordings developed at Gold Star Studios during the 1960s.

In the late 60's, Phil Spector rescued and produced the Beatles' Academy award-winning album, *Let It Be*. The 1965 song, *You've Lost That Lovin' Feelin'*, produced and co-written by Spector for The Righteous Brothers, is listed by BMI as the song with

Figure 53: The 'Pyrenees Castle' is built directly on top of a hill. Notice the water reservoir in lower right-hand corner of the photo. It was built, by French bussinessman Sylvester Dupuy, in 1927.

the most U.S. airplay in the 20th century. In 1989, Spector was inducted into the Rock and Roll Hall of Fame as a non-performer. Now, part of his long-standing legacy is murder. After a 2007 mistrial, he was convicted in 2009 of second-degree murder and given a prison sentence of 19 years to life.

The home where Phil Spector murdered Lana Clarkson is filled with fantastical legends. There are tales of wealthy hermits, Eastern gangsters, secret elevators, and ghostly apparitions. When Jennifer (the co-author of this book) visited the Alhambra Historical Museum to research the castle, she was told there were numerous ghost sittings. In fact, the castle is lightheartedly referred to as the 'ghost on the hill'. The home was built in 1927 by wealthy French businessman, Sylvester Dupuy. He'd always dreamed of owning a château similar to those in the French countryside near

Pyrenees Mountains. It took $500k to create his castle; that's more than $7 million in today's money. Dupuy made his fortune by investing in oil, land, and subdividing properties in the neighboring San Gabriel Valley. The beige castle with its red tiled roof lords over the town of Alhambra like the feudal fortresses of rural France.

Dupuy lost most of his fortune shortly before his death in 1936. The *LA Times* article, *Castle Had a Large Family Life Before Spector*, by Cecilia Rasmussen, explained much of this unusual home's history. Mr. Sylvester Dupuy died of a stroke at 58 in 1937. After World War II, his wife Anna sold the castle for huge loss at $60,000. The new owner converted the home into eight different apartments. The 'Pyrenees Castle Apartments' became home to a variety of people, including two Cal State professors who lived there for over 20 years. Anna Dupuy herself occupied one of those apartments until her death in 1949. As the years went by, the castle changed hands several times. The castle was sold once again to a woman who wanted a home for her 25 dogs. She never took up residence and the castle sat abandoned and was vandalized.

An American businessman, Cris C. Yip, who had a Hong Kong based business, bought the property in 1985 for $585k. In 1990, he spent $500k restoring the castle with deep red carpets and red velvet drapes. He installed an elaborate security system as well. However, in 1994 the Bank of Hong Kong foreclosed on it and took ownership. The home sat vacant once again until Phil Spector bought it in 1998 for $1.1 million. Phil told *Esquire* magazine that he'd bought 'a beautiful and enchanting castle in a hick town where there is no place to go that you shouldn't go.' Phil never changed the home's heavy velvet drapes and red carpet.

When Jennifer went to see the property, she brought along her five-pound Yorkshire terrier, Dolce. Dogs and cats are very sensitive to energy and, true to form, her terrier yelped a high-pitched nervous tone. Dolce only makes such a fuss when she is extremely frightened. Maybe she saw a ghost. However, Jennifer, too, felt the creepy energy of the castle. She examined the landforms, took her compass measurements and quickly left. The eerie energy of the château was almost palpable.

The castle is situated on a triangular-shaped lot atop a prominent hill. It is located in the heart of Alhambra, a city about 10 miles East of downtown Los Angeles. It overlooks the city of Alhambra from all directions and has 160° city views. The Pyrenees Castle was built with three-foot thick concrete walls. The land is surrounded by intimidating fortifications. The castle is like the best house in the worst neighborhood. It

sticks out like a sore thumb because it's far grander than the modest homes in the area.

After Phil Spector was convicted, he left behind his lizards, his iguanas, his decorative suits of armor, his white piano, and his collection of garden gnomes -- all at his beloved Pyrenees Castle.

Phil Spector's Life-Gua Number

Phil Spector 2005   Phil Spector 2007   Phil Spector 2008   Phil Spector 2009

Phil Spector is a 7 Life-Gua and they are known to be talkative, lively, and nervous. When channeled properly, that energy can be used productively and work to their advantage. This was very evident at the height of Phil Spector's career. At that time, he used his energy making hits and pioneering cutting-edge technology for the music industry. The 7's do well with a lot of 'stage'. The 7 Gua's are good at acting, and speaking in front of the camera or on the radio. During his court trials, Phil reveled in a return to the spotlight. He provided other staples of the Hollywood justice narrative: the rant on the steps of the courthouse, the elaborate and downright weird hairdo, the eccentric attire, the trophy wife, and the army of bodyguards.

With a strong tendency to overindulge in the pleasures of life such as food, drink, money, and sex, they must keep a balanced life. Even though he had been out of the record industry for years, he was still a celebrity. According to the book, *Tearing Down the Wall of Sound: The Rise and Fall of Phil Spector,* by Mick Brown, there were stories about him drinking heavily and pulling a gun on John Lennon and Leonard Cohen.

In an interview with Mick Brown for an article that was released two days before Lana Clarkson was killed, Phil Spector spoke about how he had not been well for years. He said he was emotionally crippled inside and that he was bipolar and a manic-depressive. He also explained that he was taking medication for schizophrenia. Phil said, "I have devils inside that fight me. And I'm my own worst enemy."

The 7 Guas can be fast-talkers, smooth talkers, or have razor-sharp tongues. They are very social, charming, and charismatic. They create stimulating, informative conversation wherever they go. During Phil's two murder trails, the judge allowed evidence of prior acts by Spector involving women and guns. A parade of women at both trials described how Spector

had turned from charming to menacing, often fuelled by alcohol and medication. His penchant for waving guns in people's faces, they recounted, suggested an accident waiting to happen.

Phil Spector was always viewed as notoriously eccentric, even in his heyday. However, as time went on, he slowly retreated into a self-imposed exile; hence the purchase of the 'castle'. Many described him as a demented control freak, tyrannical, an egomaniac, and insane genius. Phil's final legacy was to culminate into the unspeakable act of murdering, gorgeous and unattainable, Lana Clarkson.

The Home's Best Features

We were unable to locate a floor plan of the castle and it has been remodeled numerous times over the years. However, there are many features that reveal the castle's ability to deliver negative events to its occupants. With that being said, we found three features that are considered good Feng Shui.

Flying Star Chart
The castle became a Period 7 when Phil Spector bought and moved in 1998. At the time it was the prestigious *Combination of Ten* for wealth chart. In the beginning, the energy would have presented many opportunities for money. The home had prosperous energy, front and back, until 2004, Period 8. If his bed was placed on the Northwest wall, he was activating the worse energy of the home. It would have supported all that he experienced—both good and bad.

Good Ming Tang Indicated Good Opportunities for Money
The castle has a huge open space in the front of the home to greet the homeowner and visitors. This is an area where energy, or chi, can collect. This feature is excellent and good for business opportunities and money.

Front Door faced the Road Indicated Good Money and Career Luck
The home's front door faced the road and this is very auspicious in Classical Feng Shui. This feature allows the home to receive the road's vibrant yang energy. This is very fortunate and supports wealth and career luck. Phil Spector was able to capitalize on his career. Over the years, he still received hefty residuals from songs he produced and co-wrote.

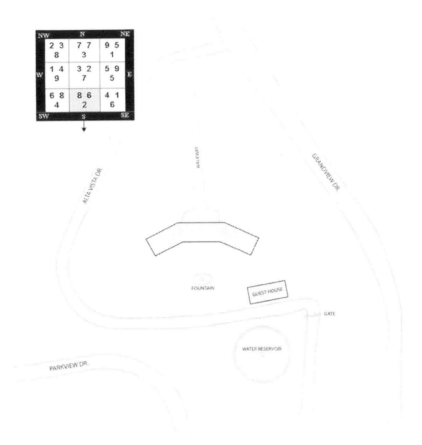

Figure 54: The triangular-shaped lot can be clearly seen from the Google Maps' ariel view. The water reservoir and the busy roads surrounding the castle are negative features.

Negative Features

Odd-shaped House Indicated Unfortunate Events

The castle was built in a strange, upside down U-shape. Odd-shaped homes rarely deliver good results or happy events. We only need to look at the home's lengthy, sordid history to see that it does not support wealth, health or relationships.

Too Many Roads Indicated Instability

Phi Spector's home was surrounded by three busy roads. This configuration will cause tremendous instability for the residents. It also indicates money loss or even bankruptcy. The history of the castle speaks of a string of people who moved in and out, with long periods of vacancy. The facts speak for themselves. The original owner lost his fortune right before his death. Another owner was foreclosed on, and the most recent owner was convicted of murder. This does not signify that good energy is prevalent in the home. Quite the opposite, actually.

Water Reservoir in Front of the House Indicated Money Loss and Instability

When a water reservoir is built too close to a home, the energy can become overwhelming. Keep in mind that this reservoir supplied water to an entire city. This feature can cause money loss, health issues, and support alcoholism. The water reservoir was built in 1932, about five years after Sylvester Dupuy moved into his much-dreamed-of castle. Six years after the arrival of the water reservoir, Sylvester Dupuy lost his fortune and died shortly thereafter. He only lived nine years in his beloved castle.

Home Built on Top of the Hill Indicated Money Loss and Being Vulnerable

It is ill-advised to build a home directly on top of a huge mountain or hill. Energy cannot be retained, and money loss can be massive. The home is vulnerable to the elements—the winds, mudslides, hurricanes, earthquakes, tornados, or whatever is native to the environment. People who live in such homes are themselves vulnerable to corporate takeovers, infidelity, financial ruin, and underhanded business partners and employees. Considering the history of the castle, it's no wonder people didn't thrive. The castle might have brought out the worst in Phil Spector. Negative allegations about him abounded. He was an abusive addict whom his ex-wife, Ronnie, called a "psychopathic monster". Over the decades, his obsession with guns was well documented.

Death and Emptiness Lines/Degrees Indicated Ghosts and Bankruptcy

When this home was built in 1927, there weren't sophisticated construction techniques available like we have today. They relied heavily on the rising and setting sun. Based on Jennifer's extensive research, she determined the home is set exactly at 180°. This degree is one of four exact cardinal points – 180° (South), 270° (West), 360°/0° (North) and 90° (East). These degrees will open a 'window' of energy that allows spirits and ghosts to enter. They should be reserved for holy places such as churches, temples and synagogues. This is likely why the castle on the hill is regularly visited by ghosts.

In Feng Shui, these degrees are known as *Death and Empty Lines* or Void Lines. It is taboo to build homes and businesses on these exact degrees. If they are, they can create divorce, bankruptcy, job loss, illness, spirit apparitions, and even an untimely death. Phil was addicted to alcohol and pills, and haunted by the 1992 death of his son from leukemia. Profoundly lonely, visitors reported that he became paranoid about being left alone and would often lock the gates of the castle to stop them from leaving him.

Triangular-Shaped Lot Indicating Ghosts

Lots or land plots that have a triangular shape are known to bring disharmony and invite ghostly apparitions. They are considered very inauspicious and will support reclusiveness, drug and alcohol abuse, anti-social behavior, and paranoia.

Feng Shui Restoration

The combined, unfortunate features of the castle, the triangular lot, being built on top of the hill, the odd-shaped home design, surrounded by roads, and the water reservoir are either too costly to change or out of the homeowner's hands. The home will continue to bring money loss, ill health, visiting ghosts, and all types of disasters. However, the home could be made into a museum for the city of Alhambra. It may also serve as a county courthouse being on the 'hill'. The home's tragic history is proof that it's unsuitable for day-to-day living and that people simply won't thrive. A public building would have quite different results.

The Pyrenees Castle at 1700 Grandview Drive Today

Currently, Phil Spector's wife, Rachelle, who married him after he was charged with second-degree murder in Lana Clarkson's death, lives in the castle. According to an online article in the *Huffington Post, Phil Spector's Wife: I'm Not a Gold Digger, We Had Frequent Sex: "Rachelle Spector's motives have been questioned by some. She says it was all about love, not money, and expressed resentment toward those who call him unattractive."* Evidently, when Jennifer asked the historical museum's attendant if Rachelle Spector was seen out and about in town, she said rarely. Spector produced her debut album, *Out of my Chelle,* his first album produced in 30 years. According to Billboard charts, a music industry source for record sales, her album wasn't on the list.

Final Thoughts

The Pyrenees Castle is an interesting landmark in the city of Alhambra. Like some of the beautiful castles in Europe, it should be a public building, not a home. Dupuy had a dream and made it come to life. However, unwittingly, he set energies in motion that he knew nothing of. Without a doubt, those who needed to experience certain karmic outcomes used its energy. However, Phil Spector's unfortunate choice put the castle on the world's stage.

Chapter Fourteen
Marilyn Monroe: *The Sex Goddess*

While living in this house for less than six months, Marilyn experienced paranoia, a lawsuit by 20th Century Fox, had numerous high-profile affairs, and finally died of either a drug overdose or murder.

Feng Shui and Facts
Address: 12305 Fifth Helena Drive, Los Angeles, CA
Period 5, Southwest 3
Moved in: 1962
Facing Direction: 232°-247°
Marilyn: 4 Life-Gua
Died: August 5, 1962
Negative Formations: *Three Killings* disturbed, L-shaped house design, sloping land at the back, paranoia, and psychosis activated by the stove and bed placement.

Background on Celebrity and Property

Marilyn Monroe is perhaps the most iconic figure in American culture and the most recognizable sex symbol of all times. A true Hollywood legend and big-screen Goddess, she remains to this day the American epitome of feminine beauty and sex appeal.

Born in Los Angeles as Norma Jeane Mortenson on June 1, 1926, she was an actress, model, and singer. She gained fame playing comic 'blond bombshell' characters. Her vulnerability and innocence only added to her charm and universal appeal. Although she was a top-billed actress for only a decade, her films grossed $200 million at the time of her unexpected death. Some of her famous movies included *Bus Stop*, *Diamonds Are a Girl's Best Friend*, *Gentlemen Prefer Blondes*, *Some Like It Hot*, *The Prince and the Showgirl*, *Something's Gotta Give*, and *The Seven-Year Itch*. On August 5, 1962, she died at age 36 from an overdose of barbiturates at her home in Los Angeles.

The Brentwood hacienda at 12305 Fifth Helena Drive was purchased by Marilyn in 1962 for $77,000. The 'Helenas' is a series of 25 tiny cul-de-sacs that run from San Vicente Boulevard to Sunset Boulevard at the eastern edge of the posh Brentwood neighborhood. Although Marilyn lived in 43 different homes in her lifetime, this was the only one she owned.

Her extremely unstable childhood made her prone to a nomadic existence. It was only after she endured two psychiatric hospitalizations and two major surgeries that she vowed to find a permanent residence.  The Brentwood hacienda was to be her final move, her last home, eerily foretold on the front entrance tiles. The tiles bore a coat of arms with the Latin inscription *Cursum Perficio*, which translated means 'My journey is over' or 'I finish my journey'.

12305 Fifth Helena Drive was secluded and private. In the 1960's, this neighborhood was considered upper middle class. In the day of lavish lifestyles of the rich and famous, the home was very unassuming for a Hollywood movie star. However, it afforded her privacy and anonymity, something she deeply craved. It was a white Spanish-style house with lush, mature trees and a swimming pool. She adored it.

Although Marilyn came from humble beginnings filled with sorrow and tragedy, once she was discovered, she quickly gained enormous fame. Very much ahead of her time, Marilyn was the first public figure to reveal childhood sexual abuse. She was also the second female movie star to establish her own production company. These were amazing and courageous accomplishments particularly in light of her family background. She was, in fact, the illegitimate child of a mentally ill mother.

As an adult, Marilyn suffered through three marriages, divorces, and multiple miscarriages. In light of having severe endometriosis, she finally accepted she would never have children. She truly was a "candle in the wind" – exposed and vulnerable. Her deep insecurity stemmed from being raised in a succession of foster homes and orphanages due to her mother's chronic mental illness. Her unhealthy attachments and personality disorders stemmed from sexual abuse, neglect, and the absence of a stable parental figure.

Marilyn sought help for these issues and had daily visits with Ralph Greenson, a psychoanalyst to Hollywood's elite. He lived nearby in Brentwood. Marilyn's marital and sexual connections were with some of the most famous men of her day – Joe DiMaggio, Arthur Miller, Frank Sinatra, and John F. Kennedy. These scandals still create gossip and speculation today, while being either romanticized or vilified.

Marilyn's Life-Gua Number
Marilyn Monroe was a 4 Life-Gua and they are known to be indecisive, flexible, and malleable. She was often quoted as saying, *"Is that who you want me to be?"* She was

not only unsure of who she was, but also of her place in the world. The 4 Gua's have easy-going personalities and may be controlled by their partners. She was notorious for her succession of famous lovers. Rumors persisted about an alleged affair with President John F. Kennedy, as well as his brother, Robert Kennedy.

The 4 Life-Guas are often attracted to the arts, entertainment, or writing and may have movie star looks or qualities. Marilyn was a true Hollywood movie star. She would set the standard for generations to come with her gorgeous face and figure coupled with her open, sweet sexuality. These Gua's have a gentle spirit and this was obvious with Marilyn's shy and reserved nature when not in the spotlight. She was often said to identify with her public and felt detached from her own celebrity status.

The Home's Best Features

Flying Star Chart was a Parent String Formation

The house was a prestigious *Parent String Formation* (Period 5, Southwest 3) which is purported to bring triple good fortune if activated correctly. If you recall, Anna Nicole Smith also had a *Parent String* home. It requires a 'mountain' in front and water at the back. The front, high stucco walls served as Marilyn's 'mountain' and she had a large, free-form swimming pool at the back. This was one of the best features of the home. It would have brought incredible good luck and perhaps would have outweighed some of the negative aspects if the *Three Killings*

had not been disturbed that year with construction. How she disturbed the *Three Killings* is explained in detail later in this chapter. With that being said, the home was situated in a beautifully serene neighborhood with charming and vibrant energy.

The Pool Placement

The pool activated the current wealth energy (5 facing star) which was extremely fortunate. During Period 5 (1944-1964), activating this energy by a large body of water such as a swimming pool, indicated abundant wealth and great fortune. The 5 star is only good in Period 5. Otherwise, it can harm the occupants in every way. Activated at the right time, it is so powerful that the ancient Chinese called it the 'king-maker' energy.

Rumors swirled that Marilyn had an affair with the American king, President John F. Kennedy. In the public's view, this was confirmed when she breathlessly sang *Happy Birthday, Mr. President* at his 45th birthday party. Her famous tribute to the President was on May 19, 1962, only three months after moving into her Brentwood hacienda.

Marilyn was introduced to the American royal family through her friend and fellow actor, Peter Lawford. At the time, he was married to Patricia Kennedy. Only after a brief acquaintance, Marilyn had the privilege of entering the inner sanctum of

'Camelot'[4]. This was the world of the super-powerful and super-rich. With the pool activating the *5 facing star*, she received extraordinary results! Never before, or since, has a celebrity received so much attention after singing happy birthday to the President of the United States of America.

Kitchen Location

In the Eight Mansion systems, kitchens should be located in one of the negative sectors to 'burn up' bad luck. Marilyn's kitchen was located in the West (-80). This would have supported regaining her health and attracting loyal relationships.

The Master Bathroom/Toilet

Due to the nature of toilets, they should be located in negative sectors of the house. Marilyn's master bathroom was very well placed (-90). This would have been very auspicious for wealth.

Negative Features

The Shape of the House Indicated Issues with Money, Relationships, and Health

As we have mentioned previously, odd- or extreme-shaped homes usually spell trouble. Marilyn's house was an L-shape home design. There were three missing sectors, the North, South, and Southwest sectors. This means that some of her best sectors were not represented in the house. The North, her wealth sector (+90), and the South, her health area (+80), did not exist. Not being able to utilize these areas was unfortunate because they would have supported her.

Odd or extreme-shaped homes generally indicate issues in all three categories of Feng Shui (prosperity, health, and relationships).

---

[4] Camelot was the nickname of the Kennedy's reign in power—the players were young, beautiful, and powerful. Reminiscent of King Arthur, Queen Guinevere and the round table of knights in the old legend, President Kennedy's court was idyllic.

Although Marilyn enjoyed being in the spotlight at the President's birthday party, she left Washington to return to the movie set of *Something's Got to Give*. Shortly thereafter, 20th Century Fox filed a $500k lawsuit against her. Fox stated that she only worked 12 days out of 35 days of production. At this point, the house was beginning to show its less auspicious side.

Sloping Land Indicated Money Loss, No Support, and Alcoholism

At the back of the property, beyond the pool, the land sloped sharply downward. In the book, *Cursum Perficio: Marilyn Monroe's Brentwood Hacienda*, the author, Gary Vitacco-Robles, describes a scene in which she looks down the hill at her neighbors. This would suggest that this area had no fence or retaining wall. If that was the case, it would have indicated issues with money loss. Her career would have also suffered. While the drop-off was not as drastic as the one at Anna Nicole's home, it could still create loss of wealth, alcoholism, drug use, instability, and 'no support' in the world. There are many ways this could have affected her life; career and health would have been at the top of the list.

And this is exactly what happened. It is true that Marilyn was absent a number of production days while filming *Something's Got to Give*. However, it was due to an upper respiratory infection that was confirmed by her physicians. Fox Studios, on the other hand, would allege that Marilyn's performance was affected by drug use. They further stated that only seven minutes of useable film had been captured. However, hours of surviving footage have most people believing that it was some of her best work ever. In a political move, Fox Studios suspended Marilyn.

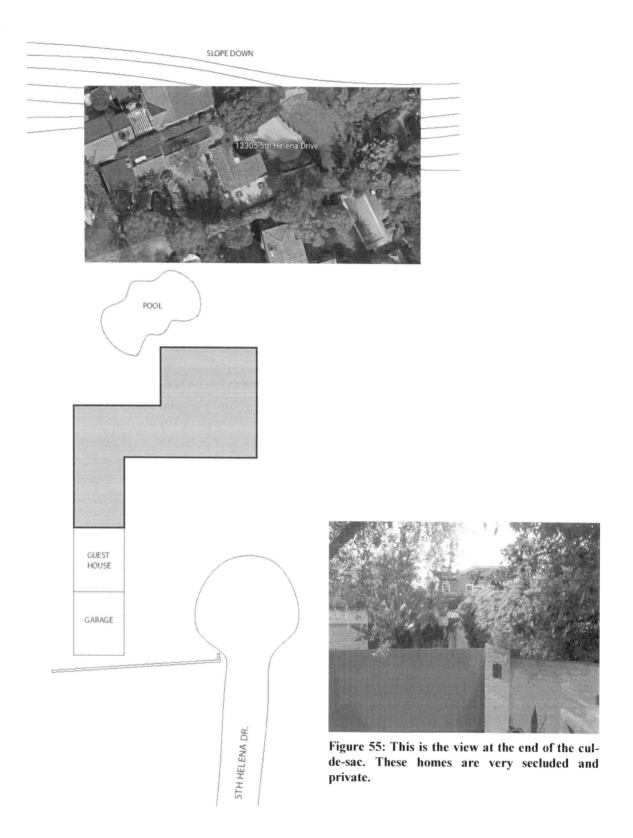

SLOPE DOWN

12305 5th Helena Drive

POOL

GUEST
HOUSE

GARAGE

5TH HELENA DR.

Figure 55: This is the view at the end of the cul-de-sac. These homes are very secluded and private.

Marilyn's health was also affected with the sloping land at the back. She was prescribed barbiturates by her psychiatrist, Greenson, for depression, anxiety, insomnia, and psychosis. She was diagnosed as borderline paranoid schizophrenic and was institutionalized twice for this condition. Marilyn was addicted to a pharmacopoeia of drugs and often drank too much. These were dangerous combinations that did nothing but deepen her insecurity and mental imbalance. It was rumored that she often arrived late for work and drank heavily. Her unreliability and inability to work when needed forced Fox Studios to suspend her. They ultimately fired her on June 8, 1962. Being suspended or fired from lucrative roles plagued her entire career. The lack of 'support' at the back of her home did not help matters.

The Master Bed Placement

Marilyn's bed was placed in the worst direction possible for her (-90). It indicated divorce, no descendants, bankruptcy, death, and business failures. The Flying Stars would have brought her mixed luck (2, 5). The *5 facing star* was superior energy at the time, but the *2 mountain star* would have harmed her health and well-being. The 2 'sickness' star would have activated depression, reproductive problems, widowhood, unwanted abortions, and cancer. Sadly, she suffered from endometriosis and had multiple miscarriages. Marilyn was very open about her desire to have children but was unable to carry a child to full term. No doubt this, too, contributed to her depression. She was medicated for this as well as other emotional issues. She suffered physically as well as emotionally, and had two serious surgeries. One was on her gall bladder and the other on her pancreas. This is unusual for a woman who was only in her 30's. It's so interesting that the descriptions for the *2 mountain star* and the -90 accurately portrayed what

happened in Marilyn's life—including no descendents.

The Front Door Indicated Health Problems

While the front door faced Southwest, not her best direction, in *Advanced Eight Mansions* it would have supported her. However, the *8 facing star* was not good in Period 5. It would have indicated accidents involving the bones, dislocation of the bones, bone and nerve disease, a sweet talker, flirting, and nose and stomach cancer.

Patio Doors to Pool Indicated Lawsuits, Arguments, and Conflict

There was a Northwest-facing door in the bedroom near the pool which activated conflict and lawsuits. As mentioned earlier, Fox Studios filed a lawsuit against Marilyn. After renegotiating her contract with them, the lawsuit was eventually dropped. In a phone call to one of the executives at Fox, she said, *"Imagine a Marilyn Monroe who actually comes to the set on time."* Legal action from such a powerhouse as Fox Studios would have been very distressing, and the door direction supported the lawsuit energy.

Other 'conflicts' came from her relationships. On the day of her death, it was rumored that Robert Kennedy arrived at Marilyn's home in the afternoon. They had a violent argument in which she told him that she felt used and passed around. Eventually, she ordered him out of her house. This confrontation upset her so much that she immediately summoned her psychiatrist, Dr. Greenson, for a 90-minute session. It's likely that he injected her with barbiturates to calm her down. Soon afterwards, she talked with her stepson, Joe DiMaggio Jr., and her friend Jeanne Carmen. No one expressed a belief that she was depressed or on drugs, or ready to commit suicide.

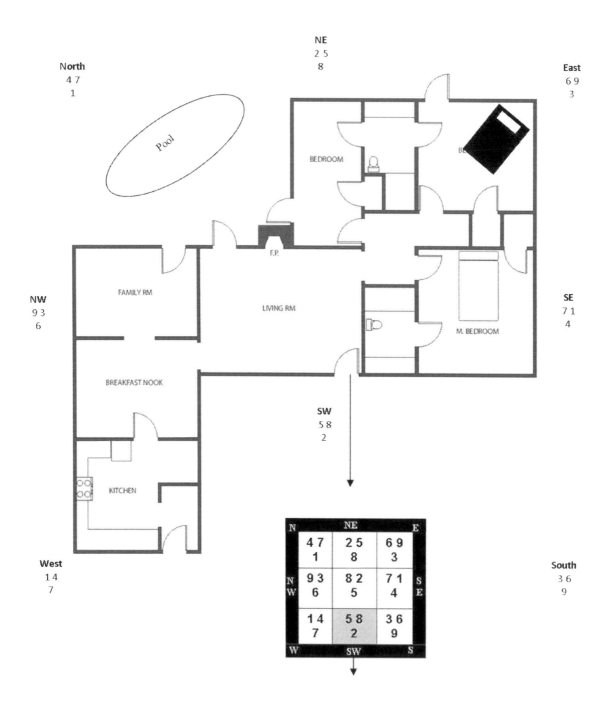

Figure 56: The floor plan of Marilyn's Period 5, SW 3 Hacienda. The pool was located in the North. Her bed placement was on the Northeast wall of her master bedroom.

If you believe any of the conspiracy theories surrounding Marilyn's death, the energy in this home would have supported those, too. In the article, *New Details of Marilyn Monroe's Life and Death,* those close to Marilyn feared foul play. The DiMaggio family has long held the belief that Marilyn was not alone on the day she died. In fact, Lee DiMaggio was on the phone with her when he heard her scream a name, and then she dropped the phone. Lee's daughter, June, said her mother took that name to her grave because of fearing for her safety.

In the early 1970s, Marilyn's home was acquired by actors Michael Irving and Veronica Hamel (*Hill Street Blues*). During a remodel, the couple discovered and removed a sophisticated government-grade eavesdropping and telephone tapping system that extended into every room of the house. Wow! But not surprising because the 3, 9 combination in the Northwest indicates 'very cunning and wicked people.'

The Kitchen and Stove Indicated Paranoia, Alcoholism, and Affairs

Marilyn's stove was sitting on the Northwest and a *9 mountain star.* This would have activated mental problems, psychosis, paranoia, miscarriages, and heart and eye problems. In the book, *Cursum Perficio: Marilyn Monroe's Brentwood Hacienda,* the author says that Marilyn's housekeeper cooked daily for the movie star. Using the stove daily would have fully activated the energy. A writer from *Life* magazine, Richard Merryman, interviewed Marilyn for six hours at her private residence just before her death. In Vitacco-Robles' book, he wrote, *"Merryman's impression is that 'the house was saturated in paranoia' with an eerie 'me-against-the-world' quality."*

The knob direction of the stove activated the Southeast (7,1). This would have supported a split personality, love affairs, romantic encounters, alcoholism, heart disease, thievery, quarrels, accidents, drowning, family members in trouble with the law, gangsters, and robberies. Those in her sphere were aware that Marilyn drank in order to cope with her haunting past. She had numerous romantic encounters, often with co-stars, three failed marriages, and was always yearning for lasting love.

The DiMaggio family told *Playboy* contributor Lisa DePaulo that Monroe and Joe DiMaggio had planned to remarry. Monroe had already bought a dress and selected her china. DiMaggio had a ring for her and there was talk that they might adopt a child. *"If she was remarrying Joe DiMaggio, the love of her life, is she going to take her life four days before?"* DePaulo asked on the TV show, *Good Morning America.*

Three Killings Indicated Money Loss, Illness, Robbery, and Fatalities

Every year there are four sha, or negative energies, that visit different areas of everyone's home. They are the *5 Yellow Star, Grand Duke Jupiter, Year Breaker,* and *Three Killings.* In 1962, the year that Marilyn moved into her hacienda, these malevolent energies were visiting the South, Southwest, Northeast, and North, respectively. It is taboo to disturb these sectors with deep digging, demolition, or construction. The *Three Killings* is the most dangerous to disturb.

If the *Three Killings* area is disturbed, it can cause betrayals, robbery, loss of money, injuries, illnesses, and fatalities. When Marilyn moved into her home, she did extensive renovations. She slowly transformed the hacienda into her dream home. According to the book, *Cursum Perficio*, *"Cabinetmaker Ray Tolman removes the gas heating stubs in each room by drilling into the solid twelve-inch thick concrete walls. He is subsequently hospitalized for a heart attack precipitated by his vigorous work."*

That type of drilling could have activated all four of the negative sectors. The author continues describing the makeover: *"Marilyn also plants a tree in the walled patio between the kitchen and guest house. She hires Mexican brick masons to build a low wall around the tree, and gardener Mr. Tateishi plants white azaleas beneath the tree. The brick masons also pave paths in the garden courtyard where herbs will grow in clay pots."*

While planting flowers or herbs would not have disturbed the *Three Killings*, all the other construction in-progress would have. We believe that, coupled with the other negative home features, Marilyn's numerous construction projects were the catalyst to the perfect storm that contributed to her demise.

Feng Shui Restoration

The House Shape
There was plenty of land to add rooms to the house to give it a more square and uniform shape. This would have filled in those missing sectors and given Marilyn great support. Unfortunately, subsequent owners have added a garage and guesthouse, making the shape even more extreme.

Sloping Land at the Back
We would have recommended that this area have a solid wall to prevent the energy from 'falling away' from the home. It is missing the all-important 'back support' known as the *Black Turtle* (aka the *Dark Warrior*). The wall would have offered Marilyn more support in the world, instead of betrayals, back-stabbing, and money loss.

The Stove Location
We would have recommended relocating the stove to sit on the Southwest (*5 mountain star*) and face the knobs Northeast (*5 facing star*). This would have provided Marilyn with some much-needed wealth and career luck.

The Master Bed Placement
We would have moved Marilyn's bedroom to the East sector of the house, her personal

relationship area (+70). The bed direction should have also been in the East (6, 9). The bed would have been angled in the corner (see the floor plan in Figure 56). This would have supported a good relationship with a stable older man, like a father figure. This placement and location would have attracted more fame but with a much better outcome in her relationships.

12305 Fifth Helena Drive Today

On the day of Marilyn's death, the Nunez family placed a sales contract on the house with their realtor. About six other realtors had also 'sold' the house on the same day.

While the estate remained in probate, a bidding war ensued which resulted in legal intervention. A judge ruled that the property would be sold at a purchase price 10% over the highest bid. In September 1963, the Nunez family became the owners and purchased many of the home's contents, including Marilyn's Hoover vacuum cleaner. In 1997, they auctioned many of her furnishings and possessions.

On May 31, 2017, Marilyn's white hacienda, which was on the market for $6.9 million, was bought for $7.25 million. Prior to this sale, the pool was in the exact location. All past changes to the home have been aesthetic. The facing direction of the home and the doors remain unchanged. Structurally, everything remains the same as when Marilyn lived there. In the 1970's, the new owners added a garage, guesthouse, and a cabana. It remains to be seen what the latest 2017 owners will do and how they may alter the famed, white hacienda.

Final Thoughts

It's hard to say how many millions of people were touched by Marilyn Monroe's life. Literally hundreds of books have been written about her, and new generations continue to discover and emulate her. She left a powerful legacy for future Hollywood movie stars. Had she remained with us, her life may have not had the same impact. She will be forever etched in our memories as someone who exuded innocence, beauty, and vulnerability.

Her movies are well-preserved in the Hollywood archives. Marilyn's memorabilia still commands some of the highest in the world for movie star greats. Her final stop, the Brentwood hacienda, proved to be disastrous. Considering the life she endured, it's not surprising that she chose a home gift-wrapped in fatal Feng Shui. Perhaps, it was by design. While the energy for tragedy was there, this would not have been every homeowner's experience.

This quote made by Marilyn Monroe in 1961 is very telling and hints at the beautiful, sensitive soul that she was: *"In Hollywood a girl's virtue is much less important than her hair-do. You're judged by how you look, not by what you are. Hollywood's a place where they'll pay you a thousand dollars for a kiss, and fifty cents for your soul. I know, because I turned down the first offer often enough and held out for the fifty cents."*

For two decades, Joe DiMaggio had flowers delivered to Marilyn's grave twice a week.

Chapter Fifteen
Brittany Murphy: *The Girl, Interrupted*

While living in this house for six years, Brittany struggled with her career, health, suffered two broken engagements, finally married and ultimately died of pneumonia, anemia, and multiple drug intoxication. Her husband died five months later in the same house.

Feng Shui and Facts
Address: 1895 Rising Glen Road Los Angeles, CA
Period 7, South 1
Moved in: 2003
Facing Direction: 157°-172°
Brittany Murphy: 1 Life-Gua
Simon Monjack: 4 Life-Gua
Brittany **died:** December 20, 2009
Simon **died:** May 23, 2010
Negative Formations: *Eight Roads of Destruction, Eight Killing Mountain Forces,* extreme house design, the pool activated lawsuits and conflict and the stove activated disasters of all types.

Background on Celebrity and Property

In an exclusive Hollywood Hills neighborhood, two young people died less than six months apart. Years later, the *Daily Mail* would suggest that the house was 'cursed'. Nevertheless, in 2003, actress Brittany Murphy bought 1895 Rising Glen Road, a five-bedroom, five-bath, 8,000-square-foot home from singer Brittany

Spears. She paid $3,850,000 for the Mediterranean style home that was built in 1997. The home was situated in the exclusive community of Sunset Hills. It is a small enclave of expensive homes that cling to the dramatically rising hillside. This is a well sought-after neighborhood, one of the most prestigious in Hollywood Hills, and filled with celebrities.

Brittany Murphy was born Brittany Bertolotti on November 10, 1977 in Atlanta, Georgia. Her star rose quickly and began at the tender age of 9, with theatre acting. By the time she turned 13, she had already signed on with a manager and was acting in commercials. When she played Tai in *Clueless,* her career really took off. That role garnered her attention in the industry and, as a result, she continued to work non-stop.

Brittany landed serious dramatic roles in movies like *Girl Interrupted, Don't Say a Word, 8 Mile, Riding in Cars with Boys, Sin City,* comedic roles in *Just Married, Little Black Book,* and *Uptown Girls.* She was the voice of Gloria in *Happy Feet* and lending the voice of Luanne in *King of the Hill.* A little known fact was that she had a broad range of talents. They included acting, singing and dancing; aka the 'triple threat'.

Having grown up in Edison, New Jersey, her infectious giggle became one of her endearing trademarks. The Hollywood standard of 'thin' began to wear on her and

media photos showed her wasting away as she succumbed to the pressure. Throughout the years, rumors of drug use and eating disorders haunted her but she denied them all. Towards the end, her career was dwindling. She was accepting roles in indie films, cartoons and other less visible projects. Her frustration was mounting as she desired roles where her talents could be showcased. In May 2007, Murphy married British screenwriter Simon Monjack in a private Jewish ceremony in Los Angeles.

On December 20, 2009, Brittany Murphy died in her Hollywood Hills home of pneumonia, anemia, and multiple drug intoxication. Five months later on May 23, 2010, her husband, Simon, was also found dead in the same home of acute pneumonia and severe anemia. Is it a coincidence that two young people died in the

same home, five months within each other and with very similar symptoms? No, it's not. The Feng Shui of this home will reveal clues as to what happened.

Brittany's home was the most extreme design of all of our celebrities. It's a strange, tri-level house surrounded by mountains in every direction. To reach the property requires negotiating a steep incline. The entire home's setting is somewhat disconcerting. One good California mudslide and another house would have swallowed it up.

Brittany and Simon's Life-Gua Numbers

Brittany Murphy was a 1 Life-Gua and they are known for their intelligence, ability to make money, and sex appeal. They may be hard to pin down, have secrets or even lead a secret life. While they appear to be calm on the surface, they can be very emotional, high strung, moody, and anxious. Alex Ben Block retells his experiences with Brittany, in his article *The Last Days of Brittany.* Alex said that while Brittany lacked a higher education, she soaked up knowledge and was self-educated. Her interests ranged from politics to science to the intricacies of the entertainment industry. Brittany kept a relatively low profile, especially after her surprise wedding to Simon Monjack in 2007. Her personal life was relatively low-key, except for the rumors of an eating disorder and drug use, which were unsubstantiated. Simon Monjack, born August 5, 1969 was a 4 Life-Gua. They're known to be easy-going, flexible and indecisive. The 1 and 4 Guas are considered a very auspicious match and can be very sweet and romantic. Their relationship would have involved intellectual conversations, a sensual connection, and deep understanding of each other. The 1 Life-Guas like to support and care for the 4 Life-Guas. Author Alex Ben Block described how Brittany was always taking care of Simon due to his numerous health issues. Their first year of marriage was filled with creative pursuits and the relationship blossomed. Simon took hundreds of photos of Brittany. He played the piano at night while she lay beneath the baby grand listening.

The Home's Best Features

Perfect Land Embrace
The home, literally, had mountains in every direction. This means the 'land embrace' was fully represented with a good *Dragon, Tiger,* and *Black Turtle.* With energy being retained, many opportunities for career, money luck, relationships, and health would have been available.

Front Door Indicated Money Luck
The oddly placed front entrance faced Northwest. This direction had the *1 facing star* and would have indicated good money luck. However, they may have always entered the home via the interior garage door. This door also had good energy which faced North (6 facing star).

The Toilet Locations Indicated Money Luck and Stability
Due to the nature of toilets, they should be located in negative sectors (-60, -70, -80, -90). The master bedroom toilet was very well-placed in the West (-60). There was also one located in the West upstairs on the third floor office.

Negative Features

Extreme House Design Indicated Money Loss, Confusion, and Instability
In comparison to the other celebrity homes analyzed in this book, Brittany's house had the most bizarre and extreme design of them all. It's obvious that it had numerous additions since 1997 when it was built. Unfortunately, extreme designs deliver very bad results. Additionally, the home had multiple levels jutting off into different directions. These are two very negative features that would cause multiple issues. Money loss would be apparent from the extreme design alone. The weird multi-levels would support disjointed/delusional thinking, confusion, and migraine headaches. In the article *The Last Days of Brittany Murphy* by Alex Ben Block, he wrote, *"a lot of what Simon told me - about his family, education, marriage and career - was exaggerated or simply fabricated."*

Period 7 Flying Star Chart Indicated Loss and Robbery
Brittany bought her home in 2003; this was the last year of Period 7. Once we entered Period 8 on February 4, 2004, the good luck ended for this house. The 7 energy is only good in its own Period. Otherwise, it will bring a sense of hopelessness, robbery (literally and figuratively), and loss. She experienced a loss of reputation, several failed romances and engagements, and lucrative movie roles. In fact, *Sin City,* which was released in 2005, was her last movie.

Figure 57: Brittany Murphy's Period 7, South 1 property had the most extreme design of all the celebrity homes. This design is notorious for causing money loss, confusion, issues with career, health, and relationships. The steep driveway formed the *Eight Roads of Destruction*. The home has been totally redesigned into a modern masterpiece.

Driveway Indicated Money Loss

The long uphill driveway leading to Brittany's home was, and remains, a negative feature. The steep driveway allows energy to escape the property. Energy must be retained in order for people to thrive. While there was an iron fence in place when Brittany owned it, energy could still flow away and down the hillside. This may explain why she struggled with landing the big, lucrative movie roles while living there. It was not her dream to do movies that went straight to videos.

Peeping Tom Energy Indicated Insecurity and Vulnerability

Directly behind Brittany's home is a large mountain with another housing tract. These homes are higher up and have a 360° view of Los Angeles. They would have a clear view of her property as well. In Feng Shui, it's called the *Peeping Tom* effect and can lead to paranoia. This can cause people to feel insecure, vulnerable, and constantly being 'watched'. Brittany felt uncomfortable in her home and didn't like living there; this may have been another reason why.

Eight Roads of Destruction Indicated Disastrous Events

The pernicious *Eight Roads of Destruction* was created by the South-facing balcony door (157°- 172°) and the driveway exiting the Southeast (127°- 142°). These formations are notorious for causing money loss, bankruptcy, illness, affairs, hassles, and other destructive events. Brittany's career was suffering. She had not done a movie since *Sin City*. It was reported that Simon had several health problems. Her life was not going as expected – she lived in a house she hated, lived in a city she hated, and her career was imploding. She had the constant burden and role of caregiver. Even in the last few days, when she was not well herself, she was taking care of her mother who was a cancer survivor and suffering debilitating neuropathy. Then there was Simon who had been ailing, on and off, for three years. Simon was having seizures a month before she died. He had suffered an apparent heart attack. Everyone living in the house was feeling the negative effect of the *Eight Roads of Destruction*.

Eight Killing Mountain Forces Indicated Death and Blood-Related Accidents

The house also had another very serious, destructive formation – an *Eight Killing Mountain Forces*. This was formed by the Southeast-facing living room doors and the mountain in the North. The *Eight Killings* will bring blood-related accidents, death, illness, and crimes of passion. The accumulative energy of all the negative features are adding up and it's no wonder two young people died in the house.

Swimming Pool Activated Lawsuits, Robbery, and Conflicts

The large pool located near the master bedroom and living room activated the *3 facing star* in the Southeast. This badly placed, huge water feature would attract lawsuits, robbery, conflict, fighting, and legal hassles. Evidently, Brittany's husband Simon had a shady past.

In *The Last Days of Brittany Murphy*, the author described Simon's money issues and deceptive behavior. Aaron Richard Golub was the author of *Factory Girl*, and Simon Monjack was working on the screenplay. Evidently, he wasn't very good at the task. However, he was very good at 'spinning self-aggrandizing stories'. Golub told Simon "I really don't want to be in business with someone who is flim-flamming people. You've left a trail of people behind that are going to sue you because you took their trust finds or inheritance or conned them into investing in projects you never delivered."

Additionally, when Simon moved into Brittany's house, he didn't mention that he left his previous fiancé with thousands in unpaid rent on an L.A. apartment, or that he had written numerous bad checks. Shortly after they married, Brittany paid $10k to a casting director who had sued Simon over a bounced check. This is the 'robber' aspect of the *3 facing star* when activated.

Central Staircase Indicated Issues with Bones, Joints, and Spine

In Feng Shui, it is taboo to have a staircase in the dead center of a home. Brittany's home had this feature and it would have caused several problems with the bones, joints, skeletal system, and spine. She lived in the house long enough for some of these to manifest.

Stove Placement Indicated Death, Cancer, Money Loss, and Fame

The stove was located in the West of the kitchen (5 mountain star) and the knobs activated the East (4 facing star). Having a stove located on a *5 mountain star* would indicate cancer, bankruptcy, death, disease, and disasters. However, the stove knobs would have activated fame energy. Brittany's health was fragile; she even had a heart murmur. She was getting paranoid about the public and film industry learning about her medical problems. According to Alex Ben Block, Simon stoked that paranoia in order to gain control over her. It's fascinating because Simon suffered from a minor heart attack in this home and they both died of anemia as one of the causes of death.

Master Bed Placement Indicated Health Issues

The master bed was likely placed on the North wall of the room (8,6). This placement would have allowed a good view of the pool and mountains. As it turns out,

the North is a good direction for them both. However, the annual *5 Yellow Star* visited the North in 2009. Normally, the 8, 6 stars are considered supportive energy. However, because the home was a Period 7 and had so many serious negative features, it is worth examining the negative aspect. In the 81 combinations, it states, 'These stars signify being childless, accidents, loss of wealth, no sons or descendants, mental instability, and the dislocation of the joints or bones'. When there are a number of negative features, the *5 Yellow Star* can deliver an enormous amount of destructive energy. The ancient text describes the 5 star as 'Lawsuits by the government, five people in the house will die disaster, calamity, catastrophe, lawsuits, setbacks, disease, death, grave misfortune. A parent hurts the son; five males can die in the house, rebellious, an extremist, the butcher, eccentric, and lots of lawsuits.'

On the day Brittany died, she had taken an anti-depressant (fluoxetine aka Prozac), an anti-seizure drug (klonopin), and an anti-inflammatory (methylprednisolone). Simon had also given her a beta blocker and Vicoprofen to ease menstrual pain. Even with all this medication, Brittany showed no signs of getting better. She often suffered with laryngitis and it was worse in the last 10 days of her life than it had ever been. To compound things, Brittany was weakened by her irregular menstrual cycles and suffered with anemia. Doctors discovered that her red blood count was drastically low. Even with all these dangerous signs, she had not seen a doctor for six weeks. On the last night of her life, she desperately gasped for breath, the lack of oxygen turned her lips blue and, finally, her lungs filled with fluid and killed her. While the *5 Yellow Star* does not always support such a dramatic end to life, if there is serious negative energy elsewhere, it can.

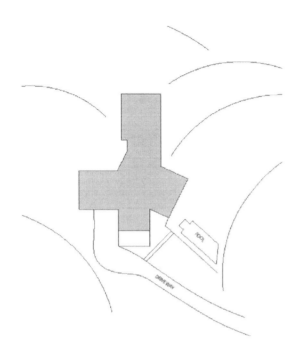

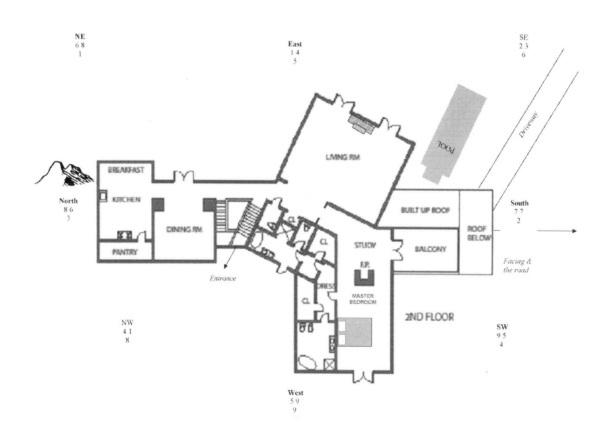

NE
6 8
1

East
1 4
5

SE
2 3
6

North
8 6
3

South
7 7
2

*Facing &
the road*

NW
4 1
8

SW
9 5
4

West
5 9
9

BREAKFAST

KITCHEN

DINING RM.

PANTRY

LIVING RM.

POOL

Driveway

BUILT UP ROOF

ROOF
BELOW

BALCONY

STUDY

F.P.

PRESS

CL.

CL.

CL.

Entrance

MASTER
BEDROOM

2ND FLOOR

Feng Shui Restoration

Since the Hollywood Hills area is an affluent neighborhood, owners could afford to have excellent Feng Shui if desired. The best recommendation we could give is to start over with a drastic renovation. The house shape/design was detrimental. There was an *Eight Roads of Destruction* and *Eight Killings*, the pool activated lawsuits, and the stove activated bankruptcy and disease. Also, it may have had a serious black mold problem. This was one of the theories of Brittany and Simon's untimely and unusual death. With all this in mind, starting fresh would be the best option and this is exactly what happened. It got a major makeover in 2016.

The Hollywood Hills Home Today

After the death of Brittany Murphy in 2009, her mother Sharon put the house on the market multiple times. She was unable to find a buyer until 2011 when she sold it for just under $3 million. After a major renovation, it was listed in 2016 for $19 million. There were no takers. It was reduced and finally sold on February 26, 2017 for $14,500 million. The old Mediterranean style was gone and replaced with a super-sleek modern masterpiece. In 2016, the *Daily Mail* featured a headline entitled *'Cursed' Hollywood Hills home that once belonged to Britney Spears and later Brittany Murphy gets a massive makeover and a new mojo as it hits the market for $19.75 million'*. The article says the house is barely recognizable after a 'ground up' renovation. It boasts five bedrooms, 6.75 baths, and 9,400 square feet of sleek finishes and floor-to-ceiling glass walls. "It's been totally transformed," said a source familiar with the previous home. "Hopefully all of that bad mojo is finally gone."

Final Thoughts

Alas, the Hollywood Hills home had several detrimental features. It was instrumental in the abrupt and mysterious deaths of Brittany Murphy and Simon Monjack. The area is hauntingly beautiful with lofty views of the world below. When Jennifer, the co-author of this book, went to visit Brittany's home, she felt the vibrant energy of the neighborhood, but peril too. She could not imagine herself living in a home that appears precariously placed over the mountain's edge, as so many were.

It's so interesting that Brittany began to despise the house she bought years earlier. Perhaps it was the unhappy events that kept creeping into her life. She suffered through several failed romantic relationships. In late 2002, Murphy began dating Ashton Kutcher, her co-star in *Just Married*. Once she was engaged to talent manager Jeff Kwatinetz. She became engaged to Joe Macaluso in December 2005, a production assistant she met while working on the film *Little Black Book*. In August 2006, they ended their engagement. Certainly, this would have been enough, yet she endured gossip and rumors about her weight, plastic surgeries, health, and possible drug use.

Her deepest instincts were telling her that the home no longer worked. She often complained to her husband that she'd rather stay at the Beverly Hills Hotel than go home. However, they continued to live in the house. Her gut feelings were not a fluke and were closer to what Oprah Winfrey calls "a whisper" that gives us warning. Who knows, if she would have sold the home, she may still be with us and her life uninterrupted. Was it karma or destiny? Only the soul knows for sure.

Conclusion on Celebrities

The celebrities that we examined had extraordinary lives and unusual, dangerous or bizarre homes. Several celebrity homes shared the most hazardous Feng Shui formations. It is rare to find one of them in a home, much less several. Even in our combined 30 years experience, these homes were a revelation. Much more could have been discovered had we been able to walk the 'corridors' of these extraordinary homes.

As you've seen, there were many factors that contributed to the energy culminating into death, murder or suicide. In Feng Shui, it is always multi-layered. This would explain why a seemingly normal home could host a horrific event. And remember, not all the homeowners had the same fate, karma, or destiny. However, it is always wise to find out the history of a home prior to purchase. It's safe to say, that if the tenants who previously lived in the home had difficulties, the next homeowner may experience them as well. In fact, the landforms (roads, mountains, water) can outlast any Period and foretell the fortune or misfortunes of the occupants.

The celebrity homes spanned from Period 5 to the current Period of 8. Most of the homes we examined were **Period 7 (1984-2004)**. These homes were owned by O.J. Simpson, Nicole Brown Simpson, Phil Hartman, Brittany Murphy, Phil Spector, José and Kitty Menendez, and Michael Jackson's Neverland Ranch. Sharon Tate's home was the only **Period 6** property. Only two were **Period 8,** that of Anna Nicole Smith and Michael Jackson's luxury rental. The oldest home was Marilyn Monroe's **Period 5** home. It's interesting that each Period or 'Age' will usher in specific types of energies and opportunities.

The following descriptions were derived from the ancient texts and written by Grandmaster Zhang Zhung San; we've made a few comments and observations. The 'Period' descriptions are so accurate, even though written over four hundreds of years ago!

Period 5 (1944-1964): *The King-Maker Energy*
"This period is not ruled by a trigram, but it represents centralized power and the extremist. It is only good during its period; otherwise, it is considered dangerous. This energy is known as the king-maker. It denotes massive fortunes and supreme power. This energy produces famous and important people in society"

Period 6 (1964-1984): *Technology Begins*
"This period is ruled by the Chien trigram. It represents ambitions, knowledge, classy people, and experience. It also denotes outstanding advancements in science and technology." Microsoft created Windows during this time period but launched the retail version of Microsoft Windows on November 20, 1985. This technology changed our world forever.

Period 7 (1984-2004): *The Glamorous Age*
"This period is ruled by the Dui trigram. It represents reform, condemnation, scrutiny, and dignity. It also denotes great orators, communication, astronomers, celebrities, beauty, and glamorous lifestyles. This time Period can see the rise of women; it also denotes metaphysics, spiritualism and a rise in consciousness (*the New Age movement was huge during this time*). It is only good in its time period; otherwise, it indicates disputes and robbers".

Period 8 (2004-2024): *The Great Age of Change*

"This period is ruled by the Gen trigram. It represents a time of restitution, karmic laws, and limits. It also denotes the birth of a religious leader, wealth, young people meeting with success, uncovering the truth, and the strengthening of family values. This time Period indicates young men rising to great success or power."

In this great *Age of Change*, the growth and influence has moved from the West to the Northeastern part of America with New York, Washington, Boston and other prominent cites taking the lead in Period 8. This Period uncovers falsehoods and foundations built on untruths. It ultimately brings great wealth, a resolution to past mistakes and karma, and a rectification of excesses. The focus of this period is also on earth and land, including housing, real estate, large- and small-scale construction, mining, and conglomerates. At the same time, it indicates that China and other SE Asians countries may rise in global influence and riches.

While Feng Shui (*Earth Luck*) is a powerful tool for enhancing harmony, prosperity, longevity and good relationships—it's not a fix-all. Nothing is. Appropriately, there is nothing on the planet that may interfere with a person's free will and choices (*Man Luck*). Equally untouchable is our *Heaven Luck*, for this is our individual karma, mission or Soul's directive.

With that being said, no matter the Period, all of our celebrities left a powerful legacy. Keeping them in the conversation, keeps them alive. It was our privilege to examine their homes and perhaps make evident the wisdom of Classical Feng Shui.

Want more proof as to the power of Feng Shui? Read *Jennifer's Story: A Life's Journey* in the next chapter. Find out how she overcame some of life's challenges and discovered Feng Shui.

Chapter Fifteen
Jennifer's Story: *A Life's Journey*

Everyone who's attained mastery in Feng Shui has a story. My own teacher, Denise, tells her introduction began with a friend holding up a book in Houston's premier metaphysical store. Eva Wong was taught by her two uncles in Hong Kong. Prolific Feng Shui author, Lillian Too, was a martial arts student and friend of Grandmaster Yap Cheng Hai in Kuala Lumpur; she interviewed him for many of her earlier books.

For me, it was by accident; by divine direction or rather serendipitously that I discovered my life's work and passion. It is also what compelled me to write this rather unusual book about famous people whose lives ended in tragedy. I found it when I least expected it and at a time when it was most needed. When I did find Classical Feng Shui, it would be in casual conversation, and it would change my life forever.

Once introduced to me, I realized that Feng Shui so deeply resonated with me, that *this* is what I had been searching for without being able to express or even describe it. When Feng Shui unfolded its mysteries to me, I began to learn the real meaning of life. All the courses of events that had taken place up until that moment were seemingly written in stone left for me to discover.

I never understood why every time I went to the mall, I wanted to rush out of there and always left feeling exhausted. Or why my best friend's beach house made me feel good until I learned about how energy affects us, and even influences behavior and events in people's lives.

As a very young child, I was acutely aware of and could often 'see' energy. I knew things before I was told. I often woke up in the middle of the night scared out of my wits because an apparition was in my room. Did everyone see these things? Apparently not, and I never told my parents what was happening to me. I was so overwhelmed with terror at times that I would high-tail it to my parent's room. Nowadays, this would be easily described as a child that was naturally psychic and sensitive to energy. But in the late seventies and early eighties, these things were not openly discussed. The new age movement wasn't big then and seeing spirits wasn't readily admitted unless you were a nut! I did what I do best, which is pretend that it didn't happen and eventually, I stopped seeing 'things' but my senses and intuition developed in other ways.

I developed a sensitivity to all types of energy, the subtle energy in homes, my school, public buildings, animals, and people's strong emotions. In the third grade, I was invited to visit my best friend's home, a mobile home. That was not shocking, but what was, is how they lived! I had never seen that degree of filth, junk, and it plagued the entire home. Dishes were over flowing in the sink; there wasn't any part of the carpet that was visible from all the clothes and junk that littered the floor. Even though I was just a little girl, I remember thinking what could be so awful or bad that would cause these people to live this way? Well, now knowing Feng Shui, the house had no solid foundation and therefore was unstable offering no support for my friend and her family.

When energy moves it starts from the outside, in. If there is nowhere for the energy to pool, it dissipates from the site. If the energy leaves the site, it becomes very difficult for people to thrive. We humans depend on energy, from our lungs expanding, and our heart pumping to be able to live; once that energy disperses, what happens? We die. It's the same thing with the energy in a home or business, in some cases you can literally die but in most, it makes life very difficult. When something is unstable it causes chaos and of course, like the celebrities we chose, and myself were experiencing that and more.

Figure 58: Jennifer, eight months pregnant, with her future husband, Tommy.

My childhood home was situated with a road coming directly to the front door, in Feng Shui this is known as a *T-Juncture*. These are considered highly toxic to the people who live in such homes. What make these formations so bad and harmful, is that it directs too much energy/chi to the house. These homes are notorious for causing problems with health, relationships, and money. T-juncture homes are equivalent to the feeling you have when you over eat and you feel like vomiting as a result.

Our home was a very severe *T-Juncture* home because the road and sidewalk were directly aligned to the front door. In this home, my parents divorced, they went bankrupt, I was hospitalized a couple of times, once for pneumonia and another time because I was hit by a car, my parents fought non-stop, and my sister and I fought uncontrollably. This house literally tore our family apart, in addition to depleting the family's wealth. My parents subconsciously chose this home because it was the catalyst for the change that they needed. This is how it happens with all of us, this is not a judgment. We choose homes that will give us a particular experience. When we are complete and the 'life lesson' or karma is done, we find ourselves selling or leaving the property.

After years of struggling and realizing that this was not the life I was born to lead, I hit a wall when my mother passed away of esophageal cancer in 1999. I got a call early on the morning of July 12, 1999. I already knew and had a strong premonition what the call was about. Yet, as I hung up the phone with the doctor and called my dad, I must have been in a state of shock because I very calmly told him that my mother was dead. The line went silent for a while and then he finally choked out that he was coming to get me and that he would take me to the hospital to go see my mother one last time. When I saw her dead, lifeless body in the hospital room, I knew that person was not my mother. Her energy, her essence was gone. What was left behind was a very sick vessel that no longer resembled who my mother was. This person lying in the hospital bed was not the vibrant woman who had given birth to me, loved me and guided me my whole life. Right then and there I realized that our energy and essence is what makes us who we are, without it we are just an empty shell.

We're not our appearance, or our best features or even our worst features. We are the souls that inhabit our bodies for a short time. The energy/essence of my mother was my rock, my mentor, and my salvation. I knew that regardless of what happened around me or to me, she was the one constant that would be there to pick up the pieces. I wasn't sure what was worse, the fact that her suffering was over and I didn't have to see her in a dilapidated state anymore or the fact that she was gone.

I spent the next ten years after my mother passed in pure misery. The first six months, I could hardly get out of bed. If it wasn't for my sister, I am not sure how I would have been able to survive another day without my mother. My sister was my "rock of Gibraltar," unmovable, solid and steady. She never gave up on me. When I had vowed to end it all, she was there to pick up the pieces. When I had given up, she kept pushing me and propelling me forward. The defining moment in any relationship is who is standing by your side when things are tough. She never left my side.

Having to feel those deep emotions that plagued my every move was not comfortable or manageable at the time, so I did what I do best which is pretend that it

didn't exist. I went from job to job, searching, seeking, and trying to find what it was that I was looking for. I was never able to pin down a dream or goal for very long because something else would come along that I could use as a distraction. I sailed through graduate school, hoping that it would distract me long enough to forget where I had come from. I dated men that were emotionally unavailable because guess what, I was emotionally unavailable. I allowed myself to be treated in the same way that I felt, invisible and unworthy. I lived life absent mindedly often bumping into other cars when I parked or drove.

I was guilty of committing to events or activities with friends when I had already committed to other people. I spent time with people that I was uninterested in because I didn't want to be alone. I pursued jobs, people, things, that I wasn't passionate about because it took up time and forced me to be with people. Basically, I spent a lot of time self-sabotaging. Regardless of all the diversionary tactics that I used, I could never shake the feeling that I felt more alone in a room full of people than by myself. I guess I got tired of pretending that my mother was on vacation and would be coming back, when one day I woke up, and I was tired of the pain and the misery. I vowed to pull myself out of it. That's when I began searching for answers. I immersed myself into spirituality because it gave me great comfort. They say when you let go of what you are, you become what you might be. I started letting go...

It wasn't until I found a Buddhist therapist, that I found my way. Yes, he was a psychologist and he was Buddhist. Weird, I know, but it's a true story. I had no idea that he was Buddhist when I walked into his office. He was a referral from my insurance company. He recommended books, like *The*

Power of Now from Eckhart Tolle, and *The Tibetan Book of Living and Dying* by Sogyal Rinpoche. He gave me exercises to do to help empower me and to strengthen my soul. He inspired me to seek out and explore every alternative therapy that was valuable. I was a guinea pig for myself. I wanted to find what would make me feel better, physically, emotionally, and spiritually without having to use prescription drugs. After two years of being on anti-depressants and feeling completely numb and unable to dream, I was able to get off the medication and reclaim my life. The journey that I began when I met him was so profound that I will be forever grateful.

My bad Feng Shui experiences are not uncommon because we all have a narrative. Indeed, some stories are worse than others, but we all feel the same pain and heartache at some point in our lives. My narrative changes because one isolated event forced me to reevaluate my life and determine if it was worth saving. After spending years on a spiritual mission, I came to the place of where things drastically changed for the better. They say it's darkest before the dawn and I find this to be true. I found myself working at a job where I was dissatisfied. I was in an all too familiar place. In the past I would work at a job for a year, two or even three and then something happens where I can no longer tolerate it anymore and I would quit, get fired or laid off. Sometimes I felt like I was reliving the same day over and over again, like in the movie *Groundhog's Day*. Other times, it was tolerable and I felt happy because I was of service. However, there was always something that was consistent. I always seemed to attract the same type of bosses. People who were over-demanding perfectionist, never satisfied with anything I did. I had these types of bosses for years; just thinking of them makes my chest tighten. Through the years though, I learned how to deal with these types of demanding people. I worked really hard always proving myself to them because I had a lot to prove to myself.

In my last employment, I learned that the only answer that they really wanted to hear is yes because when you're dealing with the truly elite you no longer have an opinion that matters, how to be invisible in a room when things were being said that were inappropriate to hear, how to approach them for vacations, and time off, and how to pretend that I loved my job. As it turned out, I got really good at this. To the point where I wondered if my discomfort with my job was because of my awkwardness with myself. I spent my time away from this job taking spiritual development classes. I was still seeking at this time because I didn't know what my career was going to be. I knew that my job was temporary but when you're working and are constantly distressed it makes it hard to see the forest through the trees. I kept plugging away hoping that the classes I took would lead me to my desired career. Had I been in a position to quit, I would have in a second but I needed my job, so I stuck it out.

Figure 59: Jennifer with the world-famous 'John of God' in Brazil.

At this time an opportunity presented itself that up until this point seemed impossible. I wanted to start my own business, but didn't know where I could get the funds to do so. As it turned out my sister and I inherited my grandmother's condo and I convinced my sister to sell her portion too. I had no clue what type of business I would pursue but I knew something had to be done. So I did what any normal person would do, I gave my notice and planned a trip to Brazil to go see John of God. John of God is a world famous healer that has instantly cured people of cancer, AIDS, Multiple Sclerosis, and in fact, all diseases and afflictions. Of course, my family and some of my friends thought that I had lost my mind. But at this point in my life, I didn't give a flying leap what their concerns and opinions were. What I knew was that if I didn't start living my life, someone else would always be living it for me! Naturally, giving my notice didn't go over too well, just as I expected. Nonetheless, I stayed for another three months and took the brunt of my former employer's disappointment with my choice to leave.

My grandmother's house had still not closed escrow, which had already been delayed twice. This was in early 2008, during the real estate market crash. Getting a loan approved literally took an act of God. I was thinking that my trip to Brazil was going to be a distant dream. I had already booked my flight and was waiting for the money to hit my account so that I could get money and exchange it for the *Brazilian Real R$*. This was a spiritual sojourn. After trying a crystal bed from a practitioner nearby, I knew I had to go in person.[5]

A crystal bed cleanses and removes any negativity from your chakras, gives relief from spiritual, emotional, and physical ailments. My first experience on a crystal bed was so incredible that I decided to fly down to Brazil. I was so excited to get on with my trip, and my life, that I called the escrow company and made an inquiry into when the funds would be released, they could not give me a definite answer. Meanwhile, the other line beeped in and I quickly hung up with the title company and answered it. It was one of my good friends. I told her my dilemma and in less than ten seconds, she quickly blurted out that I could borrow money from her for my trip to Brazil.

I boarded a flight to Brazil with *Brazilian Real R$,* safely tucked away. It quickly flashed through my mind that if I got robbed, I was going to be seriously screwed and pissed. That did not happen, and it seemed that God was on my side, at least in this little adventure. I found myself in the middle of nowhere, in the tiny town of Abadiania, not knowing a single soul, and I was happier than I had been in years.

To say that the energy in Abadiania, Brazil is pristine would be an understatement. I experienced more clarity in the six, short days that I was there than in my whole, entire life put together. Each day, there was a very long line to see the famous, *John of God.* People would come from all over the world to see him and be healed. Physicians too, had heard of his phenomenal work, and came to witness firsthand how people (many who had been declared hopeless and terminal) were healed by this seemingly ordinary man. I saw parents, whose children couldn't walk, wait in line for him to heal

---

[5] Crystal beds are designed to raise human consciousness and have an inter-dimensional affect. The illuminated quartz crystals are specifically cut to rejuvenate, align and balance energy fields. The crystals are in a fixed array and positioned over the chakras. Light and color shine through each crystal in an alternating pattern that amplifies spiraling energy from the root to the crown chakra.

their babies. I witnessed people who were on their last, tenuous thread of hope, desperate and on the verge of death waiting to be healed.

I shared the line with people who had been left for dead and not given a hope in the world. The faith that these people exhibited is beyond words and in some cases more than miraculous. I admit that I had my doubts about his ability to heal. However, this skepticism fell by the wayside when I spoke to several people who had been there many times and whom John of God has personally healed.

It was customary for anyone who wanted a healing to wait in line to meet *John of God*, and then be granted permission to receive one. On the first day that I waited in line, he directed me to "current", which is where people go to meditate for four hours a day while John of God is doing his healings; the people that are meditating are holding the energy for him to do his work. It was painful, sometimes grueling and often times I was quite bored. Nevertheless, I did it because I knew that whatever I was meant to experience, I wanted it to happen then and there. On the second day, of waiting in line, I was directed to have a psychic surgery.

Basically, it meant that one of the entities or John's spirit guides at the 'Casa,' would work on whatever issue they felt needed to be addressed.[6] In my case it was to become more spiritual and to be a healer. After you have had psychic surgery, you are not allowed to speak to anyone, watch television, read, write or do anything but sleep and go to the restroom for the next

---

[6] Affectionately known as the 'Casa', this is where John of God does his healing work and psychic surgeries

twenty-four hours. This was the most difficult task asked of me. Those lonely hours that I spent by myself forced me to contemplate my life in a way that I was unable to do up until that point. I learned things about myself that I never knew, and frankly was unwilling to look at. I felt things inside of me that had lain dormant for many, many years. There were parts of my soul that were touched in a way that I had never experienced before; these aspects of my soul needed to be stirred in a new way.

This experience forced me out of hiding, so to speak. The next day I continued with the four hours of meditation and took it easy, per the entities' advice. I made friends in this distant land that had the same thing in common with me, we were all searching. Their search may have been different from mine but nonetheless it was still a search. Everyone was there to find a higher meaning for their lives whether it was through improved health or through spiritual awakening, as it was in my case. I bonded on a deep level with people that I had never meet, seen or even heard of. They were my foster family while I was in this surreal place known as Abadiania, Brazil. It is with very fond memories and reflection that I think back to that beautiful town, and how my life was lost and then found.

Immediately upon my arrival back home from Brazil, I resolved that things were going to be different. I could no longer live a life where my work was not meaningful and heartfelt. I was equally determined to break the patterns that had plagued my life for so many years. During my previous employment, I never really stood up for myself and was I taken advantage of on more occasions than I can count. I wasn't the type to stir up trouble, and besides I really needed the job. When I came back from Brazil I had decided that I would ask for the monies that were owed to me. I knew that this would be the final step for me to fully reclaim a life that was once lost and not lived to my fullest potential.

I knew that if I didn't stand up for myself now, that I would lose a golden opportunity for a lesson that needed to be learned. So what did I do? Now knowing how energy really works, I chose an apartment that, according to Feng Shui principles, indicated lawsuits. Actually, this was to my great advantage, as I needed this energy in order to have the courage to confront my employers for the money that was rightfully owned to me. They flatly refused to pay it, and so I filed a lawsuit against this injustice.

During the duration of my lawsuit, I moved to a new apartment, which I resided in for a year. Having to deal with this stressful lawsuit was my first experience with Classical Feng Shui. A former spiritual teacher of mine, recommended, that I consult with a Feng Shui professional. I took her advice and she gave me a referral. The Feng Shui consultant came and assessed the energy of my home, by taking a compass reading of the building, the front door, the construction date of the building and my birth date. She used the front door as the facing direction for my apartment. I did everything that she recommended, but what I noticed was that the people I was suing got more aggressive. They were threatening me, they hired private investigators, and said that they were willing to drain all my funds in the legal system before they paid me one penny.

Still hopeful in the power of Feng Shui, I thought if everything got worse after hiring this person, there has to be someone out there that knows Feng Shui and that can make it better. This seemed reasonable to me, so I began with an online search and discovered there were different types of Feng Shui, even the traditional methods offered quite a variety.

Feeling slightly overwhelmed, I was attracted to a person that was in Australia. After reading over her website, the information reverberated with me, this felt right. I was on the right tract. I contacted her for more information and she referred me to a colleague in the United States who could help me. Little did I know then, that she would become my teacher and a true mentor. While the lawsuit weighed heavily on my mind and heart, I really just wanted to understand Feng Shui better. I had taken some training and classes, but was more confused than ever. When I spoke to her on the phone for the first time, I vented all of my frustrations. She patiently listened and then began to explain how it all worked. I began my studies with her that same week. A few weeks later, she taught me how to change the energy in my apartment so that I could win my lawsuit. Her analysis was a bit different because her lineage used the move-in date and the building as the facing for my apartment versus the other person's style of using the construction date and taking my apartment door as the facing for my home.

My teacher, Denise Liotta-Dennis, was like an angel who swooped in and literally made it all better. I studied closely with her for almost two years. She is a mentor, an inspiration and the person that I owe my life to for imparting this beautiful ancient knowledge, known as Classical Feng Shui. Unbeknownst to me, until Denise told me, the main door in and out of the apartment activated gossiping, fighting, arguments and lawsuits. Bingo! There it was staring at me in the face, my subconscious or unconscious mind at work again.

There is no doubt in my mind now, why I would have chosen an apartment with this energy. This was another event of many that I needed to experience. Three months to the day that she Feng Shui'd my apartment, my former employers decided to settle with me. After that I was convinced that I had found the real deal, authentic Feng Shui, and my life's calling and hence started my own Classical Feng Shui business. After I won my lawsuit, I moved and found a place that had amazing energy which I 'tapped' for greater wealth, health, and relationships. My lesson was over and that apartment no longer served or resonated with me, nor did it represent who I was. Now after assessing hundreds of homes, I see how we can use the energy of a home, and then leave it, sell it or rent it to someone else when we are done. It's like this, the house no longer makes an accurate statement of who we are!

After a slew of professional lessons and finding my passion, then my personal life became a source of clearing. I left my then boyfriend of nine years because what had always been comfortable became uncomfortable and I knew deep down inside that the love I was craving was waiting for me. I had dreams about it and knew that what I was doing was maintaining my comfort level because for so long my life had always been a series of upheavals and I was tired of change. Well when I no longer could be comfortable with status quo, I took a leap of faith. It wasn't always easy and I learned a lot about myself and hard lessons through dating.

Almost six years to the day, I left my ex boyfriend, I met the man of my dreams. Within months, I was pregnant and the following year I was engaged. We will marry in the fall of 2018. Was it easy? No. Was the ride finding my dream man fun? No. Did I learn, grow, evolve, and become a more compassionate and wise person? Hell yes. The point is this, life isn't always what you think it's going to be. Your dream man or woman isn't always what you envisioned. Sometimes, you find yourself dating and you stop trusting yourself because of all the previous mistakes you made. So what do you do? You have faith and you pray long and hard that God sends you signs so that you know you're making a good decision. You stop relying on your own strength and start relying on a higher power. When I did that, my man found me. When I did that, I stopped doubting and found peace in knowing that this was a good decision. When I did that, I got all that I wanted and more. You know why? Because sometimes God, the higher power, whatever you want to call it knows what you need more than you do.

Recently, my father passed away, and now I find myself without parents. This time the loss isn't so traumatic because I've been through it before. This time it's different because I have an amazing man by my side and my baby. This book is for all the people that have suffered and wondered why and what they could do. Our hope is that you find peace in knowing that you can shift the energy and that you're not doomed to be unhappy forever. You will find peace and there is hope.

Figure 60: Jennifer and Tommy's son, Massimo, born in January 2017.

Appendix I
How to Take a Compass Direction

Some masters take the door degree from *inside* the building. Grandmaster Yap taught his students to take the compass direction—outside, face the door, and at waist level, place the Luo Pan directly on it. This results in a very accurate compass reading. A traditional hiking compass may vary a few degrees from a Luo Pan and a smart phone may vary even more. Purchase a good app that aligns with GPS as phones do not contain a magnet like a regular compass. When using a Luo Pan or hiking compass, place it at waist level and remove all metal belts and jewelry. Take several compass readings to ensure accuracy. Review *How to Determine the Facing* on page 49. Measure all exterior doors and make note the readings.

If using a traditional Luo Pan, stand outside the door and face it. Line up the head of the needle between the two red dots. Look at the 6:00 position near your waist and see the degree.

Using your smart phone to take a compass direction, put your back to the door and it will give you a digital read out similar to this image.

When using a traditional hiking compass, follow the manufacturer's directions.

Appendix II
Wu Chang Pai Lineage

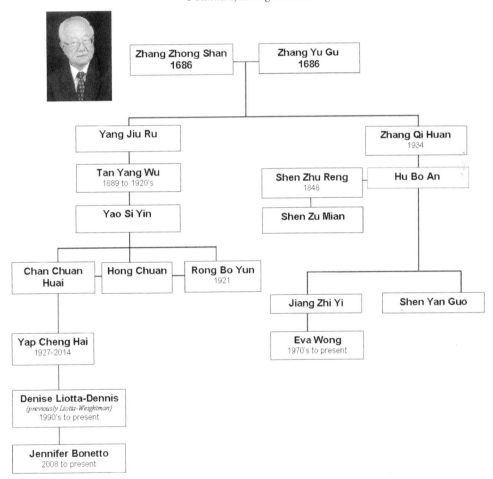

Wu Chang Pai Lineage
Founders, Zhang brothers

Appendix III: Door Tilts

Door Tilts or Re-angling: This technique is very common in Southeast Asia. It is used to take a door out of negative energy (a bad facing star) or to change the star chart—sometimes both. Remember, doors rate extremely high as to whether you will enjoy good Feng Shui or not.

Appendix IV: Flying Star Charts for Period 8

For information on how to activate Flying Star Charts, refer to the book *The Secrets of Mastering Flying Star Feng Shui: Learn how to fly, analyze, cure and enhance the stars for your home and office.*

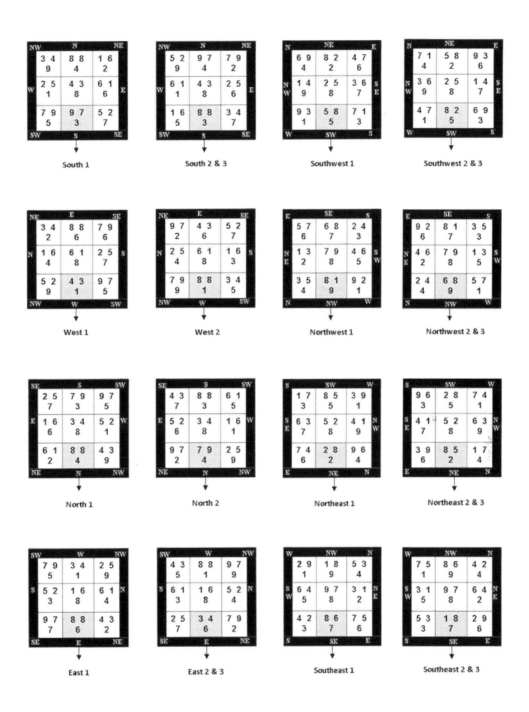

South 1   South 2 & 3   Southwest 1   Southwest 2 & 3

West 1   West 2   Northwest 1   Northwest 2 & 3

North 1   North 2   Northeast 1   Northeast 2 & 3

East 1   East 2 & 3   Southeast 1   Southeast 2 & 3

Appendix IV: Flying Star Charts for Period 7

For information on how to activate your Flying Star Charts, refer to the book *The Secrets of Mastering Flying Star Feng Shui: Learn how to fly, analyze, cure and enhance the stars for your home and office*

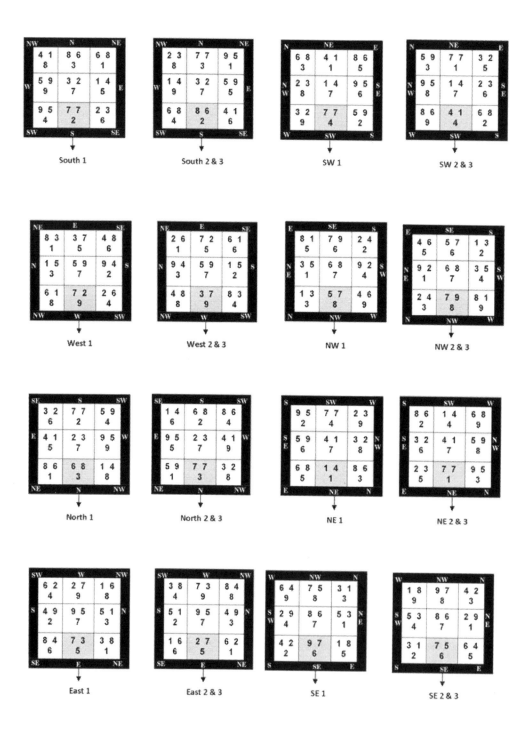

South 1   South 2 & 3   SW 1   SW 2 & 3

West 1   West 2 & 3   NW 1   NW 2 & 3

North 1   North 2 & 3   NE 1   NE 2 & 3

East 1   East 2 & 3   SE 1   SE 2 & 3

Bibliography

ABC News. *New Details of Marilyn Monroe's Life and Death.* Nov 4, 2005.

Andersen, Christopher. *Michael Jackson: Unauthorized.* Simon & Schuster, 1994.

BangShowbiz. *Michael Jackson's Los Angeles Home for Sale.* Zimbo. August 5, 2010.

Block, Alex Ben. *The Last Days of Brittany Murphy.* The Hollywood Reporter, January 19, 2011.

Brown, Mick. *Tearing Down the Wall of Sound: The Rise and Fall of Phil Spector.* Alfred A. Knopf, a Division of Random House, 2007.

Bugliosi, Vincent and Gentry, Curt. *Helter Skelter: The True Story of the Manson Murders* W. W. Norton & Company, 1994.

CNN. *She's out of his life. Lisa Marie Presley files for divorce from Michael Jackson.* January 18, 1996.

Daniel, Emeritus. *Marilyn Monroe History and Biography*. Danamo's Marilyn Monroe Pages.

Deutsch, Linda. *Letter Describes O.J. Attacks Nicole Brown Simpson Wrote That Simpson 'Beat The Holy Hell Out Of Me'.* Associated Press. Jan. 14, 1997.

Dunne, Dominick. *The Nervous Breakdown.* Vanity Fair, October 1990.

ENTERTAINMENT. *Phil Spector's Wife: I'm Not A Gold Digger, We Had Frequent Sex.* 07/07/2009, Updated Dec 06, 2017.

Greg, Alex. *'I'll rip your eyes out': Phil Hartman's second wife tells of disturbing letter from third wife Brynn Hartman, who shot the beloved comic actor in 1998 murder-suicide.* MailOnline. September 1, 2014.

Hogan, Donna and Tiefenthaler, Henrietta. *Train Wreck: The Life and Death of Anna Nicole Smith.* Phoenix Books, 2007.

Horn, John. *Jackson Sells Beatles Songs to Sony.* Associated Press. November 9, 1995.

Hilburn, Robert. *The Long and Winding Road.* Los Angeles Times. September 22, 1985

IMDb. Brittany Murphy Biography. Source http://www.imdb.com/name/nm0005261/bio.

Ishkanian, Jill. EXCLUSIVE: *'Cursed' Hollywood Hills home that once belonged to Britney Spears and later Brittany Murphy gets a massive makeover and a new mojo as it hits the market for $19.75 million.* Dailymail.com. May 13, 2016.

Johnson, David Ph.D. *What Do Agassi and the Menendez Brothers Have in Common?* Nov 30, 2009.

Kaufman, Gil. *Anna Nicole Smith Died Of Accidental Drug Overdose.* MTV News. 03/26/2007.

King, Greg. *Sharon Tate and the Manson Murders.* Barricade Books Inc., 2000.

Mandina, Cory. *Michael Jackson and his mother, Katherine, had an unbreakable bond.* McCabe, Peter and Robert D. Schonfeld. *Apple to the Core.* New York: Simon and Schuster, 1972.

Meares, Hadley. *Phil Spector's Pyrenees Castle: The Fairytale Castle that Became Home to a Nightmare.* Published by History & Society. October 4, 2013.

Michael, Scott. Findadeath.com. *Phil Hartman.* 1999-2003.

Poindexter, Joseph. *The Beverly Hills Paradise Lost.* People Magazine. March 26, 1990

Resnick, Faye and Walker, Mike. *Nicole Brown Simpson: The Private Diary of a Life Interrupted.* Dove Books, 1994.

Soble, Ron and Johnson, John. *Blood Brothers: The Inside Story of the Menendez Murders.* Penguin Books, 1994.

The Hollywood Gossip. *Neverland Ranch Pictures.* 06/26/2009.

Tracy, Dr. Ann Blake. Comments on *Zoloft Induced Suicide: A Battle for Woody.* June 19, 2005.

Van Susteren, Greta. Simpson: *'No feeling' about demolition of Rockingham estate.* CNN, July 29, 1998.

Vitacco-Robles, Gary. *Cursum Perficio: Marilyn Monroe's Brentwood Hacienda.* Writer's Club Press, 1999.

Glossary of Terms

This book includes Feng Shui terms using both Wade-Giles and Pinyin; in several instances the glossary gives both spellings. The Chinese-to-English translations also include some in Mandarin and others in Cantonese; we have chosen the ones most used by Grandmaster Yap Cheng Hai and their spellings.

72 Piercing Dragons Method: This method is used to examine the energy of a mountain; it covers 5-degree increments. However, the *72 Piercing Dragons Method* is mainly concerned with evaluating the *largest* mountain at the back of the property. The *72 Piercing Dragons Method* is attributed to the famous Master Yang Yun Song who lived during the Tang Dynasty (618–907 AD). He also created the 'Secret Verses' to accompany the 72 possible mountain measurements. These describe what the occupants may expect in the way of fortune and health, depending on the mountain's exact degree. The *72 Piercing Dragons Method* also calculates the quality of the mountain into one of five types of energy. Some have seriously negative implications with descriptions like 'fire pits'. An example of this would be a main mountain measuring between 97°-102° and the secret verses explains this 5-degree increment as indicating "Lonely, death, hunchbacks, bow-legged, and a short life-span." However many mountain directions are very auspicious, for example if the largest mountain at the back of your property is between 352°-357°, then the secret verse describes it as "Very auspicious, good children, real estate holdings, very rich and a noble government position."

The Assistant Star Water Method: This technique offers ample choices when it comes to bringing wealth luck to your site via roads or real water, which is used in conjunction with the door direction. There are twenty-four possible door directions and numerous water (virtual and real) directions from which to choose. You will get specific results depending on the choice of water direction. For example, certain water/road directions bring wealth from heaven, a high government position, riches and nobility, and good, filial children. These formulas can determine whether lawsuits, robbery, gambling, loneliness, mishaps, or quarrels are possible based on the placement. Here's an example: the door faces South (South 1, 2 or 3) and the water or road is in Southwest (SW 1, 2 or 3). The formation indicates the acquisition of a great fortune. If real water is used, the facing star in the Southwest must also be considered.

auspicious: The Chinese favor the term *auspicious*, meaning something is lucky, and good events will ensue.

Ba Gua: Also spelled as Pa Kua; an octagonal arrangement of the eight trigrams or Guas.

BaZhai: the Eight Mansion system, also spelled PaChai. This system is also known as the East-West System and Eight House Feng Shui.

Big Dipper Casting Golden Light: Known as *Jin Guang Dou Lin Jing* in Chinese and also spelled as *Kam Kwong Dou Lam King*. This style of Eight Mansions is used in this book; it is also called *Golden Star Classic*.

Black Hat Sect: A new school of Feng Shui invented in the 1980s. It was brought to the Western world by Professor Thomas Lin Yun, a Buddhist monk of the Black Hat Order of Tibetan Buddhism. Although not considered an authentic system of Feng Shui, Black Hat is the most recognized style in the world except in Asian countries, which are most familiar with traditional schools of Feng Shui.

Book of Changes: Also known as the *I Ching*.

Buddhism: is a nontheistic *(not having a belief in a god)* religion that encompasses a variety of traditions, beliefs and practices largely based on teachings attributed to Siddhartha Gautama, who is commonly known as the Buddha, meaning "the awakened one". According to Buddhist tradition, the Buddha lived and taught in the eastern part of the Indian subcontinent sometime between the 6th and 4th centuries BCE.

cardinal directions: Points of geographic orientation—North, South, East and West. The specific and exact points of these directions are 0/360, North; 90 degrees, East; 180 degrees, South; and 270 degrees, West.

Chai: House, also spelled Zhai.

Chen: One of the eight trigrams of the Ba Gua. It represents the eldest son, thunder and spring. In the Later Heaven arrangement of the Ba Gua, the Chen trigram is located in the East.

Chueh Ming: In the Eight Mansions system, this represents total loss, divorce and bankruptcy. According to Master Yap's numerical representation, it is the -90.

Chi: The vital life-force energy of the universe and everything in it; sometimes chi is referred to as *cosmic breath*. It is also spelled *ch'i* or *qi* and is pronounced *chee*.

Chien: One of the eight trigrams of the Ba Gua also spelled as *Qian*. It represents the father, the heavens, and late autumn. In the Later Heaven arrangement of the Ba Gua, the Chien trigram is located in the Northwest.

Chinese Lunar and Solar Calendars: All Feng Shui experts worth their salt use the Chinese Solar Calendar as the basis of their practice as its formulas are very time sensitive and this calendar is very accurate. This is not to say they don't celebrate the Lunar New Year, in fact, they do; the *Chinese New Year*, as well as other holidays, is extremely important. The ancient Chinese used the Solstices and Equinoxes to fix their calendar. 15° Aquarius is exactly half way between the Winter Solstice and the Spring Equinox (on the Northern Hemisphere). In the past, Chinese Lunar New Year started around the Winter Solstice. In 104 BC Emperor Han Wu Di moved the beginning of the year so that the Winter Solstice occurs in the eleventh month. Winter Solstice falls on the 15th day of Zi/Rat month, the middle of the winter, 15° Aquarius is the Sun's position. Whenever the sun reaches that position that is the Chinese Solar New Year. This could be February 3, 4, 5. The Chinese chose the 15° Aquarius as the starting point of the Spring season and the New Year. The Spring Equinox falls exactly in the middle of the Spring season; this is always on the 15th day of Mao/Rabbit month. Lunar calendar defines the lunar month on the first day of the appearance of the New Moon. A Lunar New Year begins on the 1st day of this new "moon". A lunar month is from the new moon to the next new moon. The ecliptic was divided into 12 equal divisions by the ancients. The Chinese Solar year is based on these 24 divisions called 24 solar terms. The year is divided into 24 periods of 15 days. Li Chun is the first of the 24 terms. The names of these divisions date back to the late Chou Dynasty (10450—221BC). The most important of the 24 terms is the New Year.

Chinese Zodiac: is a system that relates each year to an animal and its reputed attributes, according to a 12-year mathematical cycle. It remains popular in several East Asian countries, such as China, Vietnam, Korea and Japan.

Classical Feng Shui: Also known as Traditional Feng Shui. It is the authentic, genuine Feng Shui that has been developed and applied for hundreds, even thousands, of years in Asia. Sophisticated forms are practiced in Hong Kong, Taiwan, Malaysia, and Singapore. Classical Feng Shui is just being introduced and practiced in Western countries, and has not reached main stream status. The traditional systems of Feng Shui are the *San He*, meaning three combinations, and *San Yuan* or three cycles. All techniques, methods, and formulas will be under one or the other. Feng Shui masters and practitioners will use both systems as one comprehensive body of knowledge.

Combination of Ten Formations: The *Combination of Ten* is a special Flying Star Chart that brings wealth, opportunities, prestige, and powerful connections. To the Chinese, the number ten represents completion; ten is also considered auspicious in the Flying Star system. *Combination of Ten* charts offer the potential to double the fortune of a house, however, just like *Pearl String Formations* they must be activated specifically and correctly. The *Combination of Ten* also offers two different types of charts, 'money luck' and 'people luck'. The focus is either on the front or back of the property when activating the energy.

compass, Chinese: See Luo Pan.

Cosmic Trinity: Known in Chinese as *Tien-Di-Ren*. Three categories of luck, specifically heaven-luck, man-luck, and earth-luck. The Chinese believe heaven-luck is fixed, however, humans have control over Feng Shui (earth-luck) and personal effort (man-luck).

Dao: also spelled *Tao*, is a Chinese concept signifying the way, path, route, or sometimes known as the doctrine or principle. Within the context of traditional Chinese philosophy and religion, Tao is a metaphysical concept originating with Lao Tzu that gave rise to a religion and philosophy (Taoism). The concept of Tao was shared with Confucianism and Zen Buddhism. Within these contexts Tao signifies the primordial essence or fundamental nature of the universe. In Taoism, Chinese Buddhism and Confucianism, the object of spiritual practice is to *become one with the Tao* or to harmonize one's will with Nature in order to achieve effortless action; this involves meditative and moral practices.

direction: One of the most important aspects of determining the energy of a site or structure is.

dragon: In Feng Shui a dragon is a mountain. Dragon is a term also used for something powerful or curving, as in the mythical body of a dragon. It can apply to land and water. The Chinese so revere the dragon that it is used in multiple applications and meanings.

Early Heaven Ba Gua: This is the first arrangement of the eight trigrams; known as the *Ho Tien* or *Fu Xi* Ba Gua in Chinese. It can be easily recognized as the Chien trigram (three solid lines) and is always placed on the top. This is the arrangement used in Ba Gua mirrors to deter sha Chi.

Earth Luck: One of the three categories of luck that humans can experience; your luck will increase by using Feng Shui, also known as Earth Luck. The Chinese word for earth is *Di*.

East Life Group: In the Eight Mansions system, people are divided into the East or West group. The 1, 3, 4 and 9 Life Guas are part of the East Life Group.

Eight House: This is another name for the Eight Mansions; in Chinese it is *Pa Chai* or *BaZhai*.

Eight House Bright Mirror: In Chinese *Pa Chai Ming Jing*, is one of the eight different styles of the Eight Mansions system. This style uses the sitting direction of the house instead of the facing.

Eight Life Aspirations: Also known as the *Eight Life Stations*, these stations correspond to a point on the Ba Gua and an aspect of life—South, fame; Southwest, marriage; Southeast, wealth; North, career; and so forth. This is the work of Black Hat Sect founder Lin Yun. Eight Life Stations is not found in classic texts or part of the genuine Feng Shui of ancient practice and principles. It is neither an aspect of the Eight Mansions system nor even a derivative of that system. Some popular Feng Shui books that promote Classical Feng Shui also include the Eight Life Aspirations, which only adds to the confusion.

Eight Mansions: also known as *Eight House Feng Shui*, the *East-West System*, *BaZhai* which is also spelled *PaChai;* this system, based on your personal Gua/Kua Number, gives you the four good and four bad directions to use and mitigate in your living space or wherever you happen to be such as at a meeting, your offices, a seminar and so forth to bring good fortune.

Eight Wandering Stars: also known as the *Big Wandering Sky*, these stars are matched with the nine stars of the Big Dipper, they are as follows: Tan Lang (*Greedy Wolf* aka *Ravenous Wolf*) is matched with **Sheng Chi**; Jue Men (*Huge Door* aka *Great Door*) is matched with **Tien Yi**; Wu Chu (*Military Arts*) is matched with **Yen Nien**; Tso Fu & Fu Pi (*Left/Right Assistant* aka the *Big Dipper's Handle*) is matched with **Fu Wei**; Lu Chun (*Rewards/Salary*) is matched with **Wo Hai;** Lien Zheng (*Five Ghosts aka Chastity*) is matched with **Wu Gwei**; Wen Qu (*Literary Arts* aka *The Scholar*) is matched with **Lui Sha**; Tien Kong (*Broken Soldier* aka *Destructive Army*) is matched with **Cheuh Ming**. These nine stars and their unique energy are very important in many Feng Shui systems. More on the nine stars in Chapter Five; the Chinese names above are also the 'secret names' of the nine stars.

energy: The Chinese call energy chi (also spelled *qi*) and pronounced *chee*. Our entire universe is energy; there are many types of chi—human, environmental, and heaven (the solar system).

esoteric: Knowledge that is available only to a narrow circle of enlightened or initiated people or a specially educated group. Feng Shui is part of Chinese metaphysics and is considered esoteric.

external environment: This covers the terrain and topography, including mountains, water, and other natural formations. It also encompasses man-made features, such as roads, pools, retaining walls, highways, poles, drains, washes, tall buildings, stop signs, fire hydrants, and other structures.

facing direction: The front side of the home or building, generally where the front or main door is located and faces the street.

Feng: The Chinese word for *wind;* pronounced *fung,* although *foong* is a more accurate sound.

Feng Shui: Known as *Kan Yu* (translated as *the way of heaven and earth*) until about a hundred years ago, the Chinese system of maximizing the accumulation of beneficial chi improves the quality of life and luck of the occupants of a particular building or location. The literal translation is wind and water; however, in Classical Feng Shui wind means *direction* and water means *energy.* Pronounced *foong shway.*

Feng Shui master: One who has mastered the skills of Classical Feng Shui and/or has been declared as such by his or her teacher, or both. Most Feng Shui masters from classic traditions will belong to a lineage of their teachers. This is also known as *a lineage carrier,* meaning the master carries on the teachings and practices of his or her education. A Feng Shui master generally oversees his or her own school and students, too.

Feng Shui schools: There are two major schools or branches (not physical locations, rather they are systems) of Classical Feng Shui, San He and San Yuan; hundreds of formulas, techniques, and systems serve as sub sets of either school. If you practice Classical Feng Shui, you use the San He and the San Yuan systems as one extensive body of knowledge. See the article in the compendium for details on each school.

Flying Stars: Known as *Xuan Kong Fei Xing* in Chinese, which means *mysterious void* or the *subtle mysteries of time and space.* It is a popular Feng Shui system that is superior in addressing the time aspect of energy. Refer to Chapter Four for additional information on this vast system.

Fu Wie: The direction and location for stability as it applies to the Eight Mansions system. According to Master Yap's numerical representation, it is the +60.

Fu Xi: A sage, king and shaman who was responsible for discovering and arranging the Early Heaven Ba Gua.

Gen: One of the eight trigrams of the Ba Gua also spelled as *Ken.* It represents the youngest son, the mountain and early spring. In the Later Heaven arrangement of the Ba Gua, the Gen trigram is located in the Northeast.

grandmaster of Feng Shui: This person has been practicing and teaching for many years, belongs to a respected lineage of masters, and has at least one master among his or her pupils.

Grandmaster Yap Cheng Hai (GMY): Master Yap was born and raised in Singapore; although he did live briefly in Xiamen, China for four years. He moved to Kuala Lumpur, Malaysia in 1963 to manage his uncle's business and soon became a citizen. Although his life was full, he pursued two passions, that of Feng Shui and Martial Arts. He began practicing Feng Shui professionally in the early 60's. He has consulted with prominent figures such as members of royalty, ministers, corporations, banks, and developers. His loyal client since the sixties, Paramount Garden consulted him to plan their townships that included SEA Park, Damansara Utama and Bandar Utama. GMY is quite famous in Southeast Asia for his *Water Dragon* techniques. He learned this specialized method from Grandmaster Chan Chuan Huai in Taiwan who created several billionaires there. GMY began teaching in the late 1990's to those wishing to learn authentic, Classical Feng Shui. Denise graduated from his 2001 class as a Master right after 9/11.

Gua: Alternatively spelled *Kua* and also known as a trigram. It represents one of eight Guas of the Ba Gua, defined by a combination of three solid or broken lines.

Gua Number: Also referred to as *Ming Gua* (nothing to do with the Ming Dynasty). To determine your personal Life Gua number, use your birthday. See Chapter Three for specific instructions.

GYM Code: this is a code devised by Grandmaster Yap to easily identify your good and bad directions in the Eight Mansions system; the +90, +80, +70, +60 are your *good* directions representing wealth, health, relationships/longevity and stability respectively. The code of -90, -80, -70, and -60 represent your *bad* directions that if activated, will cause divorce/bankruptcy, bad health/betrayals, affairs/lawsuits and setbacks respectively.

Heaven Luck: One of the three categories of luck that humans can experience. The Chinese believe every human has a destiny and a fate determined by the heavens (tien). This category cannot be changed and is considered *fixed*. See also Tien-Di-Ren.

high-rise building: In the external environment, high-rise buildings and skyscrapers function as *virtual* or *urban mountains*.

Ho: The Chinese word for fire.

Ho Hai: Also known as *Wo Hai*. Part of the Eight Mansions system and can bring mishaps—nothing goes smoothly. According to Master Yap's numerical representation, this is the -60.

Hsia: pronounced *she-ah*; this is the name for the Chinese Solar Calendar based on the cycles of the Sun. The Solar Calendar regulates agriculture because the *Sun* determines the seasons; also used in all Feng Shui techniques for its accuracy. The solar year begins on February 4th or 5th, there are two possible dates is not because an uncertainly, but due to the fact that the Western calendar 'wobbles' because of the insertion of the extra day during 'leap years'.

Inauspicious: means very unlucky and in Feng Shui could indicate negative events.

I Ching: A philosophical and divinatory book based on the sixty-four hexagrams of Taoist mysticism. It is also known as the *Classic of Changes* or *Book of Changes*.

interior environment: The interior environment encompasses anything that falls within the walls of a structure, including kitchen, staircase, Master Bedroom + Family, fireplaces, bathrooms, hallways, dining room, bedrooms, appliances, furniture, and so on.

intercardinal directions: Northwest, Southwest, Northeast and Southeast.

Kan: One of the eight trigrams. It represents the middle son, the moon and mid-winter. In the Later Heaven Arrangement of the Ba Gua, it is located in the North.

Kun: One of the eight trigrams. It represents the mother, the earth and late summer. In the Later Heaven Arrangement of the Ba Gua, it is located in the Southwest.

Later Heaven Ba Gua: The second arrangement of the trigrams known as the *Wen Wang* or *Xien Tien* Ba Gua. This is used extensively in the application of Classical Feng Shui.

Li: One of the eight trigrams. It represents the middle daughter, fire and full summer. In the Later Heaven Arrangement of the Ba Gua, it is located in the South.

Life-Gua Number: a number assigned to people, based on birthday and gender, in the Eight Mansions system (BaZhai also spelled Pa Chai).

Liu Sha: In the Eight Mansions system, it also known as the *Six Killings* direction and can bring backstabbing, affairs, and lawsuits. According to Master Yap's numerical representation, it is the -80.

location: A particular place or position, differing from the concept of *direction*. For example, your living room might be located on the South side of your home (location), but your desk faces North (direction).

lunar calendar: A calendar based on the cycles of the moon.

Lung: The Chinese word for dragon.

Luo Pan: The Luo Pan is the quintessential tool of a Feng Shui practitioner. It is a compass that contains four to forty concentric rings of information. The most popular model is approximately ten inches across, square, and often constructed of fine woods. The circle part of the Luo Pan is made of brass and rotates to align with the compass itself, which is located in the center. There are three major types of Luo Pans—the *San Yuan* Luo Pan, the *San He* Luo Pan, and the *Chung He* Luo Pan (also known as *Zong He* or *Zhung He*), which is a combination of the first two. Though Luo Pans have similar basic components, Feng Shui masters do customize their own with secret information for them and their students.

Luo Shu: A square that contains nine palaces or cells with a number in each; it adds to fifteen in any direction. The Luo Shu is also known as the *Magic Square of 15*.

Magic Life-Gua: some masters call your personal Gua number by many names—Magic Life-Gua, Ming Gua, or Life Gua.

main door: This is usually the front door of the home or business. If the occupants always enter the residence from the garage, this may also be considered a main door.

Man Luck: One of the three categories of luck that a human can experience. This area of fortune is mutable and defined by individual effort, such as hard work, study, education, experience, and good deeds. The Chinese word for man is *Ren*. See Tien-Di-Ren.

Ming Dynasty: A ruling dynasty of China, which lasted from 1368 to 1644.

Ming Gua: another name for Life-Gua.

Nien Yen: This is the incorrect spelling of the *Yen Nien* (+70) in the Eight Mansions system; you will see this mistake in many Feng Shui books.

Pa Chai: the Eight Mansions system, also spelled BaZhai.

Parent String Gua Formations: Parent Strings are also referred to as *Three Combinations,* and they are the third, wealth-producing Xuan Kong Flying Star chart. These charts represent the Cosmic Trinity—heaven-earth-man or father-mother-son energies. Because of this, some Feng Shui texts hold that this prosperous chi will permeate endlessly and transcend all periods. This is actually an over-exaggeration. These charts are lucky only in their Period, which last at most twenty years. For example, the luck of the Parent String charts for Period 8 will expire in Period 9, beginning February 4, 2024.

Pearl String Formations: *Pearl Strings Formations* are also known as Continuous Bead Formations. They are special wealth-producing or relationship-supporting *Flying Star Charts* of that system. These incredible formations are said to bring great wealth and pearls, rare and expensive treasures, to the occupants. *Pearl String Formations* are based on the facing direction of a structure and always fall on the Northwest and Southeast. There are actually two types of *Pearl String Formations*, one that attracts money luck and one that fosters luck with people/relationships.

Precious Jewel Lines: The very auspicious *Precious Jewel Lines* (PJL) or *Gold Dragons* are specific compass degrees that can bring great money luck. As the name implies, they can bring precious things and "jewels" to your life. In any of the eight directions, there are there are six

PJLs from which to choose, making a total of forty-eight. An example of a Precious Jewel Line degree is 86.5, which is part of the east direction. PJLs are appropriate for any structure and have various applications. PJLs most commonly apply to doors; generally the main door of a home or business can be set to these auspicious degrees. Driveways, sidewalks, trails, entrance gates, building foundations, important interior doors, desks, and beds can also be angled toward these special degrees.

road: A route, path, or open way for vehicles. In Feng Shui, roads are *rivers* of energy, or chi and play a huge part in analyzing a site because energy is powerful. These virtual, or urban, rivers are calculated when assessing, designing, enhancing, or implementing counter measures or enhancements for a site.

San He: Also known as *San Hup*. One of the two major schools of study in Classical Feng Shui—the other is San Yuan. The San He system, excellent for tapping natural landforms, primarily addresses large-scale projects, land plots, urban developments, city planning, and master-planned communities. The system is extensive and has several practical techniques for new and existing residential spaces as well. When assessing and altering a site or a structure, San He and San Yuan can be blended for maximum results.

San Yuan: One of the two major schools of Classical Feng Shui. The Flying Stars is part of this system; it excels in techniques of timing. See the *Schools of Feng Shui* in the compendium for more details.

sector: An area inside or outside a building: South sector, North sector, and so on.

sha chi: Also known as *shar chi*. Extremely negative energy, or killing chi.

Shan: The Chinese word for *mountain*.

Sheng Chi: Part of the Eight Mansions system. It can bring life-generating energy, wealth, and opportunities. Using Master Yap's numerical representation, this is the +90.

Shui: The Chinese word for *water;* pronounced *shway.*

sitting: In Feng Shui it refers to the back of the house, as if the structure is sitting in a chair on the land or property. It is the heavy part of the house; also consider a mountain.

Sitting Star: Also known as the Mountain Star in the Flying Star system. It influences people luck, such as fertility, employees, and health.

solar calendar: A calendar based on the movements of the sun.

Southeast Asia: Countries South of China and East of India, including Thailand, Vietnam, Cambodia, Laos, Myanmar, the Philippines, and Singapore.

Tao: also known as *The Way*, and is core of Taoism (pronounced with a D sound).

tapping the energy or chi: A technique that invites the available energy from the external environment to support the occupants of a structure.

Tien Yi: Part of the Eight Mansion system. It can bring excellent health and wealth. In Chinese it means *heavenly doctor* or *the doctor from heaven watches over you*. Using Master Yap's numerical representation, it is the +80.

tilting a door: A time-honored tradition used by Feng Shui masters and practitioners to change the degree of a door and the energy of a space. The doorframe and threshold are re-angled toward the desired degree. When the door is re-hung, it is tilted on a different degree.

T-juncture: When two roads meet perpendicularly to create a *T*. The formation is toxic when a home or business sits at the top and center of that *T*.

Traditional Feng Shui: Another term for Classical Chinese Feng Shui.

Tui: Also spelled *Dui*. One of the eight trigrams that represents the youngest daughter, the lake, and mid-fall. In the Later Heaven Ba Gua it is located in the West.

Twelve Animals: Rat, Ox, Tiger, Rabbit, Dragon, Snake, Horse, Goat, Monkey, Rooster, Dog and Pig; part of the Chinese Zodiac and used extensively in Classical Feng Shui and Chinese Astrology.

water: In Feng Shui, water is the secret to enhancing wealth, prosperity, longevity, nobility, and relationships. The Chinese word is *Shui,* and it represents energy and life force. Water, according to Feng Shui, is the most powerful element on the planet.

West Life Group: In the Eight Mansions system, people are divided into the East or West group. The 2, 6, 7, and 8 Life Guas are part of the West Life Group.

Western Feng Shui: In addition to the Black Hat Sect, other schools cropped up that incorporated the principles, but not the rituals, associated with Lin-Yun's followers. As the masters of Classical Feng Shui started to teach around the world, some of the most well-acclaimed instructors and authors of Western Feng Shui began to learn Classical Feng Shui. Unwilling to give up the Western-style Feng Shui that made them famous, they mixed the old with the new, thereby adding to the confusion over authentic Feng Shui. More than half of the Feng Shui books written about the subject include a hodgepodge of both theories.

Wu Gwei: Part of the Eight Mansions system that can attract lawsuits, bad romance, and betrayals. Using Master Yap's numerical representation, it is the -70. This is also known as the *Five Ghosts* direction.

Wu Xing: Also known as the five elements of Feng Shui: wood, fire, earth, metal, and water.

Yang: Alive, active and moving energy; considered the male energy of the Yin-Yang symbol.

Yang Feng Shui: Feng Shui was first practiced for the selection of a perfect gravesite, or what is commonly known by the Chinese as Yin Feng Shui—Feng Shui for the dead. Later, techniques were developed to increase luck and opportunities for houses of the living.

Yen Nien: Part of the Eight Mansions system that can bring longevity, good relationships, and love. Using Master Yap's numerical representation, it is the +70. It is a common mistake to spell this term as Nen Yien.

Yin: Female energy, passive, and dead; the perfect complement is yang energy.

Xing Fa: An approach to assessing form and shape in the environment.

Xun: One of the eight trigrams of the Ba Gua, also spelled as *Sun*. It represents the eldest daughter, the wind and early summer. In the Later Heaven arrangement of the Ba Gua, the Xun trigram is located in the Southeast.

Jennifer Bonetto,

Feng Shui Master, MBA, Speaker, Teacher, and Author

Jennifer Bonetto is known as 'The Hollywood Feng Shui Master'. Since 2008, she has been the

soul behind her business, *Real Feng Shui SOULutions*. Jennifer is a certified Master Practitioner, Certified Master Instructor, and a fellow for the American College of Classical Feng Shui. Currently, she is part of the 400-year old Wu Chang Pai mastery lineage of Grandmaster Yap Cheng Hai, of Kuala Lumpur, Malaysia, through her teacher, American Feng Shui Master, Denise Liotta-Dennis.

Jennifer has been featured on HGTV's Season 3, Selling LA, for her Feng Shui expertise. She's the Feng Shui expert for the Aljazeera documentary, China's Home Invasion. Her background includes employment with several Fortune 500 corporations. Ms. Bonetto received an MBA from Chapman University in Orange, CA. Her business acumen and experience has helped executives and individuals achieve their goals with money, relationships and health.

Jennifer has taught and lectured extensively for special interest and event groups, the Chamber of Commerce and prestigious venues such as UC Riverside, Orange Coast, Laguna Design Center, The Art Institute of California, OWN (Oprah Winfrey Network) Studios-Los Angeles, Hilton and Hyland, RE/MAX, First Team, Coldwell Banker, Teles Properties, Real Estate Investment Expo, and the AREAA Expo.

After the loss of her mother, Jennifer was deeply moved to seek out numerous spiritual, metaphysical and esoteric practices and disciplines. Her search led her to travel to remote, Abadiania and to visit the famous healer, John of God. Jennifer is a certified Pure Barre instructor and studied yoga at a retreat in Ibiza. As an avid world traveler, she has visited over 40 countries, including China. She loves to laugh, spend time with family, friends and her fiancé Tommy and their baby son, Massimo.

Conceived by Jennifer over 9 years ago, *Hollywood's Fatal Feng Shui: An In-Depth Examination of 10 Celebrity Homes with a Tragic History* is her first Feng Shui book, published in 2018.

Denise A. Liotta-Dennis,
Feng Shui Master, Speaker, Teacher, International Author

She's known as the "fast-talkin' Texan"—an interesting and delightful oxymoron—Denise A. Liotta-Dennis is the founder and president of Dragon-Gate Feng Shui (DGFS), LLC an  international consulting firm, specializing in Classical Feng Shui site selection, planning, design, audits, and assessments for commercial and residential real estate and construction projects. In 2006, Denise founded The American College of Classical Feng Shui, the training arm of Dragon Gate, a premier platform to learn Classical Feng Shui.

Born to a Houston entrepreneurial family, Denise, who possesses a quarter century of business ownership experience, is among a rare breed of Feng Shui consultants. Denise not only resonates with all things spiritual, she talks the language and walks in the shoes of business people. Growing up in the shadow of her father's construction and real estate development companies, Denise discovered early in life an innate love of business lifestyles and entrepreneurship. Her work with Feng Shui is also an outgrowth of a natural affinity for interior design. In fact, Denise has more than twenty-five years experience working in interior design, including residential and commercial projects.

With a rapid-fire delivery that keeps audiences spellbound, wide-eyed, and on the edge of their seats, Denise—a gifted educator and speaker on Feng Shui and business topics—offers high-energy, content-rich presentations. Peppering her talks with a quaint Southwestern humor, Denise's stories are couched in the real-life foibles of entrepreneurs and those seeking a spiritual path. She shares the spiritual side of life with a practical commercial bent not found among the more esoteric practitioners common to Feng Shui. Denise has studied with four noted Feng Shui Masters from China, Malaysia and Australia, including Grand Master Yap Cheng Hai and belongs to his 400- year Wu Chang Feng Shui Mastery lineage.

Ms Liotta-Dennis' first book was released in major national and international bookstores March 8, 2013 entitled *Classical Feng Shui for Wealth and Abundance,* her second book was released January 8, 2015 entitled *Feng Shui for Romance, Sex & Relationships,* and her third book will be released in December of 2016 entitled *Classical Feng Shui for Health, Beauty & Longevity* (endorsed by Grandmaster Dr. Stephen Skinner). This book has been translated into the native languages of Czechoslovakia and Estonia.

Denise's books are sold in fine book stores in the United States, Canada, the United Kingdom, Australia, New Zealand, and Singapore. They are offered online at Walmart, Target, Barnes and Noble, Amazon, and are housed in several American libraries. International online-booksellers in Sweden, Germany, France, Poland, Japan, Italy and Denmark sell her books in English.

Her two latest books are *The Secrets to Mastering Flying Stars Feng Shui* and *Feng Shui That Rocks the House*, both were released in 2018. *Hollywood's Fatal Feng Shui: An In-Depth Examination of 10 Celebrity Homes with a Tragic History* is Denise's sixth Feng Shui book.

Classical Feng Shui for Wealth & Abundance
ISBN 978-0-7387-3353-1
$17.99

Unlock the full wealth potential of your home or office using the potent formulas and wisdom of Classical Feng Shui. Written by a Feng Shui master, *Classical Feng Shui for Wealth & Abundance* reveals authentic techniques for success with money, business, and career. In this book, beginners and advanced students will learn:

- The two most popular Feng Shui systems: Eight Mansions and Flying Stars
- Easy-to-use Get Rich Keys and your personal Life Gua number for money luck
- Wealth building formulas such as Five Ghosts Carry Treasure, Dragon Gate, and Water Dragons
- How to identify and eliminate killing chi like Eight Roads of Destruction, Robbery Mountain Sha, and Eight Killing Forces

Whether you're buying a house, creating a home, or managing a business, these ancient and powerful techniques are exactly what you need to capture prosperity and success.

Purchase this book at Barnes&Noble.com, Amazon.com and Llewellyn.com. It is also available at Barnes & Noble brick and mortar locations.

Classical Feng Shui for Romance, Sex & Relationships
ISBN 978-0-7387-4188-8
$19.99

Harness the ancient power and wisdom of Classical Feng Shui to enhance all of your relationships, from romantic pursuits to day-to-day interactions with friends, family, and coworkers. Explore real-life stories of men and women's struggles with love and relationships and how Feng Shui enabled them to overcome their obstacles. Whether you are a beginner or advanced student, Master Denise Liotta Dennis provides you with step-by-step instructions on:

- The two most popular Feng Shui systems: Eight Mansions and Flying Stars
- How to heal your house of detrimental formations that will repel romance and cause negative relationships
- Never-before-seen insights on the Life-Gua Zodiac, which helps you assess personality matches
- Other closely held secrets used by Feng Shui masters, including a variety of period charts

Classical Feng Shui for Romance, Sex & Relationships is filled with effective methods for attracting love, prosperity, and even your soul mate. Use this comprehensive guide to improve not just the energy of your living space today, but also your happiness for many years to come.
Purchase this book at Barnes&Noble.com, Amazon.com and Llewellyn.com. It is also available at Barnes & Noble brick and mortar locations.

Classical Feng Shui for Health, Beauty & Longevity
ISBN 978-0-7387-4900-6
$21.99

Improve your wellness, extend your longevity, and secure a healthy environment with the ancient power and wisdom of Classical Feng Shui. This comprehensive guide reveals ancient and modern techniques for lasting health and beauty that both beginners and advanced students can use. Providing step-by-step instruction, Feng Shui Master Denise Liotta Dennis teaches you:

- The two most popular Classical Feng Shui systems: Flying Stars and Eight Mansions
- Feng Shui's Taoist roots and a variety of health modalities from ancient and modern times
- Profound secrets of the "Heavenly Doctor" position and its importance in enhancing health
- Ways to protect your body and mind from detrimental formations, devices, and environments

With well-researched information, period charts, astoundingly accurate health predictions, and much more, *Classical Feng Shui for Health, Beauty & Longevity* will help you be happier and healthier. *Praise:* "Denise Liotta Dennis has done a great job of clearly expressing [the application of feng shui to health], going into great detail."—Grand Master Dr. Stephen Skinner

Purchase this book at Barnes&Noble.com, Amazon.com and Llewellyn.com. It is also available at Barnes & Noble brick and mortar locations.

The Secrets to Mastering Flying Stars Feng Shui
How to fly, analyze, cure and enhance the stars for your home or office
ISBN-13: 978-1985760127
$38.95

Flying Stars is the most popular, intriguing and misunderstood Feng Shui system in the world. Whether you're a practitioner or a novice, you'll be able to master and deepen your understanding of a method used for 'superior living'. This book delivers a detailed explanation of how *time* and *space* will affect all categories of Feng Shui—prosperity, relationships and health.

A fully illustrated, comprehensive and systematic home-study course that is designed for anyone who wants to put Flying Stars Feng Shui to personal, professional or practical use. With over 20 years experience, Master Liotta Dennis reveals the best tricks-of-the-trade. Step by step you are guided to shake up the energy and make-over your home or office while simultaneously learning the profound secrets of Flying Stars. **Purchase this book at Amazon.com**

Feng Shui That Rocks the House
Shake Up the Energy and Get the Life You Want
ISBN-13: 978-1986762892
$28.95

This book explains how to use the simple, yet profound Eight Mansions system. It is a more personalized Feng Shui. Learn your own Magic Life-Gua number and unlock the mysteries to a better life. While it is a compass-based formula, it is easy, effective and powerful. Designed to improve relationships, health and prosperity, you will learn the secrets passed down from Grandmaster Yap Cheng Hai from the famous Golden Star Classics. This book will teach you how to 'rock' your home and business—and finally get the life you want! You will learn:

       How to Calculate Magic Life-Gua Numbers
       The History of BaZhai (Eight Mansions)
       Your Four Good and Bad Directions
       Where to Locate your Martial Bed
       How Improve Romance and Love
       How to Jump Start Career-Luck
       Life-Gua Zodiac Personalities
       Life-Gua Compatibility (64 Combos)
       How to Evaluate Your Floor Plan
       Advanced Eight Mansion for Mixed Life Groups
       How Doors Activate Specific Types of Luck
       How to Improve Family Life

Purchase this book at Amazon.com

Made in the USA
San Bernardino, CA
22 January 2019